Earl Van Dorn

Official Reports of Battles

Embracing the defence of Vicksburg, by Major General Earl Van Dorn, and the attack upon Baton Rouge, by Major Geneal [!] Breckenridge, together with the reports of the battles of Corinth and Hatchie Bridge. Vol. 3

Earl Van Dorn

Official Reports of Battles

Embracing the defence of Vicksburg, by Major General Earl Van Dorn, and the attack upon Baton Rouge, by Major Geneal [!] Breckenridge, together with the reports of the battles of Corinth and Hatchie Bridge. Vol. 3

ISBN/EAN: 9783337325381

Printed in Europe, USA, Canada, Australia, Japan

Cover: Foto ©ninafisch / pixelio.de

More available books at **www.hansebooks.com**

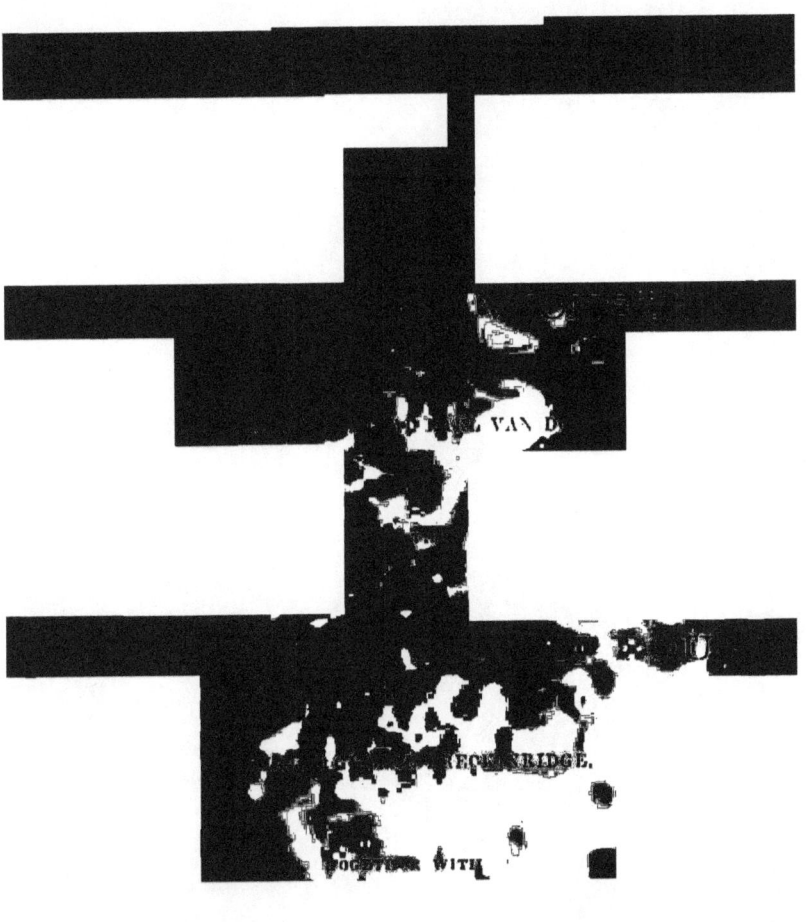

MESSAGE OF THE PRESIDENT.

RICHMOND, VA., Jan. 24, 1863.

To the House of Representatives:

I herewith transmit a communication from the Secretary of War, forwarding, for your information, copies of certain reports of military operations, being a response, in part, to your resolution of the 22d instant.

JEFFERSON DAVIS.

COMMUNICATION FROM THE SECRETARY OF WAR.

CONFEDERATE STATES OF AMERICA,
War Department
Richmond, Va., January 24, 1863.

His Excellency, THE PRESIDENT,

SIR: In response to a resolution of the House of Representatives, adopted on the 22d instant, I have the honor to enclose the following reports, viz:

1. Report of the operations at Vicksburg and Baton Rouge.
2. Report of the battles of Corinth and Hatchie Bridge.
3. Report of the expedition to Hartsville, Tenn.
4. Report of the affair at Pocotaligo and Yemassee.
5. Report of the action near Coffeeville, Miss.
6. Report of the action and casualties of the Brigade of Colonel J. M. Simonton at Fort Donelson.

Very respectfully,
Your obedient servant,
JAMES A. SEDDON,
Secretary of War.

REPORT

OF

OPERATIONS AT VICKSBURG AND BATON ROUGE.

REPORT OF MAJOR GENERAL EARL VAN DORN.

HEADQUARTERS DISTRICT OF THE MISSISSIPPI,
Jackson, Miss., September 9, 1862.

GENERAL: I have the honor to submit, for the information of the War Department, the following report of the defence of Vicksburg, and of operations in this district, up to the present time:

Pursuant to orders I assumed command of this district, and of the defences of Vicksburg, on the 27th day of June, 1862. Prior to my arrival, Major General Lovell having resolved to defend the city, had ordered a detail of his force, under the command of Brigadier General M. L. Smith, to garrison the place and construct works for its defence. I found the city besieged by a powerful fleet of war vessels and an army. The inhabitants, inspired by a noble patriotism, had determined to devote the city to destruction, rather than see it fall into the hands of an enemy who had abandoned many of the rules of civilized warfare. This voluntary sacrifice, on the altar of liberty, inspired me with the determination to defend it to the last extremity. Orders to this effect were at once issued, to which my army responded with the liveliest enthusiasm. The citizens retired to the interior, while the troops marched in and pitched their tents in the valleys and on the hills adjacent, in convenient position to support batteries and strike assailants. The batteries of heavy guns, already established by the skill and energy of General Smith, on the crest of the hills overlooking the river, were placed in complete readiness for action. Other guns were brought up from Mobile, from Richmond, from Columbus and elsewhere, and put in battery. Breckinridge's division occupied the city. Smith's brigade, which, previous to my arrival, had furnished the garrison of the place, manned the batteries, and with details from Breckinridge's division, guarded the approaches in front and on the flanks. Withers' light artillery was placed in such position as to sweep all near approaches, while Stark's cavalry watched, at a distance, on our flank on the Yazoo, and below Warrenton, on the Mississippi.

Prior to my assuming command, the attacking force of the enemy was confined to Porter's mortar fleet and Farragut's gun-boats, (with their attendant array in transports.) which had ascended the river from New Orleans. For the operations of this force in attack, and for the successful and heroic resistance made by General Smith and the troops under his command, I refer the department to the satisfactory and graphic report of that officer, herewith communicated.

The evacuation of Fort Pillow and the fall of Memphis opened the new danger of a combination between the upper and lower fleets of the enemy. This junction was effected early in July, and thus an added force of more than forty gun-boats, mortar-boats, rams and transports lay in menace before the city. On the 12th of July it opened fire, and kept up a continuous attack until the bombardment of the city ceased. Having received authority from the President to use the ram "Arkansas," as part of my force, some days prior to the 15th of July, I issued an order to Captain Brown to assume command of her, and prepare her for immediate and active service. From all reliable sources I learned that she was a vessel capable of great resistance, and armed with large offensive power. Making the order imperative, I commanded Captain Brown to take her through the raft of the Yazoo, and after sinking the "Star of the West" in the passage to go out and attack the upper fleet of the enemy to the cover of my batteries. I left it to his judgment to determine whether on reaching the city his vessel was in condition to proceed down the river and destroy the lower mortar fleet. Captain Brown properly substituted a vessel of inferior quality in place of the "Star of the West," entered the Mississippi, and on the memorable morning of the 15th of July, immortalized his single vessel, himself, and the heroes under his command by an achievement, the most brilliant ever recorded in naval annals. I deeply regret that I am unable to enrich my report by an authentic account of the heroic action of the officers and men of the "Arkansas." Commodore Lynch declines to furnish me with a report of the action, on the ground that he was an officer out of the scope of my command. The glory of this deed of the "Arkansas" stung the pride of the Federal navy, and led to the most speedy, but unsuccessful efforts of the combined fleets to destroy her. I refer the department to the accompanying report of General Smith for an accurate detail of those efforts, as also for a connected and faithful relation of the important events which make the history of the siege and defence of Vicksburg. With the failure to destroy or take the "Arkansas," the siege of Vicksburg practically ended. The attack on the batteries soon ceased, and the enemy baffled and enraged by an unexpected, determined and persistent defence, vented his wrath in impotent and barbarian efforts to destroy the city. On the 27th of July, both fleets disappeared, foiled in a more than two months' struggle to reduce the place. The casualties on our side, during the entire siege, were twenty-two killed and wounded. Not a gun was dismounted, and but two were temporarily disabled. The successful defence of Vicksburg is due to the unflinching valor of the cannoniers, who, unwearied by watchfulness night and day, stood by their guns unawed by the terrors of a fierce and continuous bombardment; to the sleepless vigilance and undaunted courage of the troops, who lay, at all hours, in close supporting distance of every battery, ready to beat back the invader so soon as his footsteps should touch the shore; to the skilful location of scattered batteries, and last, not least, to that great moral power—a high and patriotic resolve pervading and swelling the breasts of officers, soldiers and citizens, *that. at every cost, the enemy should be expelled.* I refer the department to the specific enumeration of the names of officers and men who won distinction by meritorious service during the siege, as reported by General Smith, and I heartily endorse his commendations. Satisfied that the enemy disappeared from Vicksburg, under the mortifying conviction that it was impregnable to his attack, I resolved to strike a blow before he had time to organize and mature a new scheme of assault.

The enemy held Baton Rouge, the capital of Louisiana, forty miles below the mouth of Red river, with a land force of about three thousand five hundred men, in conjunction with four or five gun-boats, and some transports. It was a matter of great necessity to us that the navigation of Red river should be opened as high as Vicksburg. Supplies, much needed, existed there, hard to be obtained from any other quarter, and strong military reasons demanded that we should hold the Mississippi at two points, to facilitate communications and co-operation between my district and the trans-Mississippi department. The capture of Baton Rouge, and the forces of the enemy at that point, would open the Mississippi, secure the navigation of Red river, then in a state of blockade, and also render easier the recapture of New Orleans. To this end I gave orders to General Breckinridge to move upon Baton Rouge with a force of five thousand men, picked from the troops at Vicksburg, and added to his command the whole effective force of General Ruggles, then at Camp Moore, making a total force of six thouand men. To ensure the success of the plan, I ordered the "Arkansas" to co-operate with the land forces by a simultaneous attack from the river. All damages sustained by the "Arkansas" from the fleets of the enemy had been repaired, and when she left the wharf at Vicksburg for Baton Rouge, she was deemed to be as formidable, in attack or defence, as when she defied a fleet of forty vessels of war, many of them iron-clads. With such effective means, I deemed the taking of Baton Rouge and the destruction or capture of enemy on the land and water, the reasonable result of the expidition. By epidemic disease, the land force under Maj. Gen. Breckinridge was reduced to less than three thousand effective men, within the period of ten days after he reached Camp Moore. The "Arkansas," after arriving within a short distance of Baton Rouge, in ample time for joint action at the appointed hour of attack, suddenly became unmanageable, from a failure in her machinery and engine, which all the efforts of her engineers could not repair. The gallant Breckinridge, advised by telegram every hour of her progress towards Baton Rouge, and counting on her co-operation, attacked the enemy with his whole effective force, then reduced to about two thousand five hundred men, drove him from all his positions, and forced him to seek protection under the cover of his gun-boats. I regret to state that the labors of General Breckinridge, in a distant field of operations, have thus far prevented him from making to me a report of his action, but enough has transpired to enable me to assure the department that the battle of Baton Rouge illustrated the valor of our troops, and the skill and intrepidity of their commander. His report will be forwarded as soon as it is received. It will be thus manifest to the departnent that an enterprise, so hopeful in its promise, met with partial failure, only from causes which were not only beyond my control, but out of the reach of ordinary foresight. I could not anticipate the sudden illness of three thousand picked men, and the failure of the "Arkansas" at the critical hour appointed to her for added honors, was a joyful surprise to the startled fleet of the enemy, and a wonder to all who had witnessed her glory at Vicksburg. Advised of the result of the expedition, I immediately ordered the occupation of Port Hudson, a point selected for its eligibility of defence, and for its capacity for offensive annoyance of the enemy, established batteries, manned them with experienced gunners, and guarded them by an adequate supporting force, holding Baton Rouge, in the meanwhile, in menace. The effect of these operations was the evacuation of Baton Rouge by the enemy, and his disappearance from the Mississippi between the capital of Louisiana and Vicksburg. The results sought by the movements against Baton Rouge, have been, to a great extent, attained. We hold two points on the Mississippi—more than two hundred miles—unmolested by the enemy, and closed to him. The navigation of the Mississippi river from the mouth of Red river to Vicksburg was at once opened, and still remains open to our commerce, giving us also the important advantage of water connection, by Red river, of the east with the west. Indispensable supplies have been, and continue to be, drawn from this source. The desired facilities for communication and co-operation between this district and the trans-Mississippi department have been established. The recapture of New Orleans has been made easier to our army.

I think it due to the truth of history to correct the error, industriously spread by the official reports of the enemy, touching the destruction of the "Arkansas." She was no trophy won by the "Essex," nor did she receive injury at Baton Rouge from the hands of any of her adversaries. Lieutenant Stevens, her gallant commander, finding her unmanageable, moored her to the shore. On the cautious approach of the enemy, who kept at a respectful distance, he landed his crew, cut her from her moorings, fired her with his own hands, and turned her adrift down the river. With every gun shotted, our flag floating from her bow, and not a man on board, the "Arkansas" bore down upon the enemy, and gave him battle. Her guns were discharged as the flames reached them, and when her last shot was fired, the explosion of her magazine ended the brief but glorious career of the "Arkansas." "It was beautiful," said Lieutenant Stevens, while the tears stood in his eyes, "to see her, when abandoned by commander and crew, and dedicated to sacrifice, fighting the battle on her own hook." I trust that the official report of Commodore Lynch will do justice to the courage, constancy and resolution of the officers and men, who were the last crew of the "Arkansas." I deem it eminently proper to say to the department, that neither the spirit which resolved to dispute at Vicksburg, the jurisdiction of the Mississippi river, nor the energy which successfully executed that resolution was *local* in its character; nor was it a spirit bounded by *State lines*, or circumscribed by *State pride*. It was a broad, catholic spirit, wide as our country, and unlimited as the independence we struggle to establish. The power which baffled the enemy, resided in the breasts of the soldiers of *seven States*, marshaled behind the ramparts of Vicksburg. Mississippians were there, but there too, also, were the men of Kentucky, of Tennessee, of Alabama, of Arkansas, of Louisiana, and of Missouri, as ready to defend the emporium of Mississippi as to strike down the foe at their own hearthstones. I incorporate, with my report, a schedule of the forces under my command at Vicksburg, as a proper contribution to the archives of the Confederacy.

General Helm.—Fourth Kentucky volunteers, Lieutenant Colonel Hynes; fifth Kentucky volunteers, Colonel Hunt; thirty-first Alabama volunteers, Colonel Edwards; fourth Alabama battalion, Lieutenant Colonel Snodgrass; thirty-first Mississippi volunteers, Colonel Orr; Hudson battery.

General J. S. Bowen.—First Missouri volunteers, Lieutenant Colonel Riley; tenth Arkansas volunteers; ninth Arkansas volunteers, Colonel Dunlap; sixth Mississippi volunteers, Colonel Lowry; second Confederate battalion; Watson's battery, Captain Bursley.

General Preston.—Third Kentucky volunteers, Colonel Thompson; sixth Kentucky volunteers, Colonel Lewis; seventh Kentucky volunteers, Colonel Crossland; thirty-fifth Alabama volunteers, Colonel Robertson; Cobb's battery, Lieutenant Gracy.

Colonel W. S. Statham.—Fifteenth Mississippi volunteers, Lieutenant Colonel Farrell; twenty-second Mississippi volunteers, Captain Hughes; nineteenth Tennessee volunteers, Lieutenant Colonel Moore; twentieth Tennessee volunteers, Colonel Smith; twenty-eighth Tennessee volunteers, Colonel Brown; forty-fifth Tennessee volunteers, Colonel Searcey; McClung's battery, Captain McClung.

General M. L. Smith.—Company of sappers and miners, Captain Winters; twenty-sixth Louisiana volunteers, Colonel DeClouett;

twenty-fifth Louisiana volunteers, Colonel Thomas; sixth Mississippi battalion, Lieutenant Colonel Balfour; twenty-seventh Louisiana volunteers, Colonel Marks; third Mississippi volunteers, Colonel Mellon; seventeenth Louisiana volunteers, Colonel Richardson; fourth Louisiana volunteers, Colonel Allen; company I, thirty-seventh Mississippi volunteers, Captain Randall; first Mississippi light artillery, Colonel Withers; regiment heavy artillery, Colonel Jackson; eighth Louisiana battalion, Pinckney; first Louisiana battalion, Major Clinch; twenty-eighth Mississippi cavalry, Colonel Stark; battalion zouaves, Major Dupiero; cavalry escort, Lieutenant Bradley.

To the members of my staff, Majors Kimmel and Stith, Assistant Adjutant Generals; to Majors Joseph D. Balfour and A. M. Haskell, Inspectors; to Surgeon Choppin, Medical Director; Surgeon Bryan, Medical Inspector; to Lieutenants Sulivan and Shoemaker, my Aids; to Lieutenant Colonel Lomax, Assistant Adjutant and Inspector General; Lieutenant Colonel J. P. Mayor, Acting Engineer; Captain A. H. Cross, Captain Thyssing, Engineer; to Colonel Fred. Tate, and to Majors Uriel Wright and Weehler, volunteer Aids, I return my thanks for the ready and efficient services rendered by them in their respective departments.

I am, sir, very respectfully,
Your obedient servant,
EARL VAN DORN,
Major General.

Since this report was written, I have received the report of Major General Breckinridge, of his operations at Baton Rouge and Port Hudson, herewith forwarded. It gives me pleasure to commend to the special notice of the department the names of all who won distinction in this service.

EARL VAN DORN, *Major General.*

MAJOR GENERAL BRECKINRIDGE'S REPORT OF OPERATIONS AGAINST BATON ROUGE, LA.

HEADQUARTERS BRECKINRIDGE'S DIVISION,
September 30th, 1862.

Major M. M. KIMMEL,
Assistant Adjutant General:

SIR: I have the honor to report the operations of a portion of my division, recently ordered from Vicksburg to Camp Moore, and Baton Rouge, Louisiana, by Major General Van Dorn:

I left Vicksburg on the 27th of July with somewhat less than four thousand men, and arrived at Camp Moore the evening of the 28th. The Major General commanding the district having received intelligence that the enemy was threatening Camp Moore in force, the movement was made suddenly and rapidly by railroad, and having but few cars, nothing could be transported except the troops, with their arms and ammunition. Brigadier General Charles Clark, who had reported for duty a few days before our departure from Vicksburg, promptly and kindly consented to accompany the expedition. Brigadier General Ruggles was already at Camp Moore, in command of a small force, with which he had kept the enemy in check. The troops were immediately organized in two divisions, General Clark taking command of the first, and General Ruggles of the second division. The rumor of an advance of the enemy in force upon Camp Moore proved to be unfounded. On the 30th of July, in obedience to a dispatch of the 29th, from the Major General commanding the district, the troops were put in motion for Baton Rouge. During the march I received information that the effective force of the enemy was not less than five thousand men, and that the ground was commanded by three gun-boats lying in the river. My own troops having suffered severely from the effects of exposure at Vicksburg, from heavy rains, without shelter, and from the extreme heat, did not now number more than thirty-four hundred men. Under these circumstances, I determined not to make the attack unless we could be relieved from the fire of the fleet. Accordingly I telegraphed to the Major General commanding the condition and number of the troops, and the reported strength of the enemy, but said I would undertake to capture the garrison, if the "Arkansas" could be sent down to clear the river, or divert the fire of the gun-boats. He promptly answered, that the "Arkansas" would be ready to co-operate at daylight on Tuesday, the 5th of August. On the afternoon of Monday the 4th, the command having reached the Comite river, ten miles from Baton Rouge, and learning by an express messenger that the "Arkansas" had passed Bayou Sara in time to arrive at the proper moment, preparations were made to advance that night. The sickness had been appalling. The morning report of the fourth showing but three thousand effectives, and deducting those taken sick during the day, and the number that fell out from weakness on the night march, I did not carry into the action more than twenty-six hundred men. This estimate does not include some two hundred partisan rangers, who had performed efficient service in picketing the different roads, but who, from the nature of the ground took no part in the action; nor about the same number of militia, hastily collected by Colonel Hardee in the neighborhood of Clinton, who, though making every effort, could not arrive in time to participate. The command left the Comite at 11 o'clock, P. M., and reached the vicinity of Baton Rouge a little before day-break on the morning of the 5th. Some hours before the main body moved, a small force of infantry, with a section of Semmes' battery, under Lieutenant Fauntleroy, the whole commanded by Lieutenant Colonel Shields, of the 30th Louisiana, was sent by a circuitous route to the road leading from Clinton to Baton Rouge, with orders to drive in any pickets of the enemy, and attack his left as soon as the action should begin in front. This service was well performed, but for details reference is made to the report of Brigadier General Ruggles, from whose command the force was detached. While waiting for daylight to make the attack, an accident occurred which deprived us of several excellent officers and enlisted men, and two pieces of artillery. The partisan rangers were placed in rear of the artillery and infantry, yet during the darkness a few of them leaked through, and riding forward encountered the enemy, causing exchange of shots between the pickets. Galloping back, they produced some confusion, which led to rapid firing for a few moments, during which Brigadier General Helm was dangerously injured by the fall of his horse, Lieutenant Todd, his aid-de-camp killed, Captain Roberts, of the Fourth Kentucky, severely wounded, several enlisted men killed and wounded, and two of Captain Cobb's three guns rendered for the time wholly useless. After General Helm was disabled, Colonel Thomas H. Hunt assumed command of his brigade. Order was soon restored, and the force placed in position on the right and left of the Greenwell Springs' road. I was obliged to content myself with a single line of battle, and a small regiment of infantry, with one piece of artillery to each division as a reserve. The enemy (expecting the attack) was drawn up in two lines, or rather in one line, with strong reserves distributed at intervals. At the moment there was light enough, our troops moved rapidly forward. General Ruggles, commanding the left, brought on the engagement with four pieces of Semmes' battery, the 4th and 30th Louisiana, and Boyd's Louisiana battalion, under command of Colonel Allen, of the 4th Louisiana, and the 3d, 6th and 7th Kentucky, and the 35th Alabama, under command of Colonel Thompson, of the 3d Kentucky. These troops moved forward with great impetuosity, driving the enemy before them, while their ringing cheers inspired all our little command.

The Louisiana troops charged a battery and captured two pieces. At this point Colonel Allen, commanding the brigade, while pressing forward with the colors in his hand, had both legs shattered, and Lieutenant Colonel Boyd received a severe wound. This produced confusion, and the enemy at the same moment throwing forward a strong reinforcement, the brigade was forced back in some disorder. It was rallied by the efforts of Colonel Breaux, Lieutenant Colonel Hunter, and other officers, and although it did not further participate in the assault, it maintained its position under a fire from the gunboats and land batteries of the enemy. During this time, Thompson's brigade, which composed the right of Ruggles' division, was behaving with great gallantry, often driving back superior forces, and towards the close of the action, took part in the final struggle from a position immediately on the left of the first division. Colonel Thompson, being severely wounded in a charge, the command devolved on Colonel Robertson, of the thirty-fifth Alabama, whose conduct fully justified the confidence of his troops. The Louisiana battery, Captain Semmes, was admirably handled throughout. The first division, under General Clark, being the second brigade, composed of the fourth and fifth Kentucky, thirty-first Mississipppi, thirty-first and fourth Alabama, commanded by Colonel Hunt, of the fifth Kentucky, and the fourth brigade, composed of the fifteenth and twenty-second Mississippi, and the nineteenth, twentieth, twenty-eighth and forty-fifth Tennessee consolidated into one battalion, commanded by Colonel Smith, of the twentieth Tennessee, together with the Hudson battery, and one piece of Cobb's battery, advanced to the right of the Greenwell Springs road. On the right, as on the left, the enemy was constantly pressed back, until after several hours of fighting he was driven to his last encampment in a large grove just in rear of the penitentiary. Here the contest was hot and obstinate, and it was here the first division suffered the greatest loss. Colonel Hunt was shot down, and upon the fall of that excellent officer, at the suggestion of General Clark, and with the consent of the officers concerned, I placed Captain John A. Buckner, Assistant Adjutant General on my staff, in command of the second brigade. In the management of his command he displayed so high a degree of skill and courage that I commend him especially to the notice of the government. General Clark pressed the attack at this point with great vigor, until he received a wound, which was supposed to be mortal, when, through some misapprehension, the second brigade began to fall back down the slope, but without confusion. Captain Buckner learning, upon inquiry from me, that I did not desire a retrograde movement, immediately, aided by Major Wickliffe,. of the fifth Kentucky regiment, (Lieutenant Colonel Caldwell, who was injured by the accident of the preceding night, having been obliged to retire,) and other regimental officers faced the brigade about and renewed the attack. At the same time Colonel Smith, commanding fourth brigade, composed of the consolidated Tennesse regiments, and the twenty-second Mississippi, Captain Hughes, was ordered forward, and moved against the enemy in fine style. In a few moments Captain Hughes received a mortal wound at the head of.

his regiment. Observing some troops on the left, partially sheltered by a shallow cut in the road, who proved to be the remnant of Thompson's brigade, and out of ammunition, I ordered them to advance to the support of the first division with the bayonet. The order was promptly obeyed, and in executing it, I happened to observe, as distinguished for alacrity, Colonel Crossland, of the 7th Kentucky, Lieutenant Colonel Goodwin, of the thirty-fifth Alabama, and Lieutenant Terry, of the 8th Kentucky, on duty with Sharp-shooters. At this critical point, Major Brown, chief commissary, and Captain Richards, one of my aids, were conspicuous in urging on the troops. In this assault we suffered considerably from the fire of the fleet until the opposing lines approached each other so closely that a regard for their own friends obliged them to suspend. The contest at and around this last encampment was bloody, but at the end of it the enemy were completely routed, some of our men pursuing and firing at them for some distance down the street running in front of the arsenal and barracks. They did not reappear during the day. It was now 10 o'clock. We had listened in vain for the guns of the "Arkansas." I saw around me not more than one thousand exhausted men, who had been unable to procure water since we left the Comite river. The enemy had several batteries commanding the approaches to the arsenal and barracks, and the gunboats had already reopened upon us with a direct fire. Under these circumstances, although the troops showed the utmost indifference to danger and death, and were even reluctant to retire, I did not deem it prudent to pursue the victory further. Having scarcely any transportation, I ordered all the camps and stores of the enemy to be destroyed, and directing Captain Buckner to place one section of Semmes' battery, supported by the seventh Kentucky, in a certain position on the field, withdrew the rest of the troops about one mile to "Ward's Creek," with the hope of obtaining water, but finding none there fit for man or beast, I moved the command back to the field of battle, and procured a very imperfect supply from some cisterns in the suburbs of the town. This position we occupied for the rest of the day.

The citizens of the surrounding and thinly settled country exhibited the warmest patriotism, and with their assistance, conveyances enough were procured to carry off all our wounded who could bear removal. A few, armed with shot guns and other weapons, had been able to reach the field in time to join in the attack. Having neither picks nor shovels, we were unable to dig graves for the burial of the dead. I still hoped for the co-operation of the "Arkansas," and, in that event, intended to renew the attack. But late in the afternoon, I learned by express that before daylight, and within five miles of Baton Rouge, her machinery had become disabled, and she lay helpless on the right bank of the river. Upon receiving this intelligence, I returned with my command to the Comite river, leaving a force of observation near the suburbs of the town. The Hudson battery, Lieut. Sweeney, and Cobb's one piece, in charge of Sergeant Hawk Peak, played their part well. I am unable to give the exact force of the enemy, but by comparing all my information with the number and size of their camps, and the extent and weight of their fire, I do not think they brought into action less than forty-five hundred men. We had eleven pieces of field artillery. They brought to bear on us not less than eighteen pieces, exclusive of the guns of the fleet. In one respect the contrast between the opposing forces was very striking. The enemy were well clothed, and their encampments showed the presence of every comfort and even luxury. Our men had little transportation, indifferent food, and no shelter. Half of them had no coats, and hundreds of them were without either shoes or socks; yet no troops ever behaved with greater gallantry, and even reckless audacity. What can make this difference, unless it be the sublime courage inspired by a just cause? The wound of Brigadier General Charles Clark being thought mortal, and the least motion causing great agony, he was left on the field at his own request, his aid, Lieutenant Yerger, remaining with him. The next morning they gave themselves up to the enemy. I cannot speak in terms too strong of the skill, coolness and courage of General Clark. He played the part of a perfect soldier. Brigadier General Ruggles conducted the attack on the left with uncommon rapidity and precision, and exhibited throughout the qualities of a brave and experienced officer. In addition to the officers of my staff already mentioned, I desire to express my acknowledgements of the zeal and gallantry of Major Wilson, chief of artillery, Major Hope, inspector general, whose horse was shot under him, Captain Nocquet, chief of engineers, Lieut. Breckinridge, aid-de-camp, and Dr. Pendleton, medical director, assisted by Dr. Weatherly, on temporary service. A number of gentlemen from Louisiana and elsewhere, rendered efficient service as volunteers, among whom were Lieutenant Colonel Pinckney, Mr. Addison and Captain Bird, of Louisiana, Lieutenant Colonel Brewer, of Kentucky, and Mr. William B. Hamilton, of Mississippi. The thanks of the army are due to the Hon. Thomas J. Davidson, for his attention to the hospitals, and to all the inhabitants of that part of Louisiana for their devotion to our sick and wounded. Colonel Pond and Major DeBaum, in command of partisan rangers, were efficient before and after the battle, in observing and harassing the enemy. The inability of General Clark, and the failure of several officers to make reports, may prevent full justice to the conduct of the first division. Any omission here, will, when brought to my notice, be embodied in a supplemental report. The report of General Ruggles is very full, as to all that occurred on the left. I send herewith a list of the officers and men specially mentioned in the division, brigade and regimental reports, for gallant conduct, with the request that it be published and the names brought to the favorable notice of the government. I transmit, also, the reports of the subordinate commanders, and the returns of the killed and wounded. It will be seen that our casualties amounted to 467. I have reason to believe that the loss of the enemy was much greater. We captured two flags and a few prisoners. Nothing was left by us but one caisson, which was so much injured as to be wholly unserviceable, one of the enemy's being brought off in its place. After the battle, the enemy, who had previously been plundering, burning houses, and other property, stealing negroes, and seizing citizens through a large region of country, never ventured to send out another marauding force. Our pickets continued to extend to the immediate vicinity of Baton Rouge, and very soon the enemy abandoned the place, and retired to New Orleans. A few days after the engagement, knowing the desire of the Major General commanding to secure a strong position on the Mississippi, below the mouth of Red river, I occupied Port Hudson with a portion of the troops under the command of Brigadier General Ruggles. The next day I received orders to remove all the troops to that point. Brigadier General Bowen, who had just arrived, was left with his command on the Comite river, to observe Baton Rouge from that quarter, to protect our hospitals, and to cover the line of communication between Clinton and Camp Moore. I directed General Ruggles to select eligible positions at Port Hudson for heavy batteries, and ordered Captain Nocquet, chief engineer, to report to him temporarily for this duty. Upon my arrival there, I found that rapid progress had been made, and some of the works under charge of Captain Nocquet, were ready to receive the guns, which the major general commanding wrote me were on the way. Port Hudson is one of the strongest points of the Mississippi, which Baton Rouge is not, and batteries there will command the river more completely than at Vicksburg. On the 19th day of August, in obedience to orders from the headquarters of the department, I moved from Port Hudson for Jackson, Mississippi, with a portion of the force, leaving Brigadier General Ruggles in command with ——— troops. In concluding this report, I have to express my obligations for the prompt and cordial support which I received at all times from the major general commanding the department.

    Very respectfully,
     Your obedient servant,
       JOHN C. BRECKINRIDGE,
          Major General.

 I omitted to mention that the fifteenth Mississippi, Major Binford, was not brought into action. This admirable regiment, much reduced by long and gallant services, was held as a reserve.
       JOHN C. BRECKINRIDGE.

REPORTS

OF

BATTLES OF CORINTH AND HATCHIE BRIDGE.

REPORT OF MAJOR GENERAL EARL VAN DORN.

HEADQUARTERS ARMY OF WEST TENNESSEE,
Holly Springs, Miss., Oct. 20th, 1862.

GENERAL: I have the honor to make the following report of the battle of Corinth:

Having established batteries at Port Hudson, secured the mouth of Red river and the navigation of the Mississippi river to Vicksburg, I turned my especial attention to affairs in the northern portion of my district.

On the 30th day of August I received a dispatch from General Bragg, informing me that he was about to march into Kentucky and would leave to General Price and myself the enemy in West Tennessee. On the 4th day of September I received a communication from General Price, in which was enclosed a copy of the dispatch from General Bragg above named, making an offer to co-operate with me. At this time General Breckinridge was operating on the Mississippi river, between Baton Rouge and Port Hudson, with all the available force I had for the field; therefore I could not accept General Price's proposition. Upon the return, however, of General Breckinridge, I immediately addressed General Price, giving my views in full in regard to the campaign in West Tennessee, and stating that I was then ready to join him with all my troops. In the meantime, orders were received by him, from General Bragg, to follow Rosencrans across the Tennessee river into Middle Tennessee, whither it was then supposed he had gone. Upon the receipt of this intelligence I felt at once that all my hopes of accomplishing anything in West Tennessee, with my small force, were marred. I nevertheless moved up to Davis' Mill, a few miles from Grand Junction, Tenn., with the intention of defending my district to the best of my ability, and to make a demonstration in favor of General Price, to which latter end, also, I marched my whole command on the 20th day of September to within seven miles of Bolivar, driving three brigades of the enemy back to that place, and forcing the return from Corinth of one division (Ross's,) which had been sent there to strengthen Grant's army.

General Price, in obedience to his orders, marched in the direction of Iuka, to cross the Tennessee, but was not long in discovering that Rosencrans had not crossed that stream. This officer, in connection with Grant, attacked him on the 19th day of September, and compelled him to fall back towards Baldwin, on the Mobile and Ohio railroad. On the 25th day of the same month I received a dispatch, by courier, from General Price, stating that he was at Baldwin, and was then ready to join me with his forces in an attack on Corinth, as had been previously suggested by me. We met at Ripley, on the 28th of Sept., according to agreement and marched the next morning towards Pocahontas, which place we reached on the 1st of Oct. From all the information I could obtain the following was the "situation" of the Federal army at that time: Sherman at Memphis with about six thousand men; Hurlbert, afterwards Ord, at Bolivar, with about eight thousand; Grant (Headquarters at Jackson,) with about three thousand; Rosencrans at Corinth with about fifteen thousand, together with the following outposts, viz: Rienzi, twenty-five hundred; Burnville, Jacinto and Iuka, about six thousand. At important bridges, and on garrison duty, about two or three thousand, making in the aggregate about forty-two thousand (42,000) men in West Tennessee. Memphis, Jackson, Bolivar and Corinth were fortified, the works mounting seige guns, the outposts slightly fortified, having field pieces. Memphis, Bolivar and Corinth are in the arc of a circle, the chord of which, from Memphis to Corinth, makes an angle with due east line about fifteen degrees south. Bolivar is about equi-distant from Memphis and Corinth, somewhat nearer the latter, and is at the intersection of the Hatchie river and the Mississippi Central and Ohio railroad. Corinth is the strongest, but the most salient point. Surveying the whole field of operations before me, calmly and dispasionately, the conclusion forced itself irresistibly upon my mind that the taking of Corinth was a condition precedental to the accomplishment of anything in West Tennessee. To take Memphis would be to destroy an immense amount of property, without any adequate military advantage, even admitting that it could be held, without heavy guns, against the enemy's guns and mortar boats. The line of fortifications around Bolivar is intersected by the Hatchie river, rendering it impossible to take the place by quick assault, and reinforcements could be thrown in from Jackson by railroad, and, situated as it is, in the angle of the three fortified places, an advance upon it would expose both my flanks and rear to an attack from the forces at Memphis and Corinth.

It was clear, to my mind, that if a successful attack could be made upon Corinth from the west and nor'hwest, the forces there driven back on the Tennessee and cut off, Bolivar and Jackson would easily fall, and then upon the arrival of the exchanged prisoners of war, West Tennessee would soon be in our possession, and communication with General Bragg effected through Middle Tennessee. The attack on Corinth was a military necessity, requiring prompt and vigorous action. It was being strengthened daily under that astute soldier, General Rosencrans; convalescents were returning to fill his ranks; new levies were arriving to increase his brigades, and fortifications were being constructed at new points, and it was very evident that unless a sudden and vigorous blow could be struck there, at once, no hope could be entertained of driving the enemy from a base of operations so convenient; that in the event of misfortune to Bragg, in Kentucky, the whole valley of the Mississippi would be lost to us before winter. To have waited for the arrival, arming, clothing and organization of the exchanged prisoners would have been to wait for the enemy to strengthen themselves more than we could possibly do. With these reflections, and after mature deliberation, I determined to attempt Corinth. I had a reasonable hope of success. Field returns at Ripley showed my strength to be about twenty-two thousand men. Rosencranz at Corinth had about fifteen thousand, with about eight thousand additional men at outposts, from twelve to fifteen miles distant. I might surprise him, and carry the place before these troops could be brought in. I therefore marched towards Pocahontas, threatening Bolivar, then turned suddenly across the Hatchie and Tuscumbia and attacked Corinth without hesitation, and did surprise that place before the outpost garrisons were called in. It was necessary that this blow should be sudden and decisive, and if unsuccessful, that I should withdraw rapidly from the position between the two armies of Ord and Rosencrans. The troops were in fine spirits, and the whole army of West Tennessee seemed eager to emulate the armies of the Potomac and of Kentucky. No army ever marched to battle with prouder steps, more hopeful countenances, or with more courage, than marched the army of Tennessee out of Ripley, on the morning of the 29th day of September, on its way to Corinth. Fully alive to the responsibility of my position as commander of the army, and after mature and deliberate reflection, the march was ordered. The ground was well known to me, and required no study to determine where to make the attack. The bridge over the Hatchie was soon reconstructed, and the army crossed at four o'clock, A. M., on the 2d of October. Adams' brigade of cavalry was left to guard this approach to our rear, and to protect the train which was parked between the Hatchie and Tuscumbia. Col. Hawkins' regiment of infantry and Capt. Dawson's battery of artillery were also left in the Bone Yard road, in easy supporting distance of the bridge. The army bivouacked at Chewalla, after the driving in of some pickets from that vicinity by Armstrong's and Jackson's cavalry. This point is about ten miles from Corinth.

At day-break, on the 3d, the march was resumed, the precaution having been taken to cut the railroad between Corinth and Jackson with a squadron of Armstrong's cavalry. Lovell's division in front kept the road on the south side of the Memphis and Charleston railroad. Price, after marching on the same road about five miles, turn--

ed to the left, crossing the railroad, and formed line of battle in front of the outer line of entrenchments, and about three miles from Corinth. Lovell formed line of battle, after some heavy skirmishing, (having to construct a passage across the dry bed of Indian creek for his artillery, under fire,) on the right and in front of the same line of entrenchments.

The following was the first order of battle. The three brigades. of Lovell's division, Villepigue's, Bowen's and Rust's in line, with reserve in rear of each; Jackson's cavalry brigade on the right in echelon. The left flank of the division on the Charleston railroad. Price's corps on the left, with the right flank resting on the same road. Maury's division on the right with Moore's and Phifer's brigade in line—Cabell's in reserve. Hebert's division on the left with Gates' and Martin's brigade in line—Colbert's in reserve. Armstrong's cavalry brigade on the extreme left, somewhat detatched and out of view. Hebert's left was masked behind a timbered bridge, with orders not to bring it into action until the last moment. This was done in hopes of inducing the enemy to weaken his right by reinforcing his centre and left, where the attack was first to be made, that his right might be forced.

At ten o'clock, all skirmishers were driven into the entrenchments, and the two armies were in line of battle, confronting each other in force. A belt of fallen timber, or abatis, about four hundred yards in width extended along the whole line of entrenchments. This was to be crossed. The attack commenced on the right by Lovell's division, and extended gradually to the left, and by half-past 10 o'clock the whole line of outer works was carried, several pieces of artillery being taken. The enemy made several ineffectual efforts to hold their ground, forming line of battle at advantageous points, and resisting obstinately our advance to the second line of detached works. I had been in hopes that one day's operations would end the contest and decide who should be the victors on this bloody field; but a ten miles' march over a parched country, on dusty roads, without water, getting into line of battle in forests with undergrowth, and the more than usual activity and determined courage displayed by the enemy, commanded by one of the ablest Generals of the United States army, who threw all possible obstacles in our way that an active mind could suggest, prolonged the battle until I saw with regret the sun sink behind the horizon as the last shot of our sharpshooters followed the retreating foe into their innermost lines. One hour more of daylight, and victory would have soothed our grief for the loss of the gallant dead who sleep on that lost but not dishonored field. The army slept on their arms within six hundred yards of Corinth, victorious so far.

During the night three batteries were ordered to take position on the ridge overlooking the town from the west, just where the hills dip into the flat extending into the railroad depot, with instructions to open on the town at four o'clock, A. M. Hebert on the left was ordered to mass part of his division on his left; to put Cabell's brigade in echelon on the left also, (Cabell's brigade being detached from Maury's division for this purpose;) to move Armstrongs' cavalry brigade across the Mobile and Ohio railroad, and, if possible, to get some of his artillery in position across the road. In this order of battle he was directed to attack at daybreak with his whole force, swinging his left flank in towards Corinth, and advance down the Purdy ridge. Lovell on the extreme right, with two of his brigades in line of battle and one in reserve with Jackson's cavalry on the extreme right on College Hill, his left flank resting on the Memphis and Charleston railroad, was ordered to await in this order, or to feel his way along slowly with his sharp-shooters until Hebert was heavily engaged with the enemy on the left. He was then to move rapidly to the assault, and force his right inwards across the low grounds south-west of town. The centre, under Maury, was to move at the same time quickly to the front, and directly at Corinth. Jackson was directed to burn the railroad bridge over the the Tuscumbia during the night. Daylight came, and there was no attack on the left. A staff officer was sent to Hebert to enquire the cause. That officer could not be found.

Another messenger was sent, and a third; and about seven o'clock General Hebert came to my headquarters and reported sick. General Price then put Brigadier General Green in command of the left wing; and it was eight o'clock before the proper dispositions for the attack at this point were made. In the mean time, the troops of Maury's left became engaged with the enemy's sharp-shooters, and the battle was brought on, and extended along the whole centre and left wing, and I regretted to observe that my whole plan of attack was, by this unfortunate delay, disarranged. One brigade after another went gallantly into the action, and pushing forward through direct and crossfire, over every obstacle, reached Corinth, and planted their colors on the last stronghold of the enemy. A hand to hand contest was being enacted in the very yard of General Rosencrans' headquarts, and in the streets of the town. The heavy guns were silenced, and all seemed about to be ended when a heavy fire from fresh troops from Iuka, Burnsville and Rienze, that had succeeded in reaching Corinth in time, poured into our thinned ranks. Exhausted from loss of sleep, wearied from hard marching and fighting, companies in regiments without officers, our troops, (let no one censure them,) gave way. The day was lost! Lovell's division was at this time advancing pursuant to orders, and was on the point of assaulting the works when he received my orders to throw one of his brigades (Villepigue's,) rapidly to the centre to cover the broken ranks thrown back from Corinth, and to prevent a sortie. He then moved his whole division to the left and was soon afterwards ordered to move slowly back, and take position on Indian Creek, and prevent the enemy from turning our flank. The centre and left were withdrawn on the same road on which they approached, and being somewhat in confusion on account of loss of officers, fatigue, thirst, want of sleep, thinned ranks, and the nature of the ground, Villipigue's brigade was brought in opportunely and covered the road to Chewalla. Lovell came in the rear of the whole army, and all bivouscked again at Chewalla. No enemy disturbed the sleep of the weary troops. During the night I had a bridge constructed over the Tuscumbia, and sent Armstrong's and Jackson's cavalry, with a battery of artillery, to seize and hold Rienzi until the army came up, intending to march to and hold that point, but after consultation with General Price, who represented his troops to be somewhat disorganized, it was deemed advisable to return by the same road we came, and fall back towards Riply and Oxford. Anticipating that the Bolivar force would move out, and dispute my passage across the Hatchie Bridge, I pushed rapidly on to that point, in hopes of reaching and securing the bridge before their arrival; but I soon learned, by couriers from Colonel Wirt Adams, that I would be too late. I nevertheless pushed on with the intention of engaging the enemy until I could get my train and reserve artillery unparked and on the Bone Yard road to the crossing at Crumb's mills, (this road branches off South from the State line road about two and a half miles West of the Tuscumbia bridge, running South or up the Hatchie.) No contest of long duration could be made here, as it was evident that the army of Corinth would soon make its appearance on our right flank and rear. The trains and reserve artillery were therefore immediately ordered on the Bone Yard road, and orders were sent to Armstrong and Jackson to change their direction, and cover the front and flank of the trains until they crossed the Hatchie, and then to cover them in front until they were on the Ripley road. The enemy were then engaged beyond the Hatchie bridge by small fragments of Maury's division as they could be hastened up and were kept in check sufficiently long to get everything off. General Ord commanded the forces of the enemy, and succeeded in getting into position before any number of our travel-worn troops could get into line of battle. It is not surprising, therefore, that they were driven back across the bridge, but they maintained their position on the hills overlooking it, under their gallant leader General Price, until orders were sent to fall back and take up their line of march on the Bone Yard road in rear of the whole train. At one time, fearing that the enemy, superior in numbers to the whole force I had in advance of the train, would drive us back, I ordered General Lovell to leave one brigade to guard the reserve to Tuscumbia bridge and to push forward with the other two to the front. This order was quickly executed and very soon the splendid brigades of Rust and Villepigue made their appearance close at hand.

The army corps of General Price was withdrawn, and Villepigue filed in and took position as rear guard to the army against Ord's forces. Rust was ordered forward to report to General Price, who was directed to cross the Hatchie at Crumb's mills, and take position to cover the crossing of the teams and artillery. Bowen was left at Tuscumbia bridge as rear guard against the advance of Rosencrans from Corinth, with orders to defend that bridge until the trains were unparked and on the road. Then to cross the bridge and burn it, and to join Villepigue at the junction of the roads. In the execution of this order, and whilst in position near the bridge, the head of the Corinth army made its appearance and engaged him, but was repulsed with heavy loss, and in a manner that reflected great credit on General Bowen and his brigade. The army was not again molested on its retreat to Riply, nor on its march to this place. The following was found to be our loss in the severest conflicts with the enemy, and on the march to and from Corinth, viz: Killed 594; wounded 2,162; prisoners and missing 2,102. One piece of artillery was driven in the night by a mistake into the enemy's lines and captured. Four pieces were taken at the Hatchie bridge, the horses being shot. Nine wagons were upset and abandoned by teamsters on the night's march to Crumb's mills. Some baggage was thrown out of the wagons, not amounting to any serious loss.

Two pieces of artillery were captured from the enemy at Corinth by General Lovell's division. One of which was brought off. Five pieces were also taken by General Price's corps, two of which were brought off. Thus making a loss to us of only two pieces. The enemy's loss in killed and wounded, by their own accounts, was over three thousand. We took over three hundred prisoners. Most of the prisoners taken from us were the stragglers from the army on the retreat.

The retreat from Corinth was not a rout, as it has been industriously represented by the enemy, and by the cowardly deserters from the army. The division of General Lovell formed line-of-battle, facing the rear, on several occasions, when it was reported the enemy was near; but not a gun was fired after the army retired from the Hatchie and Tuscumbia bridges. Nor did the enemy follow, except at a respectful distance. Although many officers and soldiers who distinguished themselves in the battle of Corinth, and in the affair of Hatchie bridge, came under my personal observations, I will not mention them to the exclusion of others, who may have been equally deserving, but who did not fall under my own eye. I have deemed it best to call on the different commanders to furnish me a special report, and a list of the names of the officers and soldiers of their respective commands who deserve special mention. These lists and special reports, I will take pleasure in forwarding, together with one of my own, when completed; and I respectfully request that they may be appended as part of my report. I cannot refrain, however, from mentioning here the conspicuous gallantry of a noble Texian, whose deeds at Corinth are the constant theme of both friends and foes. As long as courage, manliness, fortitude, patriotism and honor exist, the name of Rogers will be revered and honored among men. He fell in the front of the battle and died beneath the colors of his regiment, in the very centre of the enemy's stronghold. He sleeps, and glory is his sentence.

The attempt at Corinth has failed, and in consequence I am condemned, and have been superceded in my command. In my zeal for my country, I may have ventured too far with inadequate means, and I bow to the opinion of the people whom I serve. Yet I feel if the spirits of the gallant dead who now lie beneath the batteries of Corinth, see and judge the motives of men, they do not rebuke me, for there is no sting in my conscience. Nor does retrospection admonish me of error or of a disregard of their valued lives.

Very respectfully, sir, I am,
Your obedient servant,
EARL VAN DORN,
Major General.

REPORT OF MAJOR GENERAL PRICE OF THE BATTLES OF CORINTH AND DAVIS' BRIDGE.

HEADQUARTERS ARMY OF THE WEST, }
Holly Springs, Oct. 20th, 1862. }

MAJOR: I have the honor to submit the following report of the operations of this army, connected with the several engagements at Corinth and Davis' Bridge, of the 3d, 4th and 5th instants. Having arranged with Maj. Gen. Van Dorn to unite my forces with his for active operations, I joined him at Ripley on the 27th ultimo. My force at this time consisted of effective infantry, 10,498; effective cavalry, 2,437; effective artillery, 928 men and forty-four guns, including two 24-pounder howitzers and four rifled pieces of three and five-eighths calibre. The infantry was divided into two divisions, commanded by Brigadier Generals Maury and Hebert. Maury's division consisted of three brigades, commanded by Brigadier General Moore and Acting Brigadier Generals Cabell and Phifer. Hebert's division consisted of four brigades, commanded by Brigadier General Green and Cols. Martin, Gates and Colbert. The cavalry, except such companies as were on detached service, was under command of Acting Brig. Gen. Armstrong. The artillery was apportioned as follows, with Maury's division: Hoxton's battery, Lieut. Tobin commanding; Bledsoe's battery; McNally's battery, Lieut. Moore commanding; Lucas' battery, and Sengstack's battery. Hoxton's and Brown's battery; Sengstack's batteries were held as reserves, under command of Lieut. Burnett, acting Chief of Artillery of the division. With Hebert's division were Wade's, Landis', Guibo's, Dawson's and King's. The cavalry force, under Gen. Armstrong, reported to the Major General commanding the combined forces and afterwards acted under orders direct from him.

On the morning of the 30th ultimo we took up the line of march in the direction of Pocahontas, which place we reached on the 1st instant, and from which, we moved upon the enemy at Corinth, bivouacking on the night of the 2d instant at a point nearly opposite to Chewalla—having left one regiment of infantry and a section of artillery with the wagon train as a guard. At 4 o'clock on the morning of the 3d instant we resumed the march. My command moving on the main Pocahontas and Corinth road, in rear of Gen. Lovell's. At a point about a mile and half from the enemy's outer line of fortifications, my command made a detour to the left, with itstructions to occupy the ground between the Memphis and Charleston and Mobile and Ohio Railroads. This done, my line, Maury occupying the right and Hebert the left, with Cabell's and Colbert's brigades in reserve, fronted the enemy's works in a south-easterly direction, the right resting upon the Memphis and Charleston Railroad. While these dispositions were making, Gen. Lovell engaged the enemy upon our right; all being now ready for the attack, my line was ordered forward at about 10 o'clock, A. M. Almost simultaneously with the movement, the opposed armies became engaged in desperate conflict along the whole extent of my line. My command had scarcely cleared the position of its first formation, when entering an abatis of more than three hundred yards it became unmasked before a position naturally exceedingly formidable, and rendered trebly so by the extent of felled timber, through which it must be appproached; and the most approved and scientifically constructed entrenchment, bristling with artillery of large calibre, and supported by heavy lines of infantry. My troops charged the enemy's position with the most determined courage, exposed to a murderous fire of musketry and artillery. Without faltering they pressed forward over every obstacle, and with shouts and cheers carried, in less than twenty minutes, the entire line of works; the enemy having fled, leaving in our hands many prisoners, and two pieces of artillery; one a 4-inch Parrott gun, the other a 24-pounder howitzer. Our loss in this attack was comparatively small. This is attributable to the impetuosity with which the charge was made, and the works carried. It becomes my painful duty, in this connection, to revert to the distinguished services of two gallant officers who fell in this engagement. Col. John D. Martin, commanding a brigade of Mississippians, and Lieut. Samuel Farrington, of Wade's battery. Col. Martin, fell mortally wounded, while leading the charge against an angle in the enemy's works, exposed to the fire of enfilading batteries. The gallant bearing of this officer upon more than one bloody field, had won for him a place in the heart of every Mississippian and the admiration and confidence of his superior officers. Lieut. Farrington was struck and instantly killed by a shot from a rifled gun, while bringing one of the guns of his battery into position. This gallant soldier and courteous and chivalric gentleman, forgetful of personal interest and mindful of the necessities of the service only, resigned a lieutenant coloneley in the service of his State for a lieutenancy in the Confederate service, and gave up his life a glorious sacrifice upon the altar of his country's honor, in the seventh of the battles in which he has been conspicuous for cool, determined and effective bravery. Though young, his country mourns no more valiant defender, his command no abler commander, his friends no worthier recipient of their affection. The outer works being in our possession my line moved forward in pursuit of the retreating enemy until within about one mile of Corinth, where the enemy was encountered in position and in force. The necessary dispositions being made, my whole line again moved forward to the attack at about 3 o'clock, P. M. Here the fighting was of unparalleled fierceness along the whole extent of my line. The position of the enemy along the entire length of his lines was covered by fencing, heavy timber or underbrush. While portions of my troops advanced through open fields exposed to a deadly fire of batteries, operating over the enemy's line of infantry. Here, as in the assault upon the outer works, we had little artillery in action, it being impossible to procure such positions for my batteries as would enable them to co-operate effectively with the infantry. After continuous and most desperate fighting along the whole extent of my line, of nearly two hours duration, the enemy, notwithstanding his lines had been trebled by reinforcements, was driven from his positions and forced to take refuge in his innermost works in and around the town.

The troops of my command having nearly exhausted their ammunition in the heavy fighting through the day, were withheld from immediate pursuit, and the delay in procuring the necessary supply of ammunition forced me to close the fight for the day. My troops were withdrawn for cover, and laid on their arms during the night, in the position from which the enemy had been driven. About four o'clock on the morning of the fourth, three batteries of my command were placed in position and opened fire upon the town, under the immediate orders of the major general commanding. About daylight, orders were received to advance my whole line. In the execution of this order a delay was occasioned by the illness of Brigadier General Hebert, commanding a division. He was necessarily relieved from duty. The command devolved upon Brigadier General Green, who moved forward as soon as he could make the necessary disposition of his troops. It was after nine o'clock when my line became generally and furiously engaged with the enemy in his innermost and most formidable works, from which his infantry and artillery could jointly operate against my troops. Here, as in the previous actions, my artillery could not be effectively brought into action, and but few of the guns were engaged. The fighting, by my command, was almost entirely confined to the infantry. My men pressed forward upon the enemy, and with heavy loss succeeded in getting into the works, having driven him from them, capturing more than forty pieces of artillery, and forcing him to take refuge in the houses of the town, and in every place that would afford protection from our galling fire. He was followed and driven from house to house with great slaughter. In the town were batteries in mask, supported by heavy reserves, behind which the retreating enemy took shelter, and which opened upon our troops a most destructive fire at short range. My men held their positions most gallantly, returning the fire of the enemy with great spirit until portions of them exhausted their ammunition and were compelled to retire. This necessitated the withdrawal of the whole line, which was done under a withering fire. The attack was not resumed, and we fell back to our supply train, the men being almost exhausted from exertion and want of food and water. General Villepigue's brigade moved over to our assistance, but did not become engaged as the enemy was too badly cut up to follow us. We fell back in order to obtain water, some six miles from Corinth, where we bivouacked for the night, bringing off all of our artillery and arms, save one rifled piece which had been inadvertently driven into the enemy's line while going into battery before daylight in the morning, and had been left. We brought off, also, the two guns captured at the outer line of fortifications on the third. It is impossible for me to do justice to the courage of my troops in these engagements, nor can I discriminate between officers and commands where all behaved so nobly. This is the less necessary as the operations of my command were under the immediate observation of the major general commanding. For minute details of the actions, and particularly of the artillery, of the third and fourth instants, as well as for instances of person l and distinguished gallantry, I beg leave to refer the major general commanding to the reports of commanding officers herewith enclosed. On the morning of the fifth instant we resumed the march in the direction of Pocahontas, my command moving by division, Maury's in front, each in rear of its ordnance and supply train, except Moore's brigade which constituted the advance guard. After crossing the Tuscumbia, Moore's brigade was hurried forward to protect Davis' bridge across the Hatchie, which was threatened by an advance of the enemy. It being found that the enemy was in force, the remainder of Maury's division was ordered forward, and finally I was ordered to move up the whole of my command. Moore's brigade, with a section of the St Louis battery and Sengstack's battery were thrown across the Hatchie, but the enemy having possession of the heights commanding the crossing, as well as the position in which these troops were placed, and it being found that he was in very heavy force, it was deemed advisable to cross the Hatchie by another road, and these troops were withdrawn after serious loss to the east side of the Hatchie, where being joined by Cabell's and Phifer's brigades, and assisted by the batteries of McNally, Hogg, Landis, and Tobin, they effectually checked the advance of the enemy. Green's divisions, which had been delayed by passing the wagon train that had unparked near the Tuscumbia, arriving on the ground, was formed in line of battle, but the enemy making no further effort to advance, the whole of my command was moved off by another route, General Lovell's command being in our rear.

This was our last engagement with the enemy. In this last engagement we lost four guns, occasioned by the killing of horses. Our whole wagon train came off without molestation or loss, except of a few wagons that were broken down and had to be abandoned.

The history of the war contains no bloodier page, perhaps, than that which will record this fiercely contested battle The strongest expressions fall short of my admiration of the gallant conduct of the officers and men under my command. Words cannot add lustre to the fame they have acquired through deeds of noble daring, which, living through future time, will shed about every man, officer and soldier, who stood to his arms, through this struggle, a halo of glory as imperishable as it is brilliant.

They have won to their sisters and daughters the distinguished honor, set before them by a General of their love and admiration upon the event of an impending battle upon the same fields of the proud exclamation, "my brother, father, was at the great battle of Corinth." The bloodiest record of this battle is to come. The long list of the gallant dead upon this field will carry sorrow to the hearthstone of many a noble champion of our cause, as it does to the hearts of those who are to avenge them. A nation mourns their loss, while it cherishes the story of their glorious death, pointing out to their associate officers in this mighty struggle for liberty the pathway to victory and honor. They will live ever in the hearts of the admiring people of the government, for the establishment of which they have given their lives. Of the field officers killed, were Colonel Rogers, 2d Texas Infantry, who fell in the heart of town, of eleven wounds. Johnson, of 20th Arkansas, and Daly, of the 18th Arkansas. Lieutenant Colonels Maupin, 1st Missouri Cavalry, dismounted, and Leigh, 43d Mississippi; Majors Vaughan, 6th Missouri Infantry, Doudell, 21st Arkansas, and McDonald, 40th Mississippi. Many of my ablest and most gallant field officers are wounded, several mortally. Of this number are Colonels Erwin, 6th Missouri Infantry; Macfarland, 4th Missouri Infantry; Pritchard, 3d Missouri Infantry; Moore, 43d Mississippi, and McLean, 37th Mississippi; Lieutenant Colonels Pixler, 16th Arkansas; Hedgespeth, 6th Missouri Infantry; Serrell, 7th Mississippi Battalion; Lanier, 42d Alabama; Hobson, 3d Arkansas Cavalry; Matthews, 21st Arkansas; Campbell, 40th Mississippi, and Boone; and Majors Senteney, 2d Missouri Infantry; Keirn, 38th Mississippi; Staton, 37th Alabama; Timmins, 2d Texas; Jones, 21st Arkansas; Russell, 3d Louisiana, and Yates; and McQuiddy, 3d Missouri Cavalry. For other casualties in officers and men, I beg leave to refer to lists enclosed. I cannot close this report without recognizing the eminent services and valuable assistance of Brigadier Generals Maury, Hebert, (whose services I regret to have lost on the morning of the 4th by reason of his illness,) and Green, commanding divisions. I bear willing testimony to the admirable coolness, undaunted courage and military skill of these officers in disposing their respective commands, and in executing their orders. Through them I transmit to Brigadier General Moore, and acting Brigadier Generals Cabell, Phifer, Gates and Colbert my high appreciation of their efficient services on the field.

Their skill in manuevering their troops, and promptness and gallantry in leading them through the most desperate conflicts elicit my highest admiration. And of my troops as a body, I can say no juster or more complimentary words than that they have sustained and deepened and widened their reputation for exalted patriotism and determined valor.

To my personal staff I return my thanks for their promptness in the delivery of my orders, and their gallant bearing on the field.

All of which is respectfully submitted,
STERLING PRICE,
Major General.

Major M. M. Kinnall,
Assistant Adjutant General,
Army of West Tennessee.

MAJ. GEN. M. LOVELL'S REPORT OF THE OPERATIONS OF HIS DIVISION AT CORINTH.

HEADQUARTERS, 1ST DIVISION ARMY OF DIST. OF MISSISSIPPI,
Holly Springs, October 13th, 1862.

Major M. M. KIMMEL,

Assistant Adjutant General :

MAJOR: I have the honor to submit the following report of the part taken by my division in the recent operations around Corinth. On the 2d inst. the division repaired and crossed the Tuscumbia bridge, fifteen miles from Corinth, and moved forward, the cavalry under Armstrong and Jackson in advance. We moved to Chewalla, skirmishing lightly with the enemy several hours, and occupied the camp just abandoned, capturing some tents, quartermaster's and commissary's stores. On the 3d we moved forward, Villepigue's brigade in advance, skirmishing more heavily with a force of the enemy composed of two regiments of infantry, a section of artillery and some cavalry, until we drove them across Indian creek. At this point artillery fire became more frequent. Here we took an abandoned 12-pounder howitzer. The bridge was repaired, under fire, and I crossed the whole division, consisting of Rust's brigade on the right, Bowen's in the centre and Villepigue's on the left. The enemy occupied with his artillery a high hill at the crossing of the State line road with the Memphis and Charleston railroad, with rifle pits extending north and south, affording with the hill, a strong position for about 3,500 men. The skirmishers were there reinforced, and the whole line ordered to the assault, with reserve behind each brigade. The conflict was short and bloody. Our troops, emerging from the dense undergrowth, rushed upon the hill and rifle pits with the most determined gallantry, routed and drove off the enemy, causing them in their hasty retreat to abandon a 20-pounder Parrot gun and caisson with the limber of another gun. In this assault the following regiments are named as particularly distinguishing themselves, viz: the 9th Arkansas, Colonel Dunlop, and 3d Kentucky, Colonel Thompson, of Rust's brigade ; the 22d Mississippi, Captain Lester commanding ; Caruthers' Mississippi battalion, and the 1st Missouri regiment, Colonel Riley, of Bowen's brigade ; and the 3d Mississippi, Colonel Hurst, of Villepigue's brigade. The hill was carried mainly by the 9th Arkansas and 22d Mississippi, each vieing with the other in the dashing gallantry of their charge. The enemy's camps, half a mile beyond the position, were taken and held by the 1st Missouri regiment. Rust and Villepigue were thrown in advance, in line of battle, and Bowen's was posted on the hill until we should hear from Price's command, on our left. On our right front was a strong redoubt well flanked with infantry and with an abattis of felled timber, half a mile in width, extending around it in one direction, but with no obstructions to the north, in the direction of Price's right. This fact I communicated to the Major General commanding, and shortly afterwards the work was attacked and gallantly carried, from its right rear, by Moore's brigade, while Bowen was ordered to turn its left with his brigade from our side. Having replenished our ammunition, the whole division was moved forward and formed in line of battle on the bridge south of the railroad, Villepigue and Bowen in front and Rust in reserve. I received orders from the General commanding to move forward cautiously, feeling our way along the ridge to develop the position of the enemy.

Before advancing far, night put an end to the operations of an arduous and fatiguing, but glorious, day.

In the night, I was notified by the commanding General that early in the morning Price would open with a large battery of artillery and then attack in force with his left, and that while thus engaged, my division should pass forward and attack with vigor on our right. Accordingly, at day light, the division was moved forward, in line, along the ridge, for a mile and a half, with some very heavy firing of infantry on Villepigue's left, and artillery on Bowen's right. Rust, hitherto in reserve, moved up and occupied the centre, the line advancing until within a few hundred yards of two strong works of ten guns each, protected by heavy infantry forces. While reconnoitering these positions, with a view to the assault, I received an order from the commanding General to detach my strongest brigade to the support of Price's centre, which was being overpowered by large reinforcements of the enemy. This order was obeyed, and I was about to move the remaining brigades to the left, to close the gap made by detaching Villepigue, when the further order was received to retire, covering the retreat of the army. The division was withdrawn from under the very guns of the works without the slightest confusion, and in the most excellent order. Villepigue crossed the railroad and with his artillery, under Major Watts, put an effectual check upon the pursuit by the enemy's cavalry.

Rust's brigade was put in position on the hill carried the day before, until everything had been withdrawn across Indian creek, when he followed, bringing up the rear to Chewalla, where the division was reunited. The march was resumed on the 5th, this command acting as the rear guard to the army. Before reaching Tuscumbia bridge an order was received from the General commanding to press forward, with two brigades, to the support of Price, who was checked by large reinforcements of fresh troops at Hatchie bridge. Leaving Bowen's brigade as a rear guard on the Corinth road, Villepigue and Rust were pushed forward rapidly. The former, arriving first, was put in line of battle on the road to Hatchie bridge, to hold the enemy in check in that direction, while Rust was directed to proceed with General Price, in advance, to the crossing at Crumb's mills, where it was decided to pass the army over.

Villepigue held the enemy back with skirmishers. Bowen, however, was attacked in force, on the other road, but repelled the attack, with great slaughter to the enemy and but little loss to his own command. They were clear from the field when he crossed the Tuscumbia and burned the bridge, all the wagons having been passed over in safety. The 15th Mississippi distinguished itself particularly on this occasion. From the Hatchie to Hickory Flat (forty miles,) this division continued as the rear guard to the army, frequently forming line of battle when the enemy was reported to be coming too near, cheerfully toiling along through heat and dust and undergoing long marches, loss of sleep and want of food, with a fortitude worthy of the most unqualified admiration. Good order, discipline and subordination suffered no resolution under this severe and trying ordeal.

To the commanders of brigades, Generals Rust, Villepigue and Bowen, my thanks are especially due. Displaying their well known and approved gallantry on the field, they evinced sound judgment, discretion and ability in handling their troops, both in action and on the march, achieving signal success with small loss. The admirable condition in which the division returned to this point is the best proof of their merits. Surgeon Hawes, chief medical officer of the division, performed his duties quietly, systematically and with the utmost efficiency. Our wounded, with very few exceptions, were brought to this depot My thanks are due to the officers of my staff, Lieutenant Colonel Ivy, Captain Toutant and Captain Quitman for their assistance in the field, and in the conduct of the retreat. Being few in number, additional labor devolved upon them. Their duties were performed cheerfully, coolly and with a deliberate gallantry which caused me to repose the greatest confidence in them. The following named commanders of regiments are mentioned particularly by their brigade commanders for their courage and efficiency: Captain Ashford, 35th Alabama; Colonel Dunlop, 9th Arkansas; Captain Lester, 22d Mississippi; Colonel Riley, 1st Missouri; Colonel Hurst, 33d Missouri; Colonel Shelby, 39th Mississippi. For the names of other officers who particularly distinguished themselves, you are respectfully referred to the report of the brigade commanders herewith transmitted. Colonel Jackson, commanding cavalry brigade, acted under my orders during a portion of the time, always displaying a coolness, courage and efficiency for which he has heretofore been remarkable. The loss in my command, during the operations, was 77 killed, 285 wounded, and about 200 missing.

Respectfully submitted.

M. LOVELL,
Major General Commanding.

Report of Killed, Wounded and Missing in 1st Division of the Army of West Tennessee, near Corinth, Miss., on 3d, 4th and 5th Oct., 1862.

	Killed.	Wounded.	Missing.
1st brigade, Gen. Rust,	25	117	83
2d " " Villepigue,	21	76	71
3d " " Bowen,	26	92	40
Cavalry brigade, Col. Jackson,	1		
Bat'n. of Zouaves, Maj. Dupierre,	2		14
Totals,	77	285	208

RECAPITULATION.

Killed,	77
Wounded,	285
Missing,	208
Grand total,	570

HOLLY SPRINGS, Miss., October 15th, 1862.

OFFICIAL REPORT OF BRIGADIER GENERAL A. RUST, OF OPERATIONS NEAR CORINTH, ON 3D, 4TH, AND 5TH OCTOBER, 1862.

Head Quarters, 1st Brigade, 1st Division,
District of Mississippi, Holly Springs, Oct. 13, 1862.

Colonel: In response to Major General Lovell's circular of this date, I have the honor to submit the following report of the operations of my brigade near Corrinth, on the second, third and fourth inst. Moving from the Hatchie on Thursday, the second, my brigade in advance, when within eight miles of Corinth our cavalry came up with the enemc and reported his presence. In obedience to orders I immediately formed my brigade in line of battle, and threw forward two companies of the ninth Arkansas regiment as skirmishers. Advancing rapidly, encountering no opposition except a few straggling shots which were not responded to, we came directly upon an abandoned camp of the enemy, in which were a redoubt or two and some rifle pits. These were all abandoned, and after passing them, without halting an instant, some half mile or more, we were ordered to bivouac in line of battle. At four o'clock on the morning of the third, the division moved, General Villepigue in front, towards Corinth. When within three miles of the town, General Villepigue's skirmishers encountered those of the enemy. This was on the extreme right of the line adopted by the general commanding the division. This being my position, I immediately formed my men in front of the supposed position of the enemy, relieving General Villepigue. Major Gibson was ordered to deploy his (fourth Alabama) battalion as skirmishers, which order was promptly executed. The ninth Arkansas, Colonel Dunlop, was upon my left, and third Kentucky, Colonel Thompson, on my right. The seventh Kentucky, under Colonel Crossleve, was held in reserve.

These dispositions being made, an advance was ordered. Colonel Thompson on the extreme right, with a considerable interval between his regiment and the balance of the brigade, was purposely put in motion a short time before the other regiments were ordered forward. In a very short time the skirmishers of the opposing forces engaged each other. The engagement soon became general. On the right* the firing between Colonel Thompson, third Kentucky, and what was supposed to be two regiments of the enemy, posted on the South-side of the M. & C. R. R., was extremely animated. While following up the ninth Arkansas and thirty-first and thirty-fifth Alabama regiments in the direction whence came terrific vollies of shell, grape and cannister, I sent a staff officer to Colonel Thompson to know if he could continue to advance against the apparent odds opposed to him. He was pressing steadily forward, but was apprehensive his right might be turned. I instantly ordered the reserve regiment, seventh Kentucky, to his support. Officers and men seemed impatient for the order, and rushed impetuously forward, but only reached the scene of conflict to witness the flight of the enemy from it. Meanwhile the left wing advanced through a heavy fire of artillery and musketry towards the enemy's battery and the infantry that (behind trenches) supported it. The dense forest through which we passed, while it lasted, was a partial protection. As we emerged from it, with an unbroken line, in full view of the enemy in his strong position, beyond a deep cut in the railroad, not more than sixty yards distant in a straight line, the officers and men were subjected to a test that it is rarely the lot of soldiers to undergo. They were equal to the occasion. For a moment it appeared that the entire line would be swept away. The gaps that the enemy's artillery ploughed through the ranks, were closed up with the coolness and steadiness of veterans of a hundred fields. On my left Captain D. H. Norwood and Lieuts. Kennebrew and Moore fell, killed, and Lieuts. Ken and Baily, of the ninth Arkansas regiment, wounded, while on my right Captain Fulton was killed, and Captain Mitchell and Lieutenants Hunter, Lawler and Collice, of the thirty-fifth Alabama regiment, were severely wounded, bravely leading, and by their example inspiring their men with their own unquailing courage. In a few seconds I here lost over a hundred men and officers. To have halted or hesitated would have brought certain destruction upon my command. I ordered bayonets fixed and a charge made upon the battery. The order was obeyed with cheers and yells, and by making a detour to the left, to avoid the deep cut in the railroad, the ninth Arkansas was soon in possession of the enemy's strong position, (we had assaulted and taken one fine gun which the enemy was unable to get off) closely followed by the thirty-fif h Alabama, under Colonel Crump. After advancing some three hundred yards down the railroad, I halted and reformed my men and marched again to the South-side of the railroad, and remained in position until a fort and large camp in front of us was evacuated, in consequence of a most determined attack, by a portion of General Price's command, on their rear. Late in the evening I was ordered forward, and bivouacked in line of battle in the midst of the forts and camps of the enemy, and inside of an abattis which extended entirely around their exterior line of defence.

On the morning of Saturday, the fourth, the whole division advanced in line of battle towards the fortifications of the enemy on College Hill; General Villepigue on the left, General Bowen on the right, in front, and my own brigade following close in the rear as a reserve, to support either or both as occasion might require. When within two or three hundred yards of several forts, behind which long lines of infantry behind formidable looking breast-works, with abatis again in front, were plainly visable. The enemy opened a most rapid fire from their artillery, which my entire command sustained with the most gratifying steadiness, not an officer or man leaving his position or exhibiting, so far as I could perceive, the least discomposure. About nine and a half o'clock I moved my brigade to the front and left of the advance line occupied by General Bowen, who was ordered far to the right, and General Villepigue was withdrawn to reinforce a portion of General Price's line, which, after the most stubborn and heroic resistance to greatly superior numbers, of what was afterwards known to be fresh troops, was wavering. In a very short time it was announced by the major general commanding, that our friends on the left had been compelled to give way and abandon the field, and I was ordered to fall back to the position first taken from the enemy, near where the road from Chewalla to Corinth crosses the railroad, and there form line of battle in the most advantageous position to cover the retreat of our army. In perfect order, but as quickly as possible, I selected a line of great strength, with skirmishers displayed on a line a mile in extent and three quarters of a mile in advance of my main line, from which I could repel an advance of the enemy upon the two roads, and the railroad leading to Corinth, and awaited the withdrawal of our forces. Remaining exactly forty minutes after Colonel Riley passed, I moved my brigade in the direction taken by our retreating columns until I came to the field hospital, where I found eight wounded soldiers, only three of whom were willing to be moved. Two of them I had carried beyond the reach of the enemy on litters, the third was able to ride on a caisson. I then continued my march without again confronting the enemy during the entire retreat. The good conduct of officers and men in performing the responsible duty of rear guard to a retreating army, cannot be too highly commended. There was not a semblance of panic or disorder, or even unusual excitement during the entire retreat, upon which my brigade marched in better order and with more deliberation than it had done at all before, or has done since. The signal good conduct which they displayed on the field of battle or in the face of dangers and death, and the fortitude and constancy with which they sustained themselves afterwards under privations and hardships and sufferings, more trying to the soldier than the most appaling dangers, are, I trust, only an earnest to the country of what she may expect from them in the future. In conclusion it is only necessary to say of the third Kentucky, that Colonel Thompson and the men and officers under him, fully sustained the reputation they had won on other fields. The only regret of Colonel Crosslove and his men, of the seventh Kentucky, when ordered to the support of the third, was that this regiment stood so little in need of it. The conduct of the thirty-fifth Alabama, commanded by Captain Ashford, though deprived by illness of their accomplished Colonel, (Robertson) could not have been improved by the presence of any officer. The fourth Alabama battalion, under Major Gibson, deployed as skirmishers, performed well the part allotted to to them. The ninth Arkansas, under Colonel Dunlop, who was conspicuous for the activity and gallantry displayed in keeping his men in line, and moving steadily forward in the face of the deadly fire of the enemy's artillery, won the applause and admiration of all who witnessed its conduct. Its colors were borne by their intrepid sergeant, John. M. Pearce, upwards and onwards without faltering during the hottest of the fire, while his comrades were falling thick and fast around him. When all behaved so well, the commanding general will not hazard injustice by mentioning those who particularly attracted his notice. I regret that a sense of duty to the service and of justice to the balance of the brigade, will not allow me to bestow the same unmixed praise upon the thirty-first Alabama regiment. A portion of this regiment, in spite of the gallantry of their colonel and his efforts to make them do their duty, following the example of some of its commissioned officers, behaved disgracefully. At a most critical moment it broke in disorder and all efforts to restore it were unavailing. I called the attention of their colonel to the misconduct of several officers, whose example was evidently demoralizing to the men, and ordered them to surrender their swords and leave the field. Upon their earnest entreaties to be tried again, I permitted them to retain their swords and remain, with the hope and belief that hereafter their conduct may be in harmony with the brave members of the same regiments, whose conduct could not suffer by comparison with other commanders in the brigade.

I withhold their names, though there can be no controversy as to the regiments that were first in the strong position abandoned by the enemy and in possession of the Lady Richardson which in their flight they left behind them. It is due to the right wing of General Bowen's admirable brigade, the twenty-second Mississippi, under Lieutenant Colonel Lester, to acknowledge that their advance upon our left and the right of the enemy's battery, attracted a portion of its fire, in concert with our advance greatly facilitated its capture, entitled them to a full share of the honor.

I would here express my obligations to Captain Fall and Lieutenants Anderson, Ayers and Bertrand, of my staff, for the prompt and intelligent manner in which they executed my orders. Lieutenant Sweeny, in command of the Hudson Battery attached to my brigade, had no opportunity to participate in the action, but executed quickly and cheerfully every order addressed to him.

Casualties on the field and upon the retreat, twenty-five killed, one hundred and seventeen wounded and eighty-three missing.

The dense forest of heavy timber and thick undergrowth, under cover of which the brigade advanced until within a few rods of the enemy's battery, accounts for the comparatively small number of killed and wounded.

       (Signed,)   A. RUST,
    Brigadier General commanding First Brigade,
     First Division, Army of the District of Miss.

(Official copy,)
  EDWARD IVY, *Lieut. Col. and A. A. G.*

OFFICIAL REPORT OF BRIGADIER GENERAL JOHN S. BOWEN OF PART TAKEN BY HIS BRIGADE IN THE ACTIONS OF THE 3D, 4TH AND 5TH, AT AND NEAR CORINTH, MISSISSIPPI.

HEADQUARTERS 3D BRIGADE, LOVELL'S DIVISION,
Holly Springs, October 12, 1862.

To Lieutenant Colonel EDWARD IVEY,
    Assistant Adjutant General:

SIR: I have the honor to forward herewith reports from my several commands in regard to the part taken by them in the actions of the third, fourth and fifth instants, at and near Corinth. It will be seen that, passing over the deployments between Chewalla and the creek west of Corinth, where the enemy's outposts were driven in with little or no resistance, this brigade first formed line of battle to the east of Cypress creek, with Rust's brigade on its right and Villepigue's on the left. A heavy line of skirmishers, composed of the first Missouri regiment and the Mississippi battalion of sharpshooters proceeding in advance, supported by the twenty-second and fifteenth Mississippi regiments in line, and the sixth Mississippi regiment (Colonel Lowry) and Watson battery (Captain Bursley) in reserve.

The line advanced steadily, forcing back the enemy's sharpshooters into their entrenchments, and, pushing on, charged their works, capturing their battery at the salient near the railroad and driving their entire infantry force from the trenches. Rust's and Villepigue's carrying the trenches in front of them about the same time, rendered the work comparatively easy for my brigade. The twenty-second Mississippi regiment (Captain Lester commanding) deserves special mention for their gallant charge on this occasion. The Mississippi battalion of sharpshooters (Captain Caruthers commanding) were conspicuous for their coolness and courage, also for joining the twenty-2d Miss. regiment in the charge in which they captured the battery. The first Missouri regiment, gathering in, charged, while deployed as skirmishers, and drove the enemy from the trenches before I could reach the position with the fifteenth Mississippi regiment, which was advancing towards the same point. The first Missouri regiment, Lieutenant Colonel Riley commanding, proceeding onward, drove the enemy from one of their encampments nearly a mile inside of their works, holding the same, under fire, until the second line of battle was formed, towards sunset, for the attack on the right. The enemy having abandoned the works our right, the second line, above above alluded to, advanced and occupied their encampments, capturing a few stragglers in the evening. On the morning of the fourth, the brigade was formed in accordance with instructions received the night before, immediately in advance of the encampment occupied, and advanced steadily with Villepigue on its left and Rust in reserve, the whole moving together. Arriving within six hundred yards of a strong redoubt, supported on the right and left by a similar work, with a formidable line of infantry entrenched connecting them, it was halted, and afer a protracted skirmish, which failed to develop the enemy's strength on the position, I determined, in absence of the major general commanding, to feel them more effectually and force them to show their strength. The Watson battery (four guns) was ordered to open the works immediately in our front, and during the second round, was answered by a terrific cannonade from the right, left and front, convincing me that the information given that there were only three guns at this point was erroneous, as I had thus developed at least twenty. The battery was ordered to the rear, and after the firing abated slightly, I moved the brigade a short distance to the rear near Rust's line, in order to take advantage of the ground and save it from a repetition of the galling fire which had opened upon them.

The brigade's loss, during this shelling, was about fifty men killed and wounded, and the whole command deserves special commendation for their coolness under fire. After remaining for some time (two hours) in the new position, our skirmishers keeping up a continuous fire on our front and right, and after Villepigue had repelled the attack made on his line and moved to the left, my brigade was ordered to the rear, while Rust formed line of battle beyond, at the salient, near the railroad crossing. The first Missouri regiment, deployed as skirmishers, covered the rear of both brigades. The command, after a successful evacuation, camped at Chewalla about sunset. Detailed, on the morning of the fifth, as the rear guard of the army, the brigade left its encampments, in rear of the train, at about ten A. M., marching slowly, very much annoyed and delayed by the wagons. At twelve M., the enemy's advance overtook us, and I formed line of battle with the Mississippi battalion and one section of artillery under Lieutenant Barlow in advance, our line then fronting the enemy. The attack was made by their cavalry and vigorously repulsed by two companies of Jackson's cavalry and the Mississippi battalion, and their rout completed by the rapid and effective fire of Lieutenant Barlow's section. Resuming the retreat we were not again molested, until compelled to halt, for several hours, at the Tuscumbia river bridge, allowing the wagons to cross. The enemy arrived at our position near the bridge about sunset. Deploying, they endeavored to turn my left in order to cut me off from the bridge, at the same time advancing strongly on my front and centre. After heavy skirmishing, well maintained on both sides, and some artillery firing by the enemy, they advanced boldly in front of my centre opposite the fifteenth Mississippi regiment. Taking command of this regiment in person, I advanced it about fifteen paces, and then poured a deliberate, well-aimed and simultaneous volley. This fire, which was handsomely seconded by several rounds of canister by Binley's first section under Lieutenant Toledano, on our immediate right, which enfiladed their line, followed up a rapid, well-aimed and continuous file fire from the fifteenth Mississippi regiment, must have proved destructive, as the advance was not only thus checked, but their whole force fled from the field. I then crossed the Tuscumbia at my leisure, tore up and burnt the bridge, obstructed the ford near by, and joined the division about three miles beyond. My loss in the action of the Tuscumbia was two or three killed and eight or ten wounded. This brigade was subsequently detailed as the rear guard of the army, but had no other engagement with the enemy. I have the honor to transmit herewith a full list of the killed, wounded and missing in the three days' actions alluded to. The officers of my staff were present and untiring in the discharge of their respective duties. In addition to the assistance given by my adjutant general, Captain Hutchinson, my inspector general, Captain Percy, and Lieutenant Carter, aid-de-camp, I am indebted to Caldwell, of the Watson battery, for bearing orders in the field. All of these gentlemen were conspicuous for coolness and courage during the action and on the retreat.

In closing, I would call the attention of the division commander to the unexampled courage and endurance displayed by the troops, who, under hardships and privations which can only be appreciated by those who experienced them, never faltered in the discharge of their arduous duties. The exceptions mentioned in the report of Colonel Farrel, fifteenth Mississippi regiment, were conspicuous in a brigade which acted so well that they deserve to be immediately punished. I know of no better way of rewarding the two thousand brave men than by casting out the two or three cowards who happen to be among them. I, therefore, recommend that second Lieutenant S. T. Clark, Co. A, fifteenth Mississippi regiment, be dismissed in disgrace, and that corporal Bennett and privates Applegate and Spiney, Co. B, be drummed out of the service, and their names published with the sentence attached.

Very respectfully,

JOHN S. BOWEN,
Brigadier General commanding.

REPORT OF BRIGADIER GENERAL JOHN B. VILLEPIGUE OF OPERATIONS OF BRIGADE BEFORE CORINTH.

HEADQUARTERS 2D BRIGADE, 1ST DIVISION,
Army of District of the Mississippi, October 14th, 1862.

Lieutenant Colonel EDWARD IVEY,

Assistant Adjutant General, First Division, Army District of the Miss.:

COLONEL: I have the honor to submit the following report of the operations of the second brigade, in the actions before Corinth on the third and fourth instants:

In approaching Corinth on the third instant, the second brigade was in advance. An outpost of the enemy was met about five miles from the fortress, and driven into the outer entrenchments without much opposition. On reaching a creek about three miles from the fortress and quite near the outer entrenchments, the march of the column was delayed for some time by the enemy's artillery and from the bridge over the creek having been destroyed. The passage, however, was effected in good time, and the brigade was engaged in heavy skirmishing with the enemy until the other brigades of the division had crossed and taken up their positions. The whole division then advanced, the second brigade being on the extreme left. The enemy were driven steadily before us until we came in view of the outer entrenchments or rifle pits. Our onward course was here checked for a short time, in consequence of the deadly fire of the enemy, and the nature of the obstructions in front of us.

After a slight pause, the thirty-third Mississippi (Colonel D. W. Hurst, commanding) charged the entrenchments, and drove the enemy from them in gallant style. In consequence of the dense thickness of the undergrowth, I had lost sight of all of my regiments except the thirty-third Mississippi, so that after capturing the entrenchments, considerable time elapsed before my scattered regiments could be collected and the line reformed. During the rest of the day the brigade was engaged in executing orders from the major general commanding the division, but was not actively engaged with the enemy. Early the following morning, the brigade advanced as directed until under the fire of the enemy's artillery, which, together with the fire from the enemy's sharpshooters, was very heavy, causing many casualties. Under the circumstances, the conduct of the troops was excellent, and could not be surpassed. Later in the morning, it became necessary to fall back from this advanced position, to defeat an attempt of the enemy to turn my left flank, which was accomplished in good order, and the enemy repulsed in gallant style, and with considerable loss. This last action having caused the whole left wing of the army to attack the enemy's right, the enemy did not again appear in my immediate front, and the brigade remained idle until ordered across the railroad to cover the movements of the left wing of the army, which had been withdrawn. While performing this service, the enemy's cavalry once appeared in sight, and it became necessary to disperse them, which was done by Major G. O. Watts, by a few rounds from one of his batteries. I wish to mention for conspicuous gallantry Colonel D. W. Hurst, thirty-third Mississippi regiment, who drove the enemy from their entrenchments, at the head of his regiment, with empty guns. Colonel W. B Shelby, thirty-ninth Mississippi regiment, who rallied his men at great personal risk from a partial disorder into which they had been thrown by a flank fire of the enemy. The following officers of my staff were with me on the field, and rendered me important service in conveying orders, etc. Captain Kinlock Falconer, Assistant Adjutant General, and Major J. P. Carr, A. C. S., and Captain Belton, A. Q. M.

I transmit the reports of the different regimental commanders, giving the detailed operations of the respective commands. I also enclose a list of the killed, wounded and missing.

I am, Colonel, very respectfully,
Your obedient servant,
JOHN B. VILLEPIGUE,
Brigadier General commanding.

REPORT OF BRIGADIER GENERAL MAURY (COMMANDING DIVISION) OF ACTION AT CORINTH AND HATCHIE BRIDGE 3D, 4TH AND 5TH OCTOBER, 1862.

HEADQUARTERS MAURY'S DIVISION,
Camp on Tippah, October 10th, 1862.

Captain J. M. LOUGHBOROUGH,
Assistant Adjutant General:

CAPTAIN: I have the honor to report that this division of the army of the West moved from Ripley towards Corinth on the 30th September, numbering 3,890 infantry, five light batteries of four guns each and 881 cavalry. On the morning of October third we moved, at daylight, from our camp near Chewalla to attack the enemy in Corinth. The division was formed in line of battle near Walker's house, North of the Memphis and Charleston railroad. Moore's brigade, with its right resting near the railroad; Phifer's brigade was formed on Moore's left, extending to Hebert's division; and Cabell's brigade was held in reserve. The line faced Corinth and the enemy's advanced line of entrenchments.

The sharp-shooters of Moore's and Phifer's brigades, under Colonels Rogers, Sherman and Bridges, soon became briskly engaged with those of the enemy, and forced them back into their entrenchments. At ten, A. M., our whole line moved forward, and the strong outworks of the enemy were carried without check. Moore and Phifer at once pushed on toward Corinth in pursuit of the retreating enemy. When within little more than a mile of the town they were halted. Moore was moved towards his right to unite with the line of Gen. Lovell, which was advancing along the South-side of the Memphis and Charleston railroad and soon encountered a heavy force of the enemy, whom, after a fierce contest, he drove before him. Soon afterwards he was reinforced by two regiments of Cabell's brigade, under Colonels Johnson and Dockery. The advance was then resumed and Moore soon became hotly engaged with the enemy, occupying a fieldwork, or entrenched camp. This he carried by assault, capturing the camp and its stores. Phifer, advancing, was met near the Mobile and Ohio railroad by a strong force of the enemy, whom, after an obstinate combat, attended with a heavy loss on both sides, he drove back into Corinth and was then halted with his left resting within four hundred yards of the Mobile and Ohio railroad, his right being a little thrown back. Cabell was sent to support Phifer's right now seperated by a wide space from Moore, and was soon afterwards withdrawn to support Hebert's, who was threatened by a flank movemet of the enemy towards his extreme left. About dark Moore was drawn in towards his left, until his line united with Phifer's; and the troops lay on their arms in these positions all night. Just before daylight, Major Burnett placed the batteries of Tobin, Sengstack and McNally upon an advanced ridge about six hundred yards from Corinth, and opened fire upon the town. One of their pieces, while taking position, being thrown by Captain Tobin rather too far beyond his support, was surprised and captured by the enemys' sharp-shooters. Captain Tobin was made prisoner at the same time. At daylight all of those guns were withdrawn, and the fire of the division was maintained by the sharp-shooters only, who, boldly and incessantly, under Rodgers, Sterman and Bridges, harassed the enemy. I had been ordered to await the attack of Hebert's division on my left before advancing to storm the town. Soon after nine o'clock the firing upon my left became sharp, and Moore and Phifer were at once advanced. Cabell's brigade was moved closer up and held in reserve. In a few minutes the fusilade became general along the whole line of the army of the West; and Cabell's brigade was ordered in to support of Gates' brigade the next on Phifer's left. The brigades of Generals Moore, Phifer and Cabell were gallantly led by their commanders to the assault of the enemy's work in the heart of Corinth. They carried them, planted their colors within them, drove the enemy from them, and held them until forced back by the overwhelming reserves of the enemy. The division was then reformed and marched back to encamp near Chewalla. Next morning it moved towards Pocahontas. When within five miles of Davis' bridge, couriers from Colonel Wirt Adams, who had been guarding that point, apprised us that the enemy was advancing in force to seize it before we could cross. Moore's brigade, now reduced to about 300 men, was pushed forward, and with the St. Louis battery and two guns taken from the enemy at Corinth, (all under Major Burnett's orders,) marched across the bridges and formed with the view of storming the heights of Metamoras; but they were too few and too late. The enemy's artillery and infantry, already in position, swept them away and were close upon the bridge before Phifer's brigade, commanded by Colonel Ross, could cross and form and meet them; (we lost four of our guns here.) Nothing remained for us now but to dispute the enemy's passage over the bridge, and to hold him in check as long as possible. This was gallantly done for more than an hour by the remnants of Moore's, Phifer's and Cabell's brigades, and by the batteries of Hogg, Sengstack Dawson, Lieutenant Moore and Lieutenant Miles, superintended by Major Burnett. They were all then ordered to retire and take up a position within the timber. This was done in good order, and the enemy not advancing, the whole division was withdrawn and put upon the march by another route, our rear being covered by General Villepigue's brigade. Last night, the division bivoucked at this point. I enclose herewith the reports of the several brigade commanders, and refer you to them for more detailed accounts of these actions than I can give. I can bear honest testimony to the fidelity and valor of the officers and troops under my command. The instances of gallant conduct would include too many for me to mention here.

But there are two men of humble rank whose conspicuous courage and energy at Davis' bridge attracted general attention and admiration. One is Earnest Goolah, chief bugler of Ross' regiment; the other is Benjamin J. Chandler, a private of Co. " C," Slemm's cavalry. I recommend them to the most favorable considerations of the General commanding as worthy of the honors due to conspicuous courage upon the battle-field. My staff officers were always prompt, intelligent and gallant.

I enclose the reports of our losses. You will observe that they have been very heavy. But, sir, we remember that our noble dead fell in the streets and in the innermost fortifications of Corinth, and that our torn colors have floated in triumph over the very stronghold of the foe.

I am, sir, very respectfully yours,
DABNEY H. MAURY,
Major General Commanding Division.

(Official Copy.)
MACERAN, *Assistant Adjutant General.*

REPORT OF BRIG. GEN. GREEN OF THE ACTIONS OF THIRD, FOURTH AND FIFTH INSTANTS.

Acting Adjutant General, Army of the West:

Sir: I have the honor to submit the following report of the part taken by that portion of the army under my command in the recent engagement at Corinth.

On the morning of the third instant, being in command of the third brigade of the first division, commanded by Brigadier General Hebert, I was ordered to take position on the left of the fourth brigade, forming a line in front of and about three or four hundred yards from the enemys' outer breast works. Scarcely was the line formed when the enemy opened upon us with great fierceness a fire of shell and grape, doing us, however, but little harm, wounding a few men. About twelve o'clock we were ordered to advance; our skirmishers being in front of our lines, soon drove the enemy's skirmishers inside of the fortifications, where they endeavored to make a stand, and opened upon us with musketry. We continued to advance rapidly; the enemy fled, and we took possession of the fortifications. The order being still to move forward, we moved in line until we came to an open field, where the enemy opened upon us a murderous fire from two batteries placed upon a hill beyond. I halted the brigade and ordered Captains Landis and Geuber with their batteries to take position and fire upon the enemy. We here had a brisk artillery fight which lasted about three quarters of an hour. Our batteries having driven those of the enemy from their position, I then advanced my brigade until I came to another field where I found the enemy in line, under the cover of a fence on the far side of the field, awaiting our approach Here we saw danger ahead, with a battery and line of infantry firing upon us from the left, and a heavy fire in front. We moved forward at double-quick across the open field to meet the enemy. Here was an unceasing fire of musketry for about one and a half hours, and as we would break the lines of the enemy they would bring fresh troops. I sent to Colonel Gates, whose brigade was not engaged, to try and relieve us of the cross fire on the left, which he did by sending to my support the second Missouri infantry, Colonel Cockerel commanding. We then soon succeeded in driving the enemy from the field, but not until we had lost many brave and gallant officers and soldiers. During this engagement I was enabled to see the whole length of my brigade, consisting of three Missouri and two Mississippi regiments, and I am proud to say there was no faltering, but all seemed eager for the combat. And nobly did they sustain it; no troops could have done better, nor could I distinguish between the regiments which behaved the most gallantly; each did vigorously the work assigned it. In this charge we lost largely in officers. Colonels Erwin and McFarland and Lieutenant Colonels Ferrell and Hedgespeth were wounded. Colonel Ferrell fell while urging his men forward; he was at least twenty yards in advance of his command. I fear he will never again be able to take the field. In him we lose a gallant officer. Lieutenant Colonel Leigh of the forty-third Mississippi fell while gallantly leading his wing of the regiment. Major McQuiddy was severely wounded. Major Vaughan of the sixth Missouri was killed. While leading this charge several officers of the line were killed, among whom were the following: Captain Taylor, Captain McKinney, Captain Graves.

After the enemy fell back and the firing ceased, we gathered up the wounded and advanced our lines some two hundred yards beyond where the enemy had fought us, and slept on our arms all night.

About daylight, leaving our skirmishers out, we fell back about one hundred yards under cover of the hill, in order to get some refreshments. Before we were done eating, the enemy opened their batteries upon us most furiously.

Just at this time I received a message from General Hebert, informing me that he was unable to take the field, and that the command of the division would devolve upon me; in a few minutes I received an order from General Price placing me in command.

The command of the third brigade now devolved upon Colonel Moore of the forty-third Mississippi regiment.

At the time of assuming command I found the brigades placed as follows: the third brigade on the left of General Phifer, its left resting near the Mobile and Ohio railroad; first brigade (Colonel Gates) on its left, fronting the railroad; the fourth brigade (Colonel McLean) on its left; and the second brigade (Colonel Colbert) in reserve. I immediately sent for the second brigade and placed it in line where the third was, and held the third in reserve. In this position we skirmished for a short time with the enemy. Receiving word from Colonel McLean (commanding fourth brigade) that there was danger of his left being turned by the enemy, and that if attempted he would be unable to prevent it, I ordered the second to move to the left of the fourth, placing the third in its original position. I then ordered a forward movement, directing the second and fourth to move forward in echelon, throwing the left forward so as to come to a charge at the same time of the night.

At the time I ordered the forward movement I sent for reinforcements, believing that we would need them, for I could see the enemy had two lines of fortifications bristling with artillery and strongly supported by infantry. Our lines moved across the railroad, advancing slowly and steadily, our skirmishers constantly fighting with those of the enemy, driving them back. When within two hundred yards the command was ordered to charge at a double quick. The whole line now moved forward with great rapidity. Officers and men all seemed eager to be foremost in reaching the fortifications, but it was a hard road to travel, climbing over logs, brush and fallen timber, while masked batteries of the enemy opened upon us at almost every step with great slaughter, but nothing daunted, the divisions pressed forward. The first brigade (Colonel Gates commanding) arriving at the fortifications drove the enemy from their entrenchments, taking about forty pieces of artillery. The fourth and second brigades having worse roads, and the distance being greater, only a portion of them were able to reach the entrenchments, and the left being in danger of being out-flanked, fell back. Lieutenant Colonel Maupin, of the first Missouri cavalry, (serving as infantry,) fell while gallantly leading his regiment in the charge on the enemy's fortifications, bearing his regimental colors. Colonel Moore I fear was mortally wounded while leading the third brigade on a charge in town; he fell near the depot and was left on the field.

Colonel McLean commanding fourth brigade was severely wounded in the charge. Major McQuiddy, who was wounded on the day before in the arm, but would not leave his command, (third Missouri cavalry,) was severely wounded in the thigh. Major Yates of the thirty-sixth Mississippi was also wounded, as was also Colonel Pritchard, of the third Missouri infantry. Reinforcements again being sent for, General Cabell came up with his brigade, but before he could get to the fortifications, Colonel Gates' ammunition was exhausted and he fell back. The fire then became terrific. General Cabell was unable to retake the fortifications, and the whole line fell back on the hill, in rear of the batteries. Here I received orders to move the division back on the hill beyond the Memphis and Charleston railroad. Before reaching that point, I received an order to continue the march until further orders.

We encamped early in the evening on the right of the road opposite. Sunday morning I was ordered to resume the march, marching in the rear of Gen. Maury's division. Before reaching the Hatchie, I received an order to push forward, "that General Maury's division had engaged the enemy on the Hatchie, and needed assistance." I pushed forward as rapidly as the men could posibly travel; when we arrived, however, we found General Cabell's force falling back in good order I was ordered to form on the left of a road in a field, behind the fence. We threw out skirmishers who soon engaged those of the enemy, and drove them back. The fourth brigade came upon a body of the enemy's skirmishers, charged and repulsed them. We here lay still for about a half an hour, the enemy in sight, every minute expecting to move forward, but, instead, we received orders to "fall back," which we did without any interruption of the enemy, though they still continued throwing shell as they had been doing all the time; here I had three or four men slightly wounded. I was then ordered to move my division out on the "Bone Yard road." At the crossing of the Hatchie I received orders to proceed to the Ripley road, and bivouack for the night, which I did in line along the road toward Pocahontas, throwing out pickets to give notice of the approach of the enemy. The next morning I resumed the march in good order towards Ripley. During the fight and on the retreat, both officers and soldiers have shown themselves as brave as the most sanguine could desire. *All did their duty well*, and were I to particularize I would not know where to begin. I cannot, however, refrain from acknowledging my obligations to Captain Wm. B. Pittman, for his promptness in carrying an order through the field when the very atmosphere seemed filled with shot, shell, grape and canister; also to Major Theo. Johnson, who acted as voluntary aid, and who conveyed orders with great dispatch through the hottest firing, regardless of danger.

       Very respectfully,
        Your obedient servant,
          MARTIN E. GREEN,
      Brigadier General, Commanding Division.

October 19th, 1862.

REPORT OF BRIGADIER GENERAL CABELL, OF THE PART TAKEN BY HIS BRIGADE IN THE ACTION AT AND NEAR CORINTH, ON THE 3D, 4TH AND 5TH INSTANTS.

HEADQUATERS CABELL'S BRIGADE,
Maury's Division, October 10th, 1862.

To Captain FLOWERREE,
Assistant Adjutant General, Maury's Division:

CAPTAIN: I have the honor to report the part taken by my command in the engagements before Corinth, on the third and fourth, and at the Hatchie bridge, on the fifth instant.

My brigade consisted of the eighteenth, nineteenth, twentieth and twenty-first Arkansas regiments, Jones' battalion of Arkansas volunteers, Rapley's battalion of sharpshooters and the Appeal battery, under Lieutenant Hogg. These regiments were small, making an aggregate of (1,367) thirteen hundred and sixty-seven effective men. On the third inst., in obedience to orders from Brigadier General Maury, commanding division, my brigade, after crossing the Mississippi and Charleston railroad, was held in reserve to support the brigades of Generals Moore and Phifer, that was ordered to advance and attack the enemy. I remained within supporting distance of the two brigades with my whole brigade until half past three o'clock, when I was ordered to send two regiments to support General Moore on the right. I sent, at once, the nineteenth Arkansas regiment, under Colonel Dockey, and the twentieth Arkansas, under Colonel H. P. Johnson, who became, after arriving on the field of battle, quickly engaged with the enemy, driving the enemy before them with great loss; our loss being small, not over five killed and ten wounded in each regiment. After these regiments had been sent off, I received an order from the division commander to move, with the remainder of my brigade, to the support of General Phifer. This order was obeyed promptly. After arring on the field I found General Phifer's brigade, although much exhausted from heat and dust, had driven the enemy within less than (800) eight hundred yards of their breastworks around the city of Corinth. I immediately formed my line of battle, threw my skirmishers to the front and engaged the enemy's skirmishers, which enabled General Phifer to withdraw his brigade. After his brigade had been withdrawn, I advanced with my skirmishers, fighting the enemy as far as I deemed it prudent with the small force I lead. I therefore contented myself with holding the position I had, and watching the movements of the enemy, my skirmishers in the meantime keeping up a brisk fire with the enemy's sharpshooters. I am confident they did terrible execution with the enemy's skirmishers. I then captured two fine ambulances and nine prisoners; the enemy during this time kept up a constant fire of grape and canister, which, although furious, did but little harm, as my loss was only two privates killed and five wounded. I was here struck myself on the foot with a spent Minnie ball, which gave me a great deal of pain at the time, but did not disable me. About sundown, after the enemy had drawn all their infantry and artillery inside the inner works, I received an order to report, with my brigade, to General Hebert, on the extreme left, to guard the crossing of a road leading from the Purdy road across to the Mobile and Ohio railroad. I reported, as directed, to General Hebert, who gave me the necessary instructions, and ordered me (by the consent of General Armstrong) to retain a section of King's artillery and Colonel McCulloch's regiment of cavalry. After making such a disposition of the forces under my command, placing out my pickets to watch the movements of the enemy, and protect our left from a flank movement of the enemy, I remained there until seven o'clock, A. M., on the fourth, when I was ordered by General Hebert to move up and report to General Green, to whom he had (being sick) turned over the command of the division. I moved up, as ordered, and reported to General Green, who ordered me to remain in supporting distance of his bridgade, at the same time informing me that I would be subject to orders from my own division commander, Brigadier General Maury. A short time had elapsed before I received an order from General Maury to move as near General Phifer as I could, taking advantage of the ground to protect my men from a terrific fire of artillery, which I was exposed to from a battery of the enemy on the south side of the Mobile and Ohio railroad. I placed my brigade on the side of a hill, protecting them as much as possible from this furious discharge of grape, canister and shell, that was kept up without a moment's cessation, sufficient to demoralize any troops except such as the troops which composed my brigade. This was within less than (700) seven hundred yards of the breastworks and the town of Corinth, where the first Missouri brigade, under Colonel Gates, was hotly engaged. About eleven o'clock, A. M., I received an order from General Maury, delivered by Captain Flowerree, Adjutant General, to move rapidly to the support of Colonel Gates, who had entered the enemy's breastworks and could not hold it for the want of ammunition. This order was received with a shout by the whole brigade, who had stood this terrible cannonading for more than an hour. Immediately after receiving the order, I moved by the left flank, at double quick, until I crossed the Moble and Ohio railroad. After crossing the railroad, through a terrible fire of artillery, I faced to the front and moved on the enemy's works, the left in the open field and the right and centre through a skirt of woods about fifty yards wide, expecting to find the Missouri brigade. This brigade had, however, fallen back taking a road on my extreme right. Instead of meeting the Missouri brigade as I had been informed I would, I found the enemy in line of battle just outside of the timber, and about three hundred yards in front of the breastworks. My left became engaged at once, after facing to the front, and the whole line in a few minutes afterwards, when I gave word "charge." As soon as the command was given, the whole line moved at double-quick, almost as one man, shouting "Butler," and driving them until they reached the crest of the enemy's breastworks, where a greater force than I had driven in sprang up, delivering a tremendous volley in the very faces of a greater part of my whole line, which was at that time subject to fire, from the left front of the bastion near the college, as well as to the artillery fire from the battery on the south side of the railroad, and on the left of the work charged. A part of the twentieth Arkansas regiment, under Colonel Johnson, went over the works inside of Corinth. The numbers of the enemy being so great in front, at the same time being exposed to such a dreadful cross fire of musketry and artillery on my flanks and rear, that my men were compelled to fall back with a very heavy loss of killed and wounded officers and men.

The courage and daring of my men, who shot the enemy down in their trenches, is beyond all praise; the ground in front of the breastworks was literally covered with the dead and wounded of both friend and foe, the killed and wounded of the enemy being nearly, if not fully, two to one. Those left presented the appearance of men nearly whipped, and convinced me that it was nothing but their reinforcements and superior numbers that kept them from a total rout. My loss, in officers especially, was, I regret to say, very great at this time; a great many, both officers and privates, were wounded and taken prisoners. I lost here three brave and valuable field officers killed— Colonel H. P. Johnson and Major Dane W. Jones, 20th Arkansas regiment, and Major Dowdle, 21st Arkansas, and Colonel Daly, 18th Arkansas, mortally wounded, (since dead.) Lieut. Colonel Matheny, 21st Arkansas, wounded. Captain Lynch, 18th Arkansas, and Capt. Atkins, Rapley's battalion, two gallant officers, were killed. [A list of the killed and wounded has been furnished.] Col. Cravens, 21st Arkansas, acted nobly and had his horse shot under him. Colonel Dockey, Lieut. Col. Disunke, Lieut. Col. Fletcher, Major Williams and Major Wilson distinguished themselves by their gallantry and daring; also, Captain Ashford, who commanded the battalion of sharpshooters, (Major Rapley being absent, sick.) After being repulsed by an overwhelming force, I received an order to fall back with what was left of my brigade, with the remainder of the army, which I did, taking all the kapsacks and blankets I could with me to the camp on Chewalla, on the south-side of the Memphis and Charleston Railroad, where we remained until the morning of the 5th. I only numbered, all told, on the morning of the 5th, previous to marching to Davis' Bridge, across the Hatchie river, five hundred and fifty (550) men. Mine was the rear brigade in the division, and was, owing to the order of march of that day, some distance in rear of the advance brigade, which became engaged with a greatly superior force of the enemy immediately after crossing the Hatchie river. When the cannonading was first heard in front, I was then crossing the Tuscumbia river, a distance of five miles. I received an order from General Maury, while crossing the river, to move rapidly to the front to the support of General Moore. I moved forward, then, as rapidly as possible, at the double-quick most of the way, until I reached the field of battle, which was then on the east side of the river, and where Gen. Phifer's brigade, with my battery of artillery, which I had sent in the advance, was hotly engaged with the enemy. I immediately, after ascertaining the position of the enemy, formed line of battle, and placed my line on the right of Gen. Phifer's brigade. The enemy opened fire on us at once; we replied instantly and continued to keep up a perfect musketry duel for about an hour, when I found my cartridges giving out. I immediately issued about ten (10) rounds of cartridges to the men and renewed the fire, which was contiued until the enemy ceased firing, (except their skirmishers,) and my cartridges had given out. I sent word to Gen. Maury that my ammunition had given out, and that I could only hope to hold the ground with the bayonet should the enemy's cavalry attempt to charge us. Gen. Maury then ordered me to fall back to the timber and get ammunition. After receiving this order, I withdrew my men in good order with a loss of not more than two killed and eight wounded, a thing unprecedented, considering the obstinacy of the fight that had been going on for nearly an hour and a half. While withdrawing my men, my horse, who had become very frantic, fell on me and injured my thigh and hip very seriously, completely paralyzing my left leg. I, however, formed my line and gave the command of the few that were left to Col. Dockey, as I was unable to walk. In this action, as well as in the engagements of Friday and Saturday, I cannot particularize. Every officer and man seemed willing and anxious to meet the enemy, and the daring and gallant charge made on the enemy's breastworks, and the obstinacy with which they stood in an open field and fought the enemy partly concealed in the woods, for an hour and a half, at Hatchie river, will bear testimony to the fact and give them a just claim to the admiration and gratitude of their State and country, and will cause them to mingle their tears with the survivors' for the *heroes who have fallen.* My personal staff, Major John King, Adjutant General; Captain Balfour, Inspector General, and Lieut. Marshall Hairston, A. D C., were all distinguished for their daring and bravery. I am under many obligations for the promptness with which they assisted me in every engagement. Also, to my volunteer aids, Lieut. Shepperd and Mr. Templeman, who were conspicuous for daring and gallantry in every engagement, under every fire. Major Hooper, Brigade Quartermaster, and Major Smith, Brigade Commissary, as well as the Surgeons of the whole brigade, deserve my especial thanks for the zeal and energy displayed in the field and everywhere during the whole expedition.

To Captain Burnett, Chief of Artillery; Lieut. Hogg, commanding Appeal Battery, with his officers and men, deserve especial notice for the skill and efficiency with which they handled the battery and poured the shot and shell into the enemy's ranks.

Before closing, I must return my sincere thanks to the officers and men who have survived, for the promptness, daring and cheerfulness with which they have executed every order, and ask them never to forget the daring and heroism of the noble dead. Arkansas, though for a time cast in gloom for her lost sons, can look with pride to the daring and gallantry of her sons and console herself with the happy thought that her soldiers are equal to any and second to none amongst those who are battling for Southern independence.

Respectfully, your obedient servant,
W. L. CABELL,
Brigadier General Commanding Brigade.

REPORT OF BRIG. GEN. MOORE OF THE ACTIONS OF THE
3D, 4TH AND 5TH INSTANTS.

HEADQUARTERS MOORE'S BRIGADE, ARMY OF THE WEST,
Camp at Lumpkin's Mill,
Near Holly Springs, October 13th, 1862.

Captain D. W. FLOWERREE,
   A. A. General:

SIR: I have the honor to submit the following report of the part taken by this brigade in the action on the 3d, 4th and 5th instants.

This brigade was composed of the following regiments, to-wit: 2d Texas, Colonel W. P. Rogers; Lyle's Arkansas regiment, Lieutenant Colonel Pennington; Boone's Arkansas regiment, Lieutenant Colonel Boone; 35th Mississippi regiment, Colonel Wm. L. Barry; 42d Alabama regiment, Colonel John W. Portis; Bledsoe's battery, Captain H. M. Bledsoe, making five regiments and one battery; total effective strength eighteen hundred and ninety-two (1892) about.

On the morning of the 3d, we formed in line of battle near the road leading from Pocahontas to Corinth, and distant about one half mile from the enemy's outer works. Our brigade here occupied the right of the line formed by Maury's division, our right resting on the Mobile and Ohio railroad and Lovell's forces on our right beyond the road. Soon Lovell's forces engaged the enemy and our brigade was ordered forward across a corn field to their support, with instructions to halt on reaching the timber on the opposite side and await further orders. On reaching the point designated, a part of the 2d Texas and one company of the 35th Mississippi were thrown forward as skirmishers, and at once engaged the enemy's sharp shooters, when they were driven back within their entrenchments. We here lost a few men and Major W. C. Simmons, commanding the skirmishers, was wounded. We were now ordered forward to assault the enemy's works. We advanced in a well preserved line of battle, considering the difficulties of the ground, and on reaching the fallen timber, in front of the enemy's entrenchments, we charged and carried the works with but little opposition, except on our left, where the 42d Alabama was exposed to a heavy fire, though their loss in killed and wounded was but eight or ten, including one officer. This regiment advanced with remarkable steadiness, this being their first engagement. Advancing about one-fourth of a mile we were halted to form a junction with Lovell's forces, now on our right, which we failed to do. Our skirmishers again soon engaged the enemy and were driven back on our line, which led to a severe but short engagement, in which we soon routed the enemy and drove them from their position. Here an unfortunate mistake was committed, the 42d Alabama firing on our skirmishers, mistaking them for the enemy, and killing and wounding several officers and men. At this time a heavy cannonading was kept up at some distance to our right from a strong work of the enemy about two hundred yards south of the Memphis and Charleston railroad. Being now reinforced by Colonel Johnson's and Colonel Dockey's Arkansas regiments we changed direction to the right, and throwing forward the left wing, moved in the direction of the firing. We soon reached the railroad, having our line nearly parallel to it, and in crossing, the enemy opened on us a most terrific fire from the brow of a hill not more than seventy-five yards distant. The enemy opposed to us with a heavy force, being formed in two lines, the front lying on the ground and the other firing over them. This awful fire staggered us but for a moment, and as soon as our line was steadied a little, we charged, drove them from the position and carried their works, capturing a few prisoners and taking a large camp with their supplies of commissary and quartermaster stores. On discovering our approach the enemy removed and saved their guns. This we found to be a strong work in a firm position, and well constructed. From the position, we judged this to be the point from which a cannonading had been kept up during the day.

Being now separated from our division, and night approaching, (it being between three and four o'clock,) we dispatched Lieutenat McFarland to report to General Maury our success, and ask for orders. In the course of half an hour, General Lovell and staff came up, and, on consultation, we agreed to form a line of battle perpendicular to the railroad, our left resting on the road, and advance towards Corinth. In about an hour his forces came up, and moved to our right. At about dusk, while awaiting for a notification from General Lovell to advance, which he said he would give when ready, we received orders from General Maury to rejoin the division and take position on Phifer's right, which brought us on the hill in sight of Corinth, about an hour and a half after dark, where we slept on our arms until morning.

At early dawn, on the morning of the 4th, our batteries having been placed in front of our lines, to open fire on Corinth, the brigade was moved by the left flank and placed in rear of Phifer's, sheltered by timber in front. When the firing from the batteries ceased, we moved forward and took position obliquely to the right and front of Phifer's. Our skirmishers were again thrown forward, and kept up a sharp engagement with the enemy until about ten o'clock. We had been previously notified by General Maury that we would advance when Hebert's division made the attack on our left—our brigade being supported by Cabell's on the right and Phifer's on the left. About ten o'clock the firing on our left became heavy, and we at once gave the command, "forward," sending Lieutenant McFarland to notify General Maury of our advance movement. We had not gone one hundred yards before the enemy seemed to discover our designs, and at once opened upon us and kept up the severest fire I ever imagined possible to concentrate on one point in front of a fortification. Yet we suffered but little, being protected by the timber, until we reached the fallen timber and open space which extended about one hundred yards in front of their works.

On reaching this point we charged and carried the enemy's works, the whole extent of our line, and "penetrated to the very heart of of Corinth," driving the enemy from house to house, and frequently firing in at the windows and driving them out. The enemy were driven from the breastworks, in great confusion, leaving their guns, some with the teams still hitched, while others had their horses cut loose and ran off. Our men brought off two or three horses which they found hitched in the streets near the Corinth House, their owners being absent The 42d Alabama, from their position in line, were brought in front of a strong bastion, the walls of which they found too high to scale, but rushing to the embrasures they fired three or four volleys, driving the enemy from their guns, and then entering the works, mounted the parapet and planted their flag on the walls. After entering the works we found ourselves opposed by an overwhelming force, and being without support and our line being broken and disordered in the assault, we had no alternative but to fall back, which was done. Our loss in this assault was very severe. Three of the five regimental commanders were either killed or wounded. I can bear testimony to the coolness and gallantry with which our men and officers made this assault. I do not believe that any troops ever displayed greater courage in so desperate a charge. This was our last engagement in the vicinity of Corinth. Our division being reformed we fell back on the road to Pocahontas and biouvacked for the night. At an early hour, on the morning of the 5th instant, our brigade was ordered to the front to act as an advanced guard, when within two or three miles of Davis' bridge, across Hatchie, we received orders to push forward, cross the bridge, form a line of battle on the right of the road, and then advance, take and hold the heights of Matamoras, which command the crossing at Davis' bridge. We pushed forward with all possible dispatch, but the men being greatly exhausted and weak for the want of food, and the previous two day's hard marching and service, when we reached the crossing and formed line we did not have more than 250 or 300 men in ranks. We formed on the right, opposite the battery established by Maj. Burnett on the left of the road. As we filed off to the right, the enemy's batteries opened on us from the hill at Matamoras. The 2d Texas being in the rear was cut off by the fire, and did not form in line with the other regiments. Our position was now in a narrow strip of woods, with open fields in front and rear, that in front extending up to the enemy's position. We had been ordered to advance with our left on the road, which would have carried us through the open fields up to the very muzzles of the enemy's guns.

Being now satisfied that the hill was occupied in force, and to advance with our small force would only prove its total annihilation, we dispatched Lieutenant McFarland to the rear for reinforcements, and to report to the Commanding General that we not only could not advance, but we thought we could not hold our pre-ent position long without assistance.

During this time the enemy continued to pour a heavy fire into the battery and woods occupied by our line, in which we lost several men killed and wounded. The batteries being soon withdrawn, the enemy soon gave us their whole attention, but we still held our position until they reached our left flank and poured into us a most destructive fire. This threw our line into some confusion; but, rallying, we moved to the left, faced the enemy and opened on them.

We had not fired more than two or three rounds before a perfect shower of balls was poured into our right flank from the direction of the corn field which was at first our front. I am satisfied that this fire came from a line which had been previously formed in the field, and had been concealed by lying down in the grass and corn. We now saw that we must either fall back or be surrounded. The order was given and the bridge being now swept by the enemy's fire, the men crossed at such points of the stream as they found to be most convenient. In crossing, many of them lost their guns. This manner of crossing caused the men to become much scattered, but as they were collected, they joined Cabell's and Phifer's brigades and continued the fight. Our loss at the bridge was considerable, making the entire loss of the brigade during the three days' fight, very heavy, as will be seen by the accompanying report. It is impossible at present to make an accurate report of the killed, wounded and missing in battle, as the 35th Mississippi dispersed after the fight at Davis' bridge, there being now present some forty men, and one line officer, Lieutenant Henry. From the best information we can obtain we are assured that many of the officers and men have gone to their homes. This conduct on their part is astonishing and unaccountable, for the regiment acted nobly and did good service during the three days' fighting. It is to be regretted that their commander, Colonel Barry was not present, he having been sent to Corinth, under flag of truce te bury the dead. He is a gallant and efficient officer, of whom his State may well be proud.

Without a single exception, to our knowledge, the officers one and all did their duty nobly during the severe engagements. If I mention one in this connection I must mention all or do injustice. Corporal J. A. Going, of the 42d Alabama, deserves particular notice. He was color-bearer, and though once shot down, he gallantly bore the flag through the fight on the 4th.

Private Morgan, of Co. H, Boone's regiment, is reported as having acted with great gallantry. The flag of Lyle's regiment was torn into tatters by the enemy's shots, and when last seen, the color-bearer, Herbert Sloane, of Co. D, was going over the breastworks, waving a piece over his head and shouting for the Southern Confederacy.

I am, Captain, very respectfully, your ob't ser't,

M. C. MOORE,
Brigadier General Commanding Brigade.

REPORT OF COL. W. H. JACKSON, CHIEF OF CAVALRY, OF OPERATIONS OF CAVALRY BRIGADE AT THE LATE BATTLE AT CORINTH.

HEADQUARTERS CAVLARY,
Army of Tennessee, Watersford, Nov. 18, 1862.

To Major M. M. KIMMELL,
  A. A. General Army of West Tenn., Abbeville, Miss. :

MAJOR: I have the honor to make report of the operations of my brigade of cavalry, (1st Mississippi cavalry, commanded by Lieut. Col. F. A. Montgomery, and my own regiment, commanded by Lieut. Col. J. G. Stocks,) at the late battle of Corinth and retreat from that place.

During the battle my brigade was divided; squadrons attached to brigades of infantry and acting on the flanks. With eight companies I made a reconnoissance south of Corinth, engaged the enemy's cavalry and repulsed them in gallant style. Returning, I advanced the command to the fortifications on College Hill, where I engaged the enemy in force after the main body of our troops had withdrawn. I then withdrew my command without serious loss and brought up the rear of the army. I was then ordered to Rienzi, under Gen. Armstrong; received orders countermanding that move on our arrival at Kossuth.

The firing having commenced at Davis' Bridge, near Pocahontas, we proceeded with both commands to the Ripley and Pocahontas road; advanced up that road to within one mile and a half of Pocahontas, threatening the enemy's rear, engaging them in a brilliant skirmish, which was a move very favorable towards saving the train of wagons. I held that position all night with my brigade, and fell back before the enemy next day. From that time the brigade was engaged in bringing up the rear of the army, skirmishing all the time with the enemy to Ripley.

Owing to unavoidable circumstances, the brigade was without rations for three days. The officers and men all behaved with coolness and gallantry, and suffered all the hardships, incident to the march, with a spirit worthy of good soldiers. Where all behaved so well, it would be difficult to mention by name. I would especially notice, however, Lieut. Henry W. Watkins, company A, Jackson's regiment cavalry; also, Corporal Brochus and privates Britton and Barton, company C, same regiment; also, Capt. Gadi Herron, Lieut. Cravens and Lieut. Foote, 1st regiment Mississippi cavalry. The latter (Lieut. Foote) engaged the enemy's advance and checked them in a most gallant manner. The report from Armstrong's brigade does not mention any one especially by name. They all behaved with coolness and gallantry.

  I am, Major, with high respect,
    Your obedient servant,
  (Signed,)   H. W. JACKSON,
    Col. and Chief of Cavalry, Army West Tenn.

GENERAL PRICE TO GENERAL VAN DORN.

HEADQUARTERS DISTRICT OF THE TENNESSEE,
Tupelo, August 4, 1862.

Major General EARL VAN DORN,
  Commanding District of the Mississippi:

GENERAL: I telegraphed you yesterday that dispatches from General Bragg make it almost impossible for me to reinforce General Breckinridge. He says, very pointedly, that West Tennessee is now open to my army, intimating that he expected me to enter it; and I do not feel at liberty to disregard such an intimation, when I consider the very important relations which this army bears to that in East Tennessee. I cannot get possession of the railroad before Thursday. It will then take at least a week to transport to this point the troops, etc., which will be brought hither preparatory to a forward movement. I regret very much that I have to submit to this unavoidable delay, and I cannot think of protracting it, except under compulsion of the greatest necessity. To attempt to reinforce General Breckinridge would protract it indefinitely. The success of the campaign depends now upon the promptness and boldness of our movements, and the ability which we may manifest to avail ourselves of our present advantages. The enemy are still transporting their troops from Corinth and its vicinity eastward. They will, by the end of this week, have reduced its force to its minimum. We should be quick to take advantage of this, for they will soon begin to get in reinforcements under the late call for volunteers. The present obstructed condition of the railroad is another reason for instant action. In fact every consideration makes it important that I shall move forward without a day's unnecessary delay. I earnestly desire your coöperation in such a movement, and will, as I have before said, be glad to place my army and myself under your command in that contingency. The very names of yourself and General Breckinridge would bring thousands to our ranks, and carry dismay to those of the enemy. You speak in your dispatch of the frightful amount of sickness in General Breckinridge's division. I fear that the sweltering heats of this latitude will soon begin to tell fearfully upon my own ranks, and am, for that reason, the more anxious to take them northward, where, too, we may gain accessions from those Tennesseeans and Kentuckians who have seen and felt the wretchedness of Northern domination.

Captain Loughbrough will deliver this communication to you, and explain more particularly the condition of things in this vicinity. Please inform me, by telegraph, of your determination, so that in the event of its being favorabe, we may concert a plan of operations.

I am, General, with the profoundest respect,
Your obedient servant,
(Signed,)   STERLING PRICE,
Major General.

M. M. KIMMEL, *Major a>d A. A. G.*

GENERAL BRAGG TO GENERAL VAN DORN.

HEADQUARTERS DEPARTMENT No 2,
Chattanooga, Tenn., Aug. 11, 1862.

Major General E. VAN DORN,
Commanding Department of the Mississippi:

GENERAL: In view of the operations from here it is very desirable to press the enemy closely in West Tennessee. We learn their forces there are being rapidly reduced, and when our movements become known it is certain they must throw more forces into Middle Tennessee and Kentucky or lose those regions. If you hold them in check, we are sure of success here; but should they reinforce here so as to defy us, then you may redeem West Tennessee and probably aid us by crossing the enemy's rear.

I cannot give you specific instructions, as circumstances and military conditions in your front may vary materially from day to day. To move your available force to Holly Springs by railroad, thence into West Tennessee, co-operating with General Price, who will move soon towards Corinth; or to move to Tupelo by rail and join Price, are suggestions only. Positive instructions, except to strike at the most assailable point, cannot be given when so little is known, and when circumstances may change daily. Of course, when you join Price, your rank gives you command of the whole force. I enclose a copy of Capt. Jones' inspection report. Many of the points in it require your immediate attention : 1st. Most important is the prompt reduction of your light artillery. You have enough for an army of 100,000 men. It is impossible to keep it all up and be effective. To keep it all ineffective must be avoided. Eight batteries of four (4) guns each is ample for your present force. As you cannnot discharge the companies without authority from the War Department, I suggest that you dismount them giving such horses and material as they have to make other corps effective, and transfer the officers and men to your heavy batteries, relieving infantry ; or you could arm them as infantry and put them in the field. Some companies, I see, are still being equipped. Put a stop to it immediately. Other parts of the report, too, require your prompt consideration, especially in the staff department. The reports from the Medical Inspector, coming in, are equally unsatisfactory.

Your short time in command and close engagement at Vicksburg have allowed you but little time for these matters, but I trust you will be able, through intell'gent and effective staff officers, in correcting some of the evils soon. It is with deep regret, I see you lose Gen. Villepigue, as I consider him equal to any officer in the service. Brig. Gen. Duncan, and perhaps others exchanged, will soon be with us, when you shall be attended to.

I am, General, most respectfully and truly yours,
 (Signed,)   BRAXTON BRAGG,
             General Commanding.

M. M. KIMMEL, *Major and A. A. G.*

GENERAL BRAGG TO GENERAL VAN DORN.

        HEADQUARTERS DEPARTMENT No. 2,
         Chattanooga, Tenn , Aug. 27, 1862.

Major General EARL VAN DORN,
   Com'dg District of the Mississippi, Jackson, Miss. :

GENERAL : We move from here immediately—later, by some days, than expected, but in time, we hope, for a successful campaign Buell has certainly fallen back from the Memphis and Charleston Railroad, and will probably not make a stand this side of Nashville, if there. He is now fortifying at that place.

General E. K. Smith, reinforced by two brigades from this army, has turned Cumberland Gap, and is now marching on Lexington. Ky. Gen. Morgan (Yankee) is thus cut off from all supplies. General Humphrey Marshal is to enter Eastern Kentucky from Western Virginia. We shall thus have Buell pretty well disposed of.

Sherman and Rosencrans we leave to you and Price, satisfied you can dispose of them, and we confidently hope to meet you upon the Ohio.

  Respectfully, your obedient servant,
            BRAXTON BRAGG,
             General Commanding.

M. M. KIMMELL.

GENERAL ARMSTRONG TO GENERAL PRICE.

       MIDDLEBURG, FIVE MILES SOUTH OF BOLIVER,
           August 30, 1862.

Major SNEED, *Assistant Adjutant General :*

Just finished whipping the enemy in from of Boliver. Ran in town. I believe they will leave the country. West Tennessee is almost free of the invaders. All needed is an advance of the infantry. They estimate their force at ten thousand. I believe they have only about six thousand. Captain Pryor will give you the details. I send seventy-one prisoners to General Villipigue—four commanding officers. There are strong works in rear of Bolivar, and I did not enter the town, as it would only have caused them to shell it, without giving me any advantage.

You will hear from us again in a day or two.
 (Signed,)   F. C. ARMSTRONG.
  A true copy,
M. M. KIMMEL, *Major and A. A. G.*

GENERAL PRICE TO GENERAL VAN DORN.

HEADQUARTER DISTRICT OF THE TENNESSEE,
Tupelo, September 2, 1862.

Major General VAN DORN,
 Commanding District of the Mississippi, Jackson, Miss.:

GENERAL: I received, last night, a dispatch of which the following is a copy:

"LIQUATCHIE VALLEY, August 29.
"To General STERLING PRICE :
"Buell's whole force is in full retreat upon Nashville, destroying their stores. Watch Ronsencrans and prevent a junction; or if he escapes you follow him closely.
            "BRAXTON BRAGG."

I feel that this order requires me to advance immediately, and I shall have my whole command ready to move in three days. That portion of my cavalry which did not accompany General Armstrong, has been ordered forward to Booneville, and General Little is moving his division to Guntown and Baldwin. I hope that nothing will prevent you from coming forward without delay, with all your disposable troops. Be pleased to telegraph your determination in such way, however, that it will not be understood by others, and to write to me fully by my aid-de-camp, Lieutenant Wood, who will hand this to you.

I enclose for your information copies of a letter from General Bragg, dated August 27th, and of a despatch from General Armstrong announcing the result of an engagement in front of Bolivar.

I am, General, with the greatest respect,
      Your obedient servant,
         STERLING PRICE,
           Major General.

  A true copy :
M. M. KIMMEL, *Major and A. A. G.*

FROM GEN. PRICE TO GEN. VAN DORN.

HEADQUARTERS DISTRICT OF THE TENNESSEE,
Tupelo, September 4, 1862.

Major General EARL VAN DORN,
 Commanding District of the Mississippi:

GENERAL: One of your staff officers, Colonel Lomax, having requested me to do so, I state, for your information, that I can put in the field thirteen thousand infantry, three thousand cavalry and eight hundred artillery, *effective total;* that they are supplied with transportation and ammunition, as prescribed in General Bragg's last general orders; that subsistence has been provided to the first day of October; that the commissary trains will transport seven days' provisions, and that I will have arms for all my troops, including those exchanged prisoners that General Bragg has been ordered to be sent to me. I am, General, very respectfully,
Your obedient servant,
 (Signed,) STERLING PRICE,
 Major General, Commanding.

M. M. KIMMEL, *Major and A. A. G.*

GENERAL PRICE TO GENERAL VAN DORN.

HEADQUARTERS DISTRICT OF THE TENNESSEE.
Tupelo, September 5, 1862.

Maj. Gen. EARL VAN DORN,
 Commanding District of the Mississippi, Jackson:

GENERAL: I have received your reply to my letter of the 2d instant, and regret very much that you cannot move in this direction at once.

I feel that General Bragg's instructions and the situation of affairs within my district, alike compel me to keep near the line of the road. If I move towards Holly Springs as you suggest, I not only endanger the safety of the road, which is essential to the supply of my army, but I expose my supplies of every kind, and the valuable work shops and public property at Columbus and Gainesville to destruction by the enemy. I learn that a cavalry force of theives, 17,000 strong, is even now within forty eight hours march of Columbus.

General Bragg's orders also compel me to keep close watch upon Rosencrans, and I hear that he is now at Iuka, and crossing his army at Eastport. I am, therefore, pushing my army slowly forward, and shall remove my own headquarters to Guntown on Sunday, I shall then determine by what route to advance. I shall keep you fully advised of my movements, so that we may co-operate or unite our forces as may be most advisable.

I am, General, very sincerely,
Your friend and obd't serv't,
 (Signed) STERLING PRICE,
 Major General.

M. M. KIMMEL, *Lieut. Col. and Inspector General.*

GENERAL PRICE TO GENERAL VAN DORN.

BY TELEGRAPH FROM IUKA.

SUNDAY, September 14, 1862.

To Gen. VAN DORN:

Rosencrans has gone Westward with about ten thousand men. I am ready to co-operate with you in an attack upon Corinth. My courier awaits your answer.

STERLING PRICE,
Major General.

M. M. KIMMEL.

GENERAL PRICE TO GENERAL VAN DORN.

HEADQUARTERS DISTRICT OF THE TENNESSEE,
Iuka, September 17, 1862.

Maj. Gen. EARL VAN DORN,
Commanding District of the Mississippi:

GENERAL: I entered this town with my army on last Sunday morning. The rear guard of Rosecrans' army evacuated it at my approach, and are retreating Westward. I telegraphed you immediately, proposing a combined movement upon Corinth, and sent the dispatch by special messenger to Guntown, with instructions to forward it to you immediately and to await your reply. This has not been received yet. I hope that you will answer me at once, for General Bragg has just sent me another despatch in these words:

"EN ROUTE TO KENTUCKY, September 12, 1862.

"By the proceedings of a council of war in Nashville, captured by us, it seems Rosecrans, with part of his army is there. I have anxiously expected your advance, and trust it will not longer be delayed.

"(Signed) "BRAXTON BRAGG."

I cannot remain inactive any longer and must move, either with you against Rosecrans, or towards Kentucky. The courier who takes this to you will bring your reply.

I am, very respectfully,
Your obedient servant,
STERLING PRICE,
Major General.

M. M KIMMEL, *Major and A. A. G.*

GENERAL PRICE TO GENERAL VAN DORN.

TELEGRAM.

IUKA, September 19, 1862.

General VAN DORN:

I will make the movement proposed in your dispatch of the 16th inst. Enemy concentrating against me. Please make demonstration towards Rienzi. Have written by courier. Send your telegrams to Tupelo.

  (Signed,)   STERLING PRICE,
           Major General Commanding.

M. M. KIMMEL, *Major and A. A. G.*

GENERAL PRICE TO GENERAL VAN DORN.

         BALDWIN, September 23, 1862.

To General EARL VAN DORN:

 I will leave here on Friday morning, 20th. Wrote you this morning stating that I would meet you at Ripley. As you know more of the country, if any point be better state it, and I will meet you there.

 A few days ago the enemy's strength was thirty-five thousand. I learn that they are leaving in the direction of Jackson, and whether we attack them or not before receiving our exchanged prisoners, it is important that we should unite.

  (Signed,)   STERLING PRICE,
           Major General.

M. M. KIMMEL, *Major and A. A. G.*

GENERAL BRAGG TO GENERAL VAN DORN.

     HEADQUARTERS, DEPARTMENT No. 2,
      Bardstown, Ky., Sept. 25, 1862.

For Major General VAN DORN:

 GENERAL: We have driven and drawn the enemy clear back to the Ohio. Push your columns to our support and arouse the people to reinforce us. We have thousands of arms without men to handle them.

 Nashville is defended by only a weak division, Bowling Green by only a regiment. Sweep them off and push up to the Ohio Secure the heavy guns at these places and we will secure the Tennessee and Cumberland rivers. All depends on rapid movements. Trusting to your energy and zeal, we shall confidently expect a diversion in our favor against the overwhelming force now concentrating in our front.

Respectfully and truly yours,

BRAXTON BRAGG,
General Commanding.

M. M. KIMMEL.

REPORT

OF THE

EXPEDITION TO HARTSVILLE, TENN.

REPORT OF BRAXTON BRAGG, GENERAL COMMANDING.

HEADQUARTERS ARMY OF TENNESSEE,
Murfreesboro', Tenn., Dec. 22d, 1862.

Gen. S. COOPER,
    Adjutant and Inspector General, Richmond, Va.:

SIR: Having been informed, by acting Brig. Gen. John H. Morgan, whose cavalry brigade covered my front in the direction of Hartsville, Tenn., that the enemy's force at that point was somewhat isolated, I yielded to his request and organized an expedition under him for their attack. On the 5th instant Hanson's brigade, of Breckinridge's division, was moved forward on the road towards Hartsville and halted at Baird's Mills, a point nearly due east from Nashville, and half way to Hartsville, when it was joined by Morgan's cavalry force. Two regiments, the 2d and 9th Kentucky Infantry, with Cobb's Kentucky Artillery, moved from this point, with the cavalry, at 10, P M., on the 6th, to attack the enemy at Hartsville. Early on the morning of the same day, Hanson, with the remainder of his brigade, moved as directed on the road towards Nashville, for the purpose of a reconnoisance and to cause a diversion.

At the same time that the troops above named left their camps near here, Major General Cheatham, with two brigades, moved out on the Nashville road, halted at night at Lavergne, fifteen miles, and on the next day, in conjunction with General Wheeler's cavalry, made a strong demonstration on the enemy's front

These movements had the desired effect, and completely distracted the enemy's attention from the real point of attack. Learning that a foraging train of the enemy was on his right flank, Cheatham detached Wheeler with a cavalry force to attack it, which he did in his usual dashing and successful manner, capturing eleven wagons and fifty-seven prisoners. Under cover of these feints, Morgan, by an extraordinary night march, reached the point of his destination about sunrise, and in a short but warmly contested engagement, killed, wounded and captured the entire command of more than two thousand officers and men.

I enclose herewith the reports of General Morgan and the subordinate commanders, and take great pleasure in commending the fortitude, endurance and gallantry of all engaged in this remarkable expedition. It is a source of personal and official gratification to perceive that the Department has recognized the services of the gallant and meritorious soldier who led the expedition by confirming my previous nomination of him as a Brigadier General.

Two sets of infantry colors and one artillery guidon, taken at Hartsville, are also forwarded with this report. A third set of infantry colors was presented by its captors to the President on his recent visit to this place.

I am, sir, very respectfully,
Your obedient servant,
BRAXTON BRAGG,
General Commanding.

REPORT OF BRIGADIER GENERAL JOHN H. MORGAN, OF THE EXPEDITION AGAINST THE FEDERAL FORCES AT HARTSVILLE, TENN.

MORGAN'S HEADQUARTERS CROSS, ROADS NEAR MURFREESBORO',
December 9th, 1862.

Col. BRENT, *Chief of Staff:*

SIR: I have the honor to lay before you, for the information of the General commanding, a report of the expedition against the Federal force at Hartsville.

I left these headquarters at 10, A. M., on the 6th instant, with 1,400 men of my own command under the orders of Colonel Duke; the 2d and 9th Kentucky infantry, commanded by Col. Hunt; Captain Cobbs' battery of artillery; two small howitzers and two rifled Ellsworth guns, belonging to my own command.

At Lebanon I received information that no change had been made in the number of the Federals at Hartsville, their number being still about 900 infantry and 400 cavalry with two pieces of artillery. I found afterwards that their force had been considerably underrated.

I proceeded with the infantry and artillery to Purcell Ferry on the Cumberland river, sending the cavalry, under the orders of Col. Duke, to pass at a ford some seven miles below the point where we were to "rendezvous." I passed my troops with great difficulty, there being but one boat; and about half-past five on the morning of the 7th I arrived at Hague Shops, two miles from the Federal camp. I found that Colonel Duke with his cavalry had only just marched up, having crossed the ford with difficulty, and that one regiment of his command, 500 strong, (Col. Gano's,) had not yet reported. Major Stoner's battalion had been left on the other side of the Cumberland, with two mountain howitzers to prevent the escape of the enemy by the Lebanon road, and Col. Kenneth's regiment had been ordered to proceed to Hartsville to picket the road leading to Gallatin, and to attack any of the Federals they might find in that town, to take possession of the Castilian Springs, Lafayette and Carthage roads, so as to prevent the escape of the enemy. This reduced my force considerably; but I determined to attack and that at once; there was no time to be lost; day was breaking and the enemy might expect strong re-inforcements from Castilian Springs, should my arrival be known. Advancing, therefore, with the cavalry, closely followed by the artillery and infantry, I approached the enemy's position. The pickets were found and shot down. The Yankee bivouac first appeared to cover a long line of ground, and gave me to suppose that their number were much greater than I anticipated. On nearing the camp the alarm was sounded, and I could distinctly see and hear the officers ordering their men to fall in, preparing for resistance. Col. Duke then dismounted Col. Clarke's and Col. Chenault's regiments, in all about 750 men, drawing them up in line in a large field in the front, and a little to the right of the enemy's line which was then forming, and seeing that the artillery and infantry were in position he ordered his men to advance at the double-quick, and directed Col. Chenault, who was on left, to oblique so as to march on the enemy's flank.

His men then pressed forward, driving the Federals for nearly half a mile, without a check, before them, until their right wing was forced back upon their own left wing and centre.

Colonel Duke then ordered a halt until the infantry had commenced their attack on the Federal left wimg, which caused a retreat of the whole line. At this juncture Lieut. Col. Huffman and Major Steele, of Gano's regiment, came up with about 100 men of that regiment, who had succeed in crossing the ford, and threw their small force into the fight. My dismounted cavalry, under Col. Duke, had only been skirmishing, previously to this, for about 20 minutes; but seeing that Col. Hunt, with the infantry, was pressing hard upon the Federal's left, he ordered an advance upon the right ring and flank of their new line; it gave way and ceased, firing and soon after surrendered.

Col. Duke reports that his men fought with a courage and coolness which could not be surpassed.

Cols. Clarke and Chenault led on their men with the most determined bravery, encouraging them by voice and example.

The timely arrival of Lieut. Col. Huffman and Major Steele, and the gallant manner in which they showed themselves into the fight, had a very decided effect upon the battle at the point at which they entered. The artillery, under Captain Cobb, did most excellent service, and suffered severely from the enemies battery which fired with great precision, blowing up one of his caissons and inflicting a severe loss on that arm.

The infantry conducted themselves most gallantly; the 2d Kentucky suffering most severely.

Col. Bennett's regiment, as I said before, was not in the fight, having been sent on special service which was most efficiently performed, 450 prisoners having been taken by them, and 12 Federals killed.

Thus, sir, in one hour and a half, the troops under my command, consisting of 500 cavalry, (Col. Gano's, Col. Bennett's regiments and Major Stoner's command not participating in the fight,) 700 infantry, with a battery of artillery, in all about 1,300 strong, defeated and captured three well disciplined and well formed regiments of infantry with a regiment of cavalry, and took two rifled cannon, the whole encamped on their own ground, and in a very strong position, taking about eighteen hundred prisoners, eighteen hundred stand of arms, a quantity of ammunition, clothing, quartermasters stores and sixteen wagons. The battle was now over. The result exceeded my own expectations, but still I felt that my position was a most perilous one, being within four miles in a direct line and only eight by the main Gallatin road of an enemy's forces of at least 8,000 men, consisting of infantry, cavalry and artillery, who would naturally march to the aid of their comrades on hearing the report of our guns. I, therefore, with the sistance of my staff, got together all the empty wagons left by the enemy, loaded them with arms, ammunition and stores, and directed them immediately to Hart's Ferry.

There was no time to be lost. The pickets placed by my assistant adjutant general on the Castilian Springs road sent to report the advance of a strong body of Federals, estimated at 5,000 men.

I sent to Colonel Clarke's regiment to make a show of resistance, ordering Col. Gano's regiment, which had arrived, in support. In the meantime I pressed the passage of the Ford to the utmost.

This show of force caused a delay in the advance of the enemy who had no idea of the number of my men, and probably greatly overrated my strength and gave me time to pass the Ford with infantry, artillery and baggage wagons. The horses of my cavalry being sent back from the otherside of the Cumberland river, to carry over the infantry regiments, it was time to retreat. The enemy attacked our rear, but was kept at bay by the two regiments before specified, aided by four guns I had previously ordered to be placed in position on the south side of the Cumberland, looking forward to what was now taking place. The banks of the river, on both sides, are precipitous, and the stream breast deep, but our retreat was effected in excellent order. We lost not a man, except three badly wounded, that I was reluctantly forced to leave behind. Cavalry, infantry, guns and baggage train safely crossed, with the exception of four wagons which had been sent by another route, and which are still safely hidden in the woods, according to accounts received to day.

In justice to my brave command, I would respectfully bring to the notice of the General commanding the names of those officers who contributed by their undaunted bravery and soldier like conduct to the brilliant success which crowned the efforts of the Confederate arms.

To Colonel Hunt, of the 9th Kentucky, commanding the infantry, I am deeply indebted for his valuable assistance. His conduct, and that of his brave regiment, was perfect, and their steadiness under fire remarkable.

The 2d Kentucky also behaved most gallantly and suffered severely, sixty-two men killed and wounded, three regimental officers left dead on the field, sufficiently testified to their share in the fight, and the resistance they had to encounter.

Colonel Clarke's regiment paid also a high price for its devotion. It went into the field two hundred and thirty strong, had six officers with twenty-one non-commissioned officers and privates killed and wounded, besides six missing.

Colonel Duke, commanding the cavalry was, as he always has been, "the right man in the right place." Wise in council, gallant in the field, his services have ever been invaluable to me.

I was informed by my Adjutant General that Colonel Bennett, in the execution of the special service confided to him, and in which he so entirely succeeded, gave proofs of great gallantry and contempt of danger.

I owe much to my personal staff. Major Llewellyn, Captains Charlton Morgan and Williams and Lieutenant Tyler, acting as my *aides de camp*, gave proof of great devotion, being everywhere in the hottest fire, and Major Llewellyn received the sword of Colonel Stewart, and the surrender of his regiment. Captain Morgan and Captain Williams' horses were killed under them, and Lieutenant Tyler was severely wounded. My Orderly Sergeant, Craven Peyton, received a shot in his hip and had his horse killed by my side.

I must have forgiveness if I add, with a soldier's pride, that the conduct of my whole command deserved my highest gratitude and commendation.

Three Federal regimental standards and five cavalry guidons fluttered over my brave column on their return from the expedition. With such troops victory is enchained to our banners, and the issue of a contest with our Northern opponents, even when they are double our force, no longer doubtful.

I have the honor to be, sir, with the highest respect,
Your most obedient servant,
JOHN H. MORGAN,
Brigadier General.

REPORT OF MAJOR GENERAL BRECKINRIDGE OF THE BATTLE OF HARTSVILLE, TENN.

HEADQUARTERS BRECKINRIDGE'S DIVISION,
December 11, 1862.

Major THOS. M. JACK, *A. A. General:*

Sir: I have the honor to forward a report from Col. R. W. Hanson, commanding 1st brigade of my division, covering the report of Col. Thos. H. Hunt, who commanded the 2d and 9th Kentucky regiments and Cobb's battery, in the recent expedition (under command of Brigadier General Morgan) against Hartsville; and also, the reports of Major Hewitt and Capt. Morehead, commanding, respectively, the 2d and 9th Kentucky, and of Capt. Cobb, commanding the battery.

I beg to call attention to the officers and men specially named for gallantry, and to suggest, respectfully, that the troops engaged in this expedition deserves mention in orders for conduct, which, in fortitude and daring, has not been surpassed during the war.

Very respectfully,

JOHN C. BRECKINRIDGE,
Major General Commanding.

REPORT COLONEL R. W. HANSON OF THE BATTLE OF HARTSVILLE, TENNESSEE.

HEADQUARTERS FIRST BRIGADE,
Camp near Murfreesboro', December 11, 1862.

Colonel BUCKNER,
Assistant Adjutant General:

In pursuance of the order of General Bragg, I proceeded, with my command, on the 5th instant to Baird's mill, and remained two days, making, as directed, reconnoisance towards Nashville. General Morgan designated the second and ninth Kentucky and Cobb's battery, as the troops he desired to accompany him upon the Hartsville expedition. They were detached under command of Colonel Hunt. I enclose, herewith, his report of the battle of Hartsville, and the reports of his subordinate officers. I wish to call attention to the honorable mention that is made in Major Hewitt's and Colonel Hunt's reports of the gallant conduct of Sergeant Oldham, of the second Kentucky regiment, with the hope that the proper steps may be taken to procure for him the proper reward of his conduct. Sergeant Oldham was the color bearer of the second Kentucky regiment at the battle of Donelson, and acted with great gallantry upon that occasion. He is a suitable man for a lieutenancy, being well qualified as well as truly brave.

R. W. HANSON,
Colonel Commanding Brigade.

REPORT OF COLONEL THOMAS H. HUNT OF THE BATTLE OF HARTSVILLE.

HEADQUARTERS NINTH KENTUCKY REGIMENT,
Camp near Murfreesboro', Dec. 9, 1862.

To Captain JOHN S. HOPE,
Acting Assistant Adjutant General:

CAPTAIN: I have the honor to report that the detachment from the first brigade, Breckinridge's division, consisting of the second Kentucky regiment, Major James W. Hewitt, commanding, three hundred and seventy-five strong; ninth Kentucky regiment, Captain James T. Morehead, commanding, three hundred and twenty strong, and Cobb's battery, placed under my command, as senior officer, with orders to report to General Morgan, left Baird's mill where the brigade was in bivouac, on Saturday the sixth instant, about one and a half o'clock, P. M. Marching in the rear of the cavalry force until we arrived in the vicinity of Lebanon an exchange was made, when the infantry mounted the horses and rode five or six miles. The command reached Cumberland river about ten o'clock. The infantry, artillery and a small portion of cavalry crossed at — ferry, the balance of the cavalry crossing at a ford a few miles lower down the river. The two boats used for crossing were of small capacity and in miserable condition, but by constant bailing they were kept afloat, and by five o'clock, in the morning the command was safely over.

The march of five miles to Hartsville, (where the battle was fought,) yet to make, over bad roads for artillery, was not accomplished until after sunrise, and the purpose of General Morgan to surprise the enemy was defeated. When we approached in sight of their camp, we found their infantry already formed, occupying a very strong position on the crest of a hill with a deep ravine in front, and their artillery in battery. The troops under my command were placed in position west of the enemy's camp, while under a heavy fire from their battery, and sharpshooters thrown out from their right, but these latter were quickly driven in by the dismounted cavalry.

The second regiment having been formed on the left of the ninth, was now ordered forward to support and follow up the success gained by the cavalry skirmishers. That they had hot work to accomplish is shown by their heavy loss in killed and wounded.

In the meantime Captain Cobb, with his battery, was not idle. He was doing good execction and the enemy responded with effect, one of their shells striking and blowing up a caisson. As the ground was cleared of the enemy opposite our left, he (Captain Cobb) was ordered to take a new position with his battery in that direction, and at the same time the ninth Kentucky regiment was ordered forward to engage the enemy's left.

My whole command was now engaged. The crest of the hill was reached, and here commenced a desperate struggle, as the contestants were only from thirty to fifty paces apart, where they fought for the space of ten minutes, when the order to charge was given and most nobly was the command responded to. The enemy broke and were driven to the river cliff, where they were completely surrounded by my force in front, and the dismounted cavalry on their flanks and rear, and where they surrendered at discretion.

It was a continued success from the commencement. In about one and half hours from the time the first gun was fired they surrendered, and more prisoners were brought off than we had men in the action. Large quanties of commissary and quartermasters stores were also secured, a section of artillery and a large number of small arms with the usual supply of ammunition.

Gen. Morgan had made most skillful disposition, which, with the good fighting qualities of the troops engaged, secured success. I cannot speak in too high terms of praise of the troops, and I scarcely know which most to admire their patient endurance on the march or courage in the battle. They marched fifty miles in cold winter weather, the ground covered with snow, crossed and recrossed the Cumberland river, fought a largely superior force, strongly posted within six miles of their supports, and brought off the prisoners, all within the space of thirty hours. Captain Cobb, with his officers and men, had a most laborious time in getting their pieces and horses across the river, and it was only by the best directed exertions they succeeded at all. Where officers and men all behaved so well it is impossible for me to single out individual cases as peculiarly worthy of commendation. I cannot, however, refrain from mentioning Lieutenant Joseph Benedict who acted as my aid on the occasion. He was the right man in the right place.

I enclose, herewith, copies of the reports of Major Hewett, Captain Morehead and Captain Cobb, and would bring to your attention the fact that the former commends color sergeant John Oldham for his gallant bravery.

The following is a summary of the loss sustained by my command.

Command.	Killed.	Wounded.	Missing.
Second Kentucky regiment,	8	54	3
Ninth Kentucky regiment,	7	10	1
Cobb's battery,	3	7	0
Total,	18	71	4

Included in the above, are of the second Kentucky regiment, Chas. H. Thomas, first lieutenant, and John W. Rogers, second lieutenant,

Co. C, killed; T. M. Horne, first lieutenant, Co. A, mortally wounded second Lieutenant A J. Pryor, Co. D, Lieutenant Harding, Co. K, wounded. Of ninth Kentucky, second Lieut. Dandridge Crockett, killed, first Lieutenant J. W. Cleveland, wounded.

I am, sir, very respectfully,
Your obedient servant,
THOMAS H. HUNT,
Colonel Commanding Detachment.

REPORT OF MAJOR HEWITT, 2D KENTUCKY REGIMENT.

HEADQUARTERS 2D KENTUCKY REGIMENT,
Camp Murfreesboro', Dec. 9th, 1862.

Colonel THOMAS W. HUNT:

Sir, I have the honor to report that in pursuance of your orders I formed my regiment on the left of the ninth Kentucky, opposite the enemy's camp near Hartsville, a portion of General Morgan's cavalry being at the same time on my left. When the orders came for me to advance, I ordered my regiment forward and after passing the fence the nature of the ground was such that I deemed it advisable to deploy my regiment, and therefore gave the order to deploy. In this way we drove the enemy from heir first camp and continued to drive them until they surrendered. The officers, without an exception, behaved in the most gallant style. They were continually in advance of their men urging them forward, and where all behaved so well, it would be impossible to particularize. Each seemed to vie with the other in deeds of gallantry. The whole command, I am pleased to say, behaved in a most unexceptionable manner. I cannot conclude my report without reference to color-sergeant John Oldham, whose conduct and courage during the whole engagement elicited the encomiums of both officers and men. Append d is a list of the killed, wounded and missing, all of which I respectfully submit.

Your obedient servant,
(Signed,) JAMES W. HEWITT,
Major Commanding Twenty-second Kentucky Regiment.

Killed,	8
Wounded,	54
Missing,	3
Total,	65

REPORT OF CAPTAIN JAMES T. MOOREHEAD OF THE
BATTLE OF HARTSVILLE.

NINTH KENTUCKY REGIMENT,
Camp near Murfreesboro', Dec. 10, 1862.

To Colonel THOMAS N. HUNT,

Commanding Infantry:

SIR: At twelve o'clock, on Saturday the sixth instant, I, as senior captain, was placed, by your orders, in command of the ninth Kentucky regiment, which had, the day before, moved to Baird's mills, eighteen miles from Murfreesboro, and was, at that time, about to march against the enemy, reported to be at Hartsville, Tennessee.

The weather was excessively cold, the snow having fallen the day before to some depth and the road was very rough; notwithstanding, the men marched steadily during the day and all night, and reached the immediate neighborhood of the enemy's camp, near Hartsville, at sunrise. The enemy occupied a strong position in front of his encampment, his line of battle stretching along the crest of a hill, which was separated from our forces by an intervening hollow or ravine. Our line of battle was formed with Cobb's battery on the right, supported by the ninth Kentucky regiment directly in its rear. On our immediate left was the second Kentucky regiment and still farther to the left a portion of two regiments of dismounted cavalry, under Colonel Duke. The enemy occupied, with his sharpshooters, the woods and ravines in front of the left wing of our line, and opened a brisk fire on us. Against them the dismounted cavalry deployed as skirmishers, and soon succeeded in dislodging and driving them back upon the main body of the enemy. The second Kentucky regiment was ordered forward, and the ninth left in support of the battery. In a few minutes after, I was ordered to advance and moved the regiment, in double quick, in the direction of the main body of the enemy, going over, in our route, very rough ground, and through a deep ravine. Ascending the hill the regiment advanced to the right of the second Kentucky, halted, and immediately became engaged, at less than fifty paces, with the enemy. After fighting for a short time, I ordered a charge, which was made with such gallantry by the regiment, that the left wing of the enemy's line gave way and commenced retreating in confusion. Pressed closely by the ninth Kentucky, they passed through their camps and took refuge under the brow of a hill on the bank of the river and in rear of their artillery. The regiment continued to move rapidly on and captured the two pieces of artillery and a stand of colors, charged the line of the enemy and drove them to the brink of the river, compelling their immediate surrender. Here we captured Colonel Moore, commanding brigade, who, in reply to a question from Captain Gouch, answered that he surrendered himself and all the men around him, meaning the whole force. The battle was now fairly won, the firing had ceased save a few scattering shots here and there. I immediately formed the regiment again in line of battle, had order restored, stragglers collected, and the men kept in their places. I sent details from all the companies to look after the dead and wounded, and detailed company "H," Captain Bosche, to guard the 106th Ohio regiment captured by us. The prisoners being collected, I was ordered to detail companies "A and C," to guard them, and afterwards company "G." The regiment recrossed the river and began its march towards Lebanon, Tennessee. Too much praise cannot be given to the officers and men for their spirit and patient endurance under a march of almost unexampled hardship and rapidity, and for their gallantry and good conduct in action.

The regiment had in battle an aggregate of three hundred and twenty men. The casualties were as follows, viz:

Company A—Lieutenant Thomas McCaing, commanding.—One private wounded.

Company B—Captain Crouch, commanding.—One private wounded.

Company D—Lieut. Beale. commanding.—One private wounded.

Company G—Lieutenant Daniel, commanding.—One private missing; one private wounded.

Company H—Captain E. Bosche, commanding.—One private missing and one corporal killed.

Company I—Captain John Desha, commanding.—Three privates killed, and two lieutenants (J. W. Cleveland and W. T. Casey) and three privates wounded.

Company I—Lieutenant Gaines, commanding.—Killed, Lieutenant D. S. Crockett, and one private.

Total.—Killed, 7; wounded, 10; missing, 9.

All of which is respectfully submitted,
(Signed,) JAMES T. MOREHEAD,
Captain, commanding ninth Kentucky regiment.

REPORT OF CAPTAIN COBB.

Report of killed and wounded in Captain R. Cobb's company of Light Artillery, in the action near Hartsville, Tennessee, on Sunday, the 7th December, 1862.

Killed:—Sergeant W. E. Etheridge, Privates David Watts and Sanderfer. Total 3.

Wounded and left on the field on account of severity of wounds :—
Corporal James Donoh, Privates T. C. Carnhill, B. F. Perdue, Henry Williams. Total 4.

Wounded and not left :—Privates John Leonard, slightly, John Thomas, R F. Lear. Total 3.

Total killed and wounded, 10.

   Respectfully submitted,
  (Signed,)   R. COBB,
            Captain Commanding Battery.

A LIST of Killed, Wounded and Missing at the Battle of Hartsville, Tennessee, December 7, 1862, in the Troops commanded by Acting Brigadier General John H. Morgan.

Name.	Rank.	Co.	Killed, wounded and missing.	Remarks.
9TH KENTUCKY REGT.				
J. W. Cleveland	1st Lieut.	I.	Slightly in shoulder.	
Dandridge Crockett	2d "	"	Killed.	
W. T. Casey	3d Sergt.	"	Slightly in leg.	
Peter Kaye	Corpl.	H.	Killed.	
T. P. Winns	Private.	A.	Slightly in ankle.	
George Pash	"	B.	Severely in wrist.	
Wm. Hedger	"	D	Slightly in head.	
J. B. Gordon	"	G.	Missing.	Supposed to be killed.
Thos. Strother	"	"	Slightly in thigh.	
E. L. Ray	"	H.	Killed.	
James Michial	"	I.	Killed.	
John Smith	"	"	Killed.	
R. S. Cummings	"	"	Severely in breast and thigh.	
J. Creager	"	"	Severely in arm.	
W. B. Moss	"	"	Dangerously in mouth.	
Dennis O'Halloran	"	"	Slightly in leg.	
E. B. Messhon	"	K.	Killed.	
2ND KENTUCKY REGT.				
Thos. M. Horn	1st Lieut.	A.	Mortally wounded in breast.	Since died.
Chas. H. Thomas	"	C.	Killed.	
John W. Rodgers	2d Lieut.	"	Killed.	
A. J. Pryor	"	D.	Slightly in right arm.	
Ed. Harding	"	K.	Slightly in left leg.	
J. R. Owens	Sergeant.	A.	Slightly in left side.	
Anico West	"	D.	Slightly in right breast.	
R. T. Pryor	"	"	Dangerously in arm.	
Thos Maddox	"	E.	Killed.	
James Bark Jr	"	E.	Severely in right leg.	
James A. Reice	"	F.	Killed.	
P. H. Yancey	Corporal.	B.	Killed.	
Vite Frazier	"	C.	Severely in arm.	
Thomas Stewart	"	K.	Slightly in ankle.	
D. W. Weaver	Private.	A.	Killed.	
J. R. Brigg	"	"	Severely in leg.	
C. P. Davis	"	"	Slightly in head.	
P. H. Edwards	"	"	Mortally in breast.	
John King	"	"	Severely in right arm.	
Chas. Moore	"	"	Severely in breast.	
Thos. Rawatt	"	"	Mortally in arm.	Since died.
George Thomason	"	"	Severely in m uth.	
Hunif Winter	"	"	Severely in breast and shoulder.	
N. N. Daws	"	"	Slightly in head.	
J. B. Johnston	"	"	Slightly in side.	
N. P. Cannon	"	"	Slightly in left breast.	
Wm. Ward	"	"	Missing.	
F. R. Edwards	"	"	Missing.	
L. D. Payne	"	"	Dangerously in both legs.	
Samuel Scott	"	B.	Dangerously in right leg.	
Chas. H. Hall	"	"	Slightly in left thigh.	
M. S. Dougherty	"	"	Slightly in righ arm.	
E. S. Gordon	"	"	Slightly in right leg.	
J. P. Jones	"	"	Dangerously in foot.	
R. S. Payne	"	"	Missing.	
John A. Lee	"	C.	Slightly in leg.	
Alex. Rowley	"	"	Slightly in leg.	
George Galihen	"	"	Dangerously in head and neck.	
F. Lane	"	"	Slightly in abdomen.	
John R. Herey	"	D.	Killed.	
J. A. Pryor	"	"	Killed.	
J. Irbey	"	"	Dangerously in arm.	
Thos. F. Boay	"	"	Slightly in leg.	

LIST of Killed, Wounded and Missing—(Continued.)

Name.	Rank.	Co.	Killed, wounded and missing.	Remarks.
T. J. Jackson	Private.	D.	Slightly in hand.	
J. M. Sullivan	"	"	Slightly in leg.	
James M. Donald	"	E.	Slightly in breast.	
James Pulley	"	"	Slightly in hand and neck.	
P. C. Cunningham	"	"	Slightly in leg.	
J. Howard	"	F.	Severely in hand.	
S. Sutton	"	"	Severely in side and neck.	
R. Anderson	"	"	Severely in shoulder.	
Sam Thomason	"	"	Slightly in thigh.	
James W. Lindsay	"	"	Missing.	
Robert Raither, Jr.	"	G.	Mortally in leg.	Since died.
D. J. Brickley	"	"	Slightly in arm.	
M. Powers	"	"	Slightly in leg.	
George Hiller	"	"	Slightly in leg.	
John A. Mason	"	H.	Severely in shoulder.	
C. M. Swager	"	"	Slightly in leg.	
Garrc A Elgin	"	"	Severely in thigh and knee.	
H. P. White	"	"	Severely in both hands.	
J. H. Kinkton, Jr.	"	I.	Severely in leg.	
Wm. Brown	"	"	Severely in shoulder.	
John S. Sreet	"		Missing.	
John Harris	"		Missing.	
Frank Taylor	"		Slightly in face.	
P. L. Lewis	"		Slightly in leg.	
David Mordon	"		Slightly in leg.	

COL. GANO'S REGT. OF CAVALRY.

Name.	Rank.	Co.	Killed, wounded and missing.	Remarks.
Andrews	Sergeant.		Missing.	

COL. CLARKE'S REGT. OF CAVALRY.

Name.	Rank.	Co.	Killed, wounded and missing.	Remarks.
Coleman	Lieut. Col.		Slightly in thigh.	
W. E. Curry	Capt. Q. M.		Slightly.	
Jinddleton	Captain.	D.	Slightly.	
Price	Chaplain.	"	Missing.	
W. S. Cailer	1st Lieut.	D.	Slightly in thigh and ankle.	
Robt. Cunningham	2d Lieut.	E.	Severely in hip.	
W. S. Kendall	"	D.	Killed.	
A. Maydwell	Q. M. Sgt.		Missing.	
George Didlake	O. S.	A.	Missing.	
E. Campbell	"	E.	Severely in thigh.	
Robert M. Kansey	"	H.	Slightly.	
Wm. Merrill	2d Sergt.	A.	Missing.	
John Owen	Corporal.	E.	Slightly in thigh.	
George Roby	Private.	A.	Severely in both thighs.	
J. H. Easton	"	"	Slightly.	
Christopher Spears	"	B.	Slightly.	
Charleton	"	"	Killed.	
Henry Nicholas	"	B.	Slightly.	
Robert Baker	"	F.	Severely in neck.	
James Thomas	"	H.	Missing.	
W. H. Stan	"	"	Severely in neck.	
C. C. Brown	"	"	Slightly.	
T. J. Gilky	"	"	Mortally.	
Thos. Wilson	"	"	Severely.	
Wash Kemper	"	"	Slightly.	
Lewis Peters	"	I.	"	
J Beack	"	"	"	
W Trimble	"	"	"	
Joseph Burkley	"	"	"	
Hiram Jones	"	"	"	
Andy Gilligan	"	"	"	
Jowell Owens	"	E.	Missing.	

COL. CHENAULT'S REGT. OF CAVALRY.

Name.	Rank.	Co.	Killed, wounded and missing.	Remarks.
James Kelly	"	A.	Mortally.	Since reported dead.

LIST of Killed, Wounded and Missing—(Continued.)

Name.	Rank.	Co.	Killed, wounded and missing.	Remarks.
Colley W. Pundon	Private.	A.	Slightly.	
Thos. Duerson	"	"	"	
John Hall	"	"	"	
Thos. Buchanan	"	"	Killed.	
COL. BENNETT'S REGT. OF CAVALRY.				
Haynes	Lieut.		Slightly in shoulder.	
W. E. Griffith	Private.	D.	Slightly in finger.	
Wm. Mooter	"	"	Severely in thigh.	
Frank Buchan	"	E.	Mortally.	
COBB'S BATTERY.				
W. E. Etheridge	Sergeant.		Killed.	
James Dorob	Corporal.		Severely in hand, groin and leg.	
David Watts	Private.		Killed.	
Benj. Sandefur	"		Killed.	
Thomas Campbell	"		Severely in arm and face.	
Henry Williams	"		Severely in ankle.	
John Leonard	"		Slightly in hip.	
B. F. Purdu	"		"	
R. F. Lear	"		"	
J. C. Thomas	"		" in hand.	
GEN. MORGAN'S PERSONAL STAFF.				
Robert Tyler			Slightly in knee.	
C. Peyton			Severel,.	Left behind.

RECAPITULATION.

Command.	Killed.	Wounded.	Missing.	Total.
9th Kentucky Regiment	6	10	1	17
2d " "	8	64	6	78
Col. Gano's Regiment of Cavalry			1	1
Col. Clarke's " "	2	24	6	32
Col. Chenault's " "	1	4		5
Col. Bennett's " "	1	3		4
Cobbs Battery	3	7		10
Gen. Morgan's Staff		2		2
Total	21	114	14	149
Officers	4	11	1	16
Non-commissioned Officers	5	13	4	22
Privates	12	90	9	111
Total	21	101	14	149

A true copy from files in this office.

GEO. WM. BRENT.
A. A General.

REPORT

OF THE

BATTLES OF POCOTALIGO AND YEMASSEE.

REPORT OF BRIG. GEN. W. S. WALKER.

HEADQUARTERS THIRD MILITARY DISTRICT S. C.,
Pocotaligo, November 4th, 1862.

Brig. Gen. THOMAS JORDAN,
Chief of Staff and A. A. G.:

Sir: I have the honor to report, that about nine o'clock, on the morning of the 22d October, I was informed by my pickets that the enemy were landing in force at Mackey's Point, from twelve gunboats and transports. I was notified, at the same time, that they were ascending the Coosawhatchie river with four transports.

The command was immediately ordered under arms, to march to Old Pocotaligo. I moved in advance to the telegraph office; and made the following disposition of my forces: The Lafayette Artillery, four pieces, under Lieutenant LeBleur, and a section of the Beaufort Volunteer Artillery, under Lieutenant N. M. Stuart, were ordered to Coosawhatchie, a town two miles distant from my head quarters in McPhersonville, and five from Old Pocotaligo. Captain Wyman's company, stationed near Coosawhatchie, and five other companies of the eleventh regiment of infantry, from Harleeville, were ordered to support this Artillery. Colonel Colcock's command of five companies of cavalry, and two companies of Sharp Shooters, had been recently notified to expect an attack at Coosawhatchie, and in that event were instructed to move to its support. Major Jefford's command, of three companies of cavalry, were ordered from Green Pond to the Saltkehatchie bridge. With the blessings of a good Providence, these combinations of my forces, scattered over an extent of sixty miles, were effected in time to foil the enemy.

I also telegraphed to General Beauregard's headquarters to Brigadier General Hagood, commanding second military district, and to

Brigadier General Mercer, at Savannah, for reinforcements, requesting those from Charleston to disembark at Pocotaligo, and those from Savannah at Coosawhatchie. Captain W. L. Trenholm, who was in command of the outposts, consisting of two companies—his Rutledge Mounted Riflemen and Captain Kirk's Partisan Rangers—was ordered to withdraw the main body of the pickets, only leaving a few important posts guarded.

The force with which I first engaged the enemy consisted of two sections of the Beaufort Volunteer Artillery and the Nelson Light Artillery, eight pieces, under the command of Captain Stephen Elliott; the Charleston Light Dragoons, Captain B. W. Rutledge; first battalion cavalry, Major Morgan; Captain D. B. Heyward's company of cavalry; Captain Kirk's Partizan Rangers; Captain Allston's company of Sharpshooters; Captain Izard's company I, of the eleventh regiment of infantry, Lieutenant W. L. Campbell commanding: number in all four hundred and seventy-five (475.)

As one-fourth of the cavalry were horse holders, the force actually engaged was reduced to four hundred and five (405) men.

The force of the enemy was represented by prisoners, and confirmed by the statement of negroes who had crossed Port Royal Ferry to the main land on that day and been captured, to be seven regiments, one of which I judge went to Coosawhatchie.

I sent in advance a section of the Beaufort Volunteer Artillery, supported by Captain Allston's Sharpshooters and two companies of cavalry under Major Morgan to skirmish with the enemy, while I took position on the Mackey's Point road, near Dr. Hutson's residence, at a salt marsh skirted by woods on both sides and crossed by a causeway. After a short encounter with the enemy, in which Major Morgan, while at the head of his command, was severely wounded in the ankle, my advance force retired in good order to the main position. The Beaufort Artillery was posted in and near the road commanding the causeway, and the Nelson Artillery in an open field in the rear of the line of skirmishers and screened from the enemy by the trees in front. A dropping fire of infantry first commenced, which was soon swelled by their artillery. Owing to the close proximity of the trees fringing the other side of the swamp, I found that my artillery were suffering severely in men and horses, and, accordingly after holding my ground for three quarters of an hour, I determined to withdraw to a second position two miles and a half in rear. This was done in good order, Captain Allston's Sharpshooters and part of Co. I, eleventh infantry, covering our retreat and behaving for the most part with great spirit. At the head of the road I was joined by Captain Trenholm with the larger portion of his company and Captain Kirk's. I assigned the command of the cavalry to him, and ordered my whole force to move back across Pocotaligo bridge and take up a position among the houses and scattered trees of the hamlet.

The artillery was placed in position to command the bridge and causeway—the Charleston Light Dragoons being held in reserve. The bridge was ordered to be torn up; and this was scarcely done when the enemy appeared in sight and commenced a continuous and rapid fire of musketry and rifled guns. Lieutenant Massie, of the Nelson Artillery, could bring only one piece of his battery into action, owing to the original smallness of his company, now greatly reduced by deaths and wounds.

Two pieces of the Beaufort Artillery were silenced by the disabling of the gunners; the remaining two kept up a fire to the close of the fight. The enemy's artillery was entirely silenced and withdrawn early in the action. One piece of the Beaufort Artillery was most judiciously withdrawn during the battle and posted three hundred yards on my right, under Sergeant-Major Fuller. It was retired by a cross road unseen by the enemy, and had all the effect of a reinforcement from its new and unexpected position. It fired spherical case, and the practice was excellent.

At the crisis of the fight, I ordered up the Charleston Light Dragoons. That gallant corps came forward with an inspiriting shout and took position on my left, which wanted strengthening.

I had been notified by telegraph that reinforcements were on the way from Charleston and Savannah and Adams' run. The Nelson battalion of two hundred men, Captain Slight commanding, was the only reinforcement that arrived in time for the fight, about an hour and a half before its close.

As soon as this corps made its appearance near the field, I ordered one half to a position commanding a causeway some six hundred yards on my right, to protect my flank; and the remainder was deployed to the front to relieve my exhausted men. The arrival of this battalion gave me assurance of victory; I felt perfectly certain of success.

The two companies sent to my right under Captain Brooks were well handled; one was deployed as skirmishers, and subjected to a scattering fire. Their appearance threatened the enemy's flank, and no doubt hastened his retreat.

The enemy continued their fire until 6 o'clock, P. M., when it slackened and ceased. I then sent a squad of six men of the Rutledge Mounted Riflemen over the bridge to ascertain the position of the enemy. The bridge was in so damaged a condition that it was some time before the infantry could cross.

The cavalry were obliged to make a circuit of five miles to reach the head of the road by which the enemy had retreated. This enabled them to retire unmolested. As soon as the cavalry arrived, I sent two companies, Rutledge Mounted Riflemen, Lieut. L. I. Walker, commanding, and Captain Kirks' Partisan Rangers, to follow up the retreat. I was reluctant to send a larger force, as I did not know the result of the contest at Coosawhatchie, and from the telegraph wire being cut, was fearful it was disastrous to our arms. A locomotive was dispatched from Pocotaligo station by my aid, Mr. R. M. Fuller, and two couriers by myself to that point to reconnoitre, while I held my force at the junction of the Mackey's Point and Coosawhatchie roads, ready to operate either way. The cavalry had proceeded but two and a half miles in pursuit, when they were stopped by a bridge completely torn up and destroyed by the enemy in their flight. This could not be repaired until morning. There were abundant evidences that the retreat of the enemy was precipitate and disordered. One hundred small arms were picked up and a considerable amount of stores and ammunition. The road was strewn with the debris of the beaten foe. Forty six of the enemy's dead were found on the battlefield and roadside. Seven fresh graves were discovered at Mackey's Point. I estimated their total killed and wounded at three hundred.

The fight, from the first fire of our advance to the final retreat of the enemy lasted from half past 11 o'clock, A. M., to 6 o'clock, P. M. We have ample reason to believe that our small force not only fought against great odds, but against fresh troops brought up to replace those first engaged. The entire command had been earnestly warned in orders not to waste their fire. This caution was urged upon them during the action by the commanding officer, his aids and the company officers. I am satisfied, from my own observation, they fired with care and judgment: and yet some of our men expended *eighty* rounds of catridges in the battle. The close vicinity of the ordnance train under its energetic chief, Capt. W. W. Elliott, enabled me to keep up the supply.

I beg to express my admiration of the remarkable courage and tenacity with which the troops held their ground. The announcement of my determination to maintain my position until reinforcements arrived seemed to fix them to the spot with unconquerable resolution.

The rapid and continuous vollies of the enemy's musketry were only intermitted while fresh troops were brought up and while those engaged were retired.

The Beaufort Volunteer Artillery fought with great courage, and their pieces were admirably served. Captain Stephen Elliot, whose name is identified with the history of the defence of this coast by many a daring exploit, behaved with his accustomed coolness, skill and determination.

Capt. Trenholm, in command of the cavalry, again exhibited high qualities as a soldier on the same ground where he had won his first laurels.

Captain Edwards, Co. "B," 1st battalion cavalry, showed good conduct in the command of his company.

Lieutenant Walker, commanding the Rutledge Mounted Riflemen, displayed judgement and daring. His company were as steady as veterans, using their rifles with great precision and effect.

When the battle was hottest, I ordered Lieut. Walker to take a squad of his men and assist the Beaufort Artillery to remove one of their pieces further to the rear. This was most gallantly done under a severe fire.

Lieut. Massie, of the Nelson Light Artillery, was active and energetic in the service of his guns.

Captain Rutledge, of the Charleston Light Dragoons, was cool and collected in both fights. His gallant corps was held in reserve, and when they took up their position, came with a most inspiring cheer, which the men engaged returned, thus giving the impression to the enemy of decided reinforcements.

The government is greatly indebted to Captain Sligh, and his brave battalion for their timely aid: Captain Sligh behaved with marked coolness and courage. Captain* ———— and Lieutenant† ————— who came immediately under my notice, showed zeal and bravery. I have again to commend the conduct of Lieutenant R. M. Skinner, acting adjutant of the first battalion cavalry. He was among the foremost on the field until disabled by a severe wound in the arm.

Enclosed in Colonel Colcock's report of the engagement at Coosawhatchie, it will be seen that his command behaved with spirit and success. The most important point to defend was the railroad bridge over the Coosawhatchie river. From this the enemy were very quickly driven by our artillery fire, but they succeeded in penetrating to a point on the railroad, west of the bridge, before the cavalry arrived; one or two rails only being torn up and the telegraph wire cut, the damage was repaired in a few minutes. After the enemy had retired to their gun-boats, the cavalry under Lieutenant Colonel Johnson fired with effect upon their crowded decks.

To the following gentlemen, acting as my personal staff, I desire to express my thanks for their zeal, gallantry, and intelligent discharge of duty. Captain Hartstene, C. S. N., naval aid, Captain W. W. Elliott, ordinance officer, Captain George P. Elliott, Captain John H. Screven, Corporal D. Walker and Privates Tripp and Martin, of the Rutledge Mounted Riflemen, and private E. B. Bell, of the seventeenth battalion, S. C. V. Privates F. F. Davant and Ion Simmons, of the Charleston Light Dragoons, had their horses shot, and afterwards fought with their company on foot.

My aid, Mr. R. M. Fuller, rendered valuable service by the intelligent discharge of his duty at the telegraph office. The Messrs. Cuthbert, father and son, gave me useful assistance. Privates Tripp and Bell were seriously, and private Martin slightly wounded. Captain Hartstene's horse was wounded, and Captain Walker's killed.

The judgment, coolness and gallantry displayed by Captain Hartstene, were as conspicuous on land as he has hitherto shown on sea. I must express my indebtedness to Mr. Buckhalter, of the Charleston and Savannah railroad for valuable services, and for the resolution and courage with which he urged a train filled with troops, after the engineer had been killed, through an ambuscade of the enemy to Coosawhatchie.

When the engagement was over, ample reinforcements arrived from Savannah and Charleston. The enemy's gun-boats remained in a commanding position off Mackay's Point on the 23d, covering their embarkation. My force could not be moved nearer than two miles without being exposed to a destructive fire. A detachment of cavalry under Captain Trenholm closely watched their operations, occasionally saluted by their shells.

On the night of the 23d, sergeant Robinson, of the Rutledge Mounted Riflemen made a reconnoisance up to the extreme point, and discovered that the enemy had abandoned the main land. Early on

---

*The names of these officers, though repeatedly requested, have not yet been learned.

†The commanding officer of the battalion has received instructions to forward them to department headquarters.

the morning of the 24th, their gun-boats had disappeared. I enclose a list of the casualties, and a sketch of the positions at which the different conflicts took place.

I have the honor to be, very respectfully,
Your obedient servant,
(Signed,) W. S. WALKER,
Brigadier General commanding.

LIST OF CASUALTIES in the battle of Pocotaligo, Oct. 23, 1862.

	Killed.	Wounded.	Missing.
Company I, Eventh Infantry	2	8	2
Captain Alston's Sharpshooters	1	7	2
Nelson's Battalion	4	17	
Beaufort Volunteer Artillery	1	13	
Nelson Light Artillery	4	14	
Company A, First Battalion Cavalry		1	
" B, " " "	1	9	
" C, " " "		1	1
" D, " " "	1	2	
Rut'edge Mounted Riflemen		2	
Charleston Light Dragoons		8	
Partizan Rangers	1	2	
Marion Men, of Combahee		6	1
Aggregate	15	90	6

One Lieutenant and two men were captured while on picket, belonging to company C, First Battalion Cavalry.

RECAPITULATION.

Company I, Eleventh Infantry.—Killed, wounded and missing; all enlisted men.
Captain Allston's sharpshooters.—Wounded, Captain Allston, Second Lieu onant M. Stuart, Third Lieutenant E. P. Carter, slightly; killed one enlisted man; three wounded; two missing.
Nelson's Battalion.—All enlisted men.
Beaufort Volunteer Artillery.—All enlisted men.
Nelson Light Artillery.—Wounded, Lieutenant Massie severely; enlis'ed men, four killed; thirteen wounded.
First Battalion Cavalry.—Wounded, Major Morgan severely; Lieutenant R. M. Skinner, acting Adjutant, severely. Company A, one enlisted man wounded. Company B, one enlisted man killed; wounded, Lieutenant P. D. Rush slightly; and eight enlisted men. Company C, enlisted men; one wounded and one missing. Company D, enlisted men; one killed and two wounded.
Charleston Light Dragoons.—Enlisted men; eight wounded.
Rutledge Mounted Riflemen.—Enlisted men; two wounded.
Partizan Rangers.—Second Lieutenant W. T. Speaks killed; wounded Third Lieutenant P. E. Terry, severely; one enlisted man.
Marion Men, of Combahee.—Wounded, six enlisted men, and one missing.

REPORT OF COLONEL C. J. COLCOCKE.

HEADQUARTERS 3D REG'T CAV., S. C. V., }
Grahamville, Nov. 4th, 1862. }

Lieut. ED. H. BARNWELL, *A. A. A. General:*

Sir: A little after nine o'clock on the morning of the 22d October, it was reported to me unofficially that about day light that morning, the Aboliton fleet, consisting of fourteen steamers, with numerous barges attached, had proceeded up Broad river.

Prostrated by a protracted spell of fever, from which I had just began to convalesce, I was too weak to take the field, but resumed the command of my post. I ordered Lieut. Col. Johnson to take command of the small force at my disposal, which consisted, as you are aware, of five companies of cavalry and two companies of sharpshooters, of Major Abney's battalion, who was in command, and to proceed with the least possible delay towards Coosawhatchie, to which point I was informed that a portion of the enemy's fleet were advancing. On arriving at Bee's Creek, still four miles from Coosawhatchie, Col. Johnson was informed that a portion of the Abolition forces were landing at Seabrook's Island, in his rear, a point indicating an attack upon this place. To meet this he had to divide his command and put three companies in the vicinity of Bee's Creek Hill. This information was subsequently ascertained to be incorrect, but too late to make use of these forces in the defense of Coosawhatchie.

Proceeding with three companies of cavalry towards that point, upon arriving within two miles of it he ascertained that the enemy had already landed from a gunboat and barge lying a little below the Ocean landing, and was advancing his column towards the direction of Bee's Creek Hill. He immediately dismounted his men and formed them as skirmishers to meet the expected attack. This movement, however, was only a feint, as they soon "about faced" and advanced towards Coosawhatchie. The ground being unfavorable for a charge, the effect of which would have necessarily been attended with severe loss to the cavalry, with a prospect of little injury to the enemy, Colonel Johnson very judiciously made a detour to the left, hoping to cut them off before they reached Coosawhatchie.

About this time the train, with a portion of Colonel Ellis' regiment and Captain Chisholm's company, of Major Abney's battalion, which had been taken up within a short distance of Coosawhatchie, as they were marching along the railroad track towards that point, passed by. The enemy hearing their approach for some distance, (the two roads here running parallel and very close to each other,) availed themselves of the opportunity to ambuscade and fire into the train.

The particulars of this disastrous affair I will not refer to, as I suppose a full report of all the circumstances will be made up by the officer in command of that detachment, who succeeded the late unfortunate Major Harrison. It seems, that on arriving near Coosawhatchie, the enemy divided into two detachments, one of which ambuscaded the train as above referred to, and the other advanced to the river, for the purpose of destroying the railroad and turnpike bridges. With timely forethought, you had fortunately dispatched at an early hour that morning, for their protection, the La Fayette Artillery, Lieut. Le Bleux commanding, and a section of Capt. Elliott's battery, Lieut. Stuart commanding. These, supported by Captain Wyman's company of infantry, most gallantly repulsed the enemy in their attack on the bridges and drove them in confusion towards their other detachments, which, beyond the range of our artillery, had succeeded in cutting the telegraph wire and displacing a couple of rails on the track. About this time, the cavalry, which had to make a considerable detour over very unfavorable ground, made its appearance, and the enemy beat a hasty retreat, the cavalry pursuing. Unfortunately, the enemy had taken the precaution, in advancing, of destroying all the bridges, which so retarded the progress of the cavalry as to prevent their cutting off their retreat to their gunboat, and barges. Disappointed in this object, Col. Johnson dismounted his men and deploying them as skirmishers, advanced to within about one hundred and thirty yards of the gunboats, where, under the protection of a few trees, they poured three volleys from their rifles into the crowded decks and barges of the enemy, which must have done considerable execution. The companies composing this detachment consisted of Capts. J. H. Howard's, A. B. Estes', under the immediate command of Lieut. Peebles, and Capt. Geo. C. Heyward. Recovering from their surprise, the enemy opened a terrific fire of grape, shell and musketry, in which they were assisted by two of their gunboats stationed a half mile lower down the river, under whose enfilading fire our small force had to fall back. In this affair, I regret to inform you, we lost private Thomas B. Fripp, of Capt. Heyward's company, who fell mortally wounded, shot in three places, as gallant a soldier and true-hearted gentleman as ever fell a martyr in defending the cause of liberty. First Lieut. T. G. Buckner, of Capt. Heyward's company, was also severely, but I hope not mortally, wounded in the abdomen, and Corporal Thomas Farr, of the same company, received a flesh wound in the thigh, from which, I am happy to say, he is rapidly recovering. That the casualties were not greater, I can only attribute to the interposition of a merciful Providence, who protects those fighting in a righteous cause. For casualties occurring in Maj. Abney's command, I refer you to that officer's report, which you will find herewith enclosed.

Two hours after this train passed Grahamville another train arrived from Savannah with the 32d and —— Georgia regiments, under the command of the gallant Col. Harrison. Unfortunately, they arrived at Coosawhatchie after the enemy had retired, and thus were denied the pleasure which they seemed earnestly to desire, of having a brush with the Abolitionists.

The enemy's boats retired immediately after the skirmish, leaving in their hasty retreat, one of their splendid barges, capable of transporting seventy or eighty men.

The next morning not a sign of the Abolition fleet was to be seen in the upper waters of Broad river.

I have the honor to remain,
Very respectfully, your obedient servant,
(Signed,) C. J. COLCOCKE,
Colonel Commanding.

REPORT OF CAPTAIN ELLIOTT.

HEADQUARTERS ARTILLERY, THIRD MILITARY DISTTICT,
Department South Carolina,
McPhersonville, October 24th, 1862.

Lieutenant E. H. BARNWELL, A. A. A. General,
Third Military District, Department South Carolina:

Sir: I have the honor to submit the following report of the casualties in the artillery force under my command.

The following is a list of the casualties in two sections Beaufort Artillery, Lieutenant J. J. Rhodes, commanding:

Wounded—Sergeant J. F. Chaplin, finger shot off; Sergeant William Thomson, neck, severely; Corporal N. B. Fuller, arm, severely; Corporal E. E. Durban, hand, severely; Corporal J. J. Brown, leg, flesh; privates J. E. Tripp, abdomen, since dead; R. F. Sams, hand, severely; John Jenkins, three fingers shot off; Daniel Jenkins, head slightly; A. Budden, leg, flesh wound; E. B. Trescott, leg, severely; J F. Cuthbert, head, slightly; S. A. Sams, foot, slightly; J. D. Richardson, back, flesh wound.

Very respectfully, your obedient servant,
STEPHEN ELLIOTT, JR.,
Captain Beaufort Artillery, Commanding Artillery,
Third Military District, Department S. C.

CASUALTIES in Colonel *Walker's* immediate command in the affair near Pocotaligo, October 22, 1862.

COMMAND.	KILLED.		WOUNDED.		MISSING.		TOTAL.
	Officers.	Enlisted.	Officers.	Enlisted.	Officers.	Enlisted.	
Co. I, 11th S. C. V............		2		8	1	1	12
Charleston Light Dragoons.......				8			8
Co. B, 1st Battalion. S. C. S. S....		1		3	4	2	10
Captain Heyward's Company......				4		1	5
Nelson's Light Artillery............		4	2	13			19
Co A. 1st Battalion Cavalry.......				1			1
Co. B, 1st Battalion Cavalry		1		1	7		9
Co. C, 1st Battalion Cavalry.......				1	1	3	5
Co. D, 1st Battalion Cavalry.......		1		2			3
Partizan Rangers Capt. Kirk......	1			1	1		3
R. M. R., Lieutenant J. Walker, commanding............				2			2
	1	9	8	50	2	7	77

Report of killed, wounded and missing at Pocotaligo and Coosawhatchie.

Captain Lamkin's Virginia battery.—Killed, 4 privates; wounded, 2 officers and 13 privates.

Company B, 1st battalion South Carolina Sharpshooters, Captain T. Balton.—Killed, 1 private; wounded, 3 officers and 4 privates; missing 2 privates.

Captain Heyward's 3d cavalry.—Wounded, 4 privates; missing 1 private.

Captain Rutledge's Charleston Light Dragoons.—Wounded, 8 privates.

Company I, 11th S. C. V., infantry, Lieutenant Campbell.—Killed, 2 privates; wounded, 8 privates; missing 1 officer and 1 private.

Beaufort Light Artillery, Lieutenant J. J. Rhodes.—Killed, 1 private; wounded, 13 privates.

Company A, 1st battalion cavalry.—Wounded, 1 officer.

Company B, 1st battalion cavalry.—Killed, 1 private; wounded, 1 officer and 7 privates.

Marion Men, of Combahee, Captain Heyward.—Killed, none; wounded, none.

Rutledge's Mounted Riflemen, Lieutenant T. J. Walker.—Wounded, 2 privates.

Company C, 1st battalion cavalry, Lieutenant A. O. Banks.—Wounded, 1 private; missing, 1 officer and 4 privates.

Company D, 1st battalion cavalry, N. P. Gree.—Killed, 1 private; wounded, 2 privates.

Partizan Rangers, Captain Kirk.—Killed, 1 officer; wounded, 1 officer.

Companies B, C, D, K, Major J. J. Harrison, Coosawhatchie.—Killed, 1 officer; wounded, 7 privates.

Captain Heyward's company, 3d South Carolina cavalry.—Killed, 1 private.

Captain Howard's company, 3d South Carolina cavalry.—Killed, 1 private; wounded, 1 officer.

REPORT OF COL. ALLSON.

CAMP WALKER, McPHERSONVILLE, S. C.,
October 24, 1862.

Lieut E. H. BARNWELL, *A. A. A. G.*:

LIEUTEANT: I have to report the following casualties in this company in the engagement of the 22d inst:

Killed.—Private P. B. McDaniel.

Wounded.—Captain J. B. Allston, slight cut from ball in right fore arm and buckshot wound in fleshy part of the right buttock; Lieut. Middleton Stuart, in fleshy part of arm, (right) near the shoulder, from ball; Lieut. Caper, contusion on right hip, from fragment of shell. Privates J. A. Attaway, flesh wound in back part of neck; W. Brown, cut from ball, in calf right leg; E. Boatwright, severe contusion on right hip from ball striking his canteen; S. M. Smith, severely, in right shoulder, from ball.

Missing.—Privates W. W. Long, left severely wounded at Hatsons'; J. Walden, last seen at junction of Mackey Point, and Cosawhatchie road.

The company went into action with thirty-nine (39) enlisted men, and three commissioned officers.

JOS. BLYTHE ALLSON,
Captain Co. " B," 1st Bat. S. C. S. S.

REPORT OF COL. ELLIS.

HEADQUARTERS HARDEEVILL,
October 26th, 1862.

Col. Wm. S. WALKER:

SIR: The following are the casualties, reported in the companies of the 1st regiment which were engaged with the enemy at Coosawhatchie.

Major J. J. Harrison, commanding regiment.

Co. B, Lieut. Chaplin, commanding—Killed.—Private C. Rush, leg crushed by train, reported.

Co. C, Sergeant D. D. Leadbetter, commanding—Wounded.—Private G. W. Monroe, in foot and arm, slightly.

Co. D, Lieut. Sauls, commanding—Wounded.—Sergeant C. Cook, slightly in the face; Private G. E. Stanley, slightly in knee.

Co. H, Captain Boatwright, commanding—Wounded.—Corp'l. J. Hiers, in shoulder; Privates J. M. Hickman, in ankle, slight; J. Polk, leg fractured; W. I. Carter, in ankle, slightly.

The Abolitionists who were in ambush fired into the train at Coosawhatchie, doing the damage.

Respectfully, yours,
D. W. ELLIS,
Col. Commanding Post.

REPORT OF LIEUT. CAMPBELL

McPhersonville, South Carolina,
October 24th, 1862.

Lieut. Ed. H. Barnwell, *A. A. A. G.*:

Sir: I have to report you the following casualties in Company I, 11th Regiment South Carolina Volunteers, in the recent engagements with the enemy at "Hatson's" plantation and "old Pocotaligo," to-wit:

Killed.—Sergeant F. E. Grant, Private D. P. Campbell—2.

Wounded.—Sergeant A. I. Smoke, Privates Stephen Crosby, Wm, O. Bryan, H. Valentine, G. W. Way, Joseph Warren, G. S. Warren. James Farley—8.

Missing.—Second Lieut. E. B. Loyless, Private R. Ritter—2.

Very respectfully,
Your obedient servant,
WM. L. CAMPBELL,
1st *Lieutenant Commanding Co.*

REPORT OF CAPT. TRENHOLM.

Headquarters Cavalry,
McPhersonville, 24th October, 1862.

Lieutenant Ed. H. Barnwell,
A. A. A G., Third Military District:

Lieutenant: I have the honor to report the following list of casualties in my command on the 22d instant:

R. M. R., Lieutenant L. J. Walker, commanding.—Killed—None.

Wounded—Privates J. J. Fripp, severely; Sanders Glover slightly.

M. M. C., Captain D. B. Heyward, commanding.—Killed—Private Jasper Johns, flesh wound in thigh.

Wounded—Privates John Adams, leg amputated; Lewis Ritter, wounded in thigh; W. T. Remley, wounded in arm.

Missing—W. D. Jordan.

Co. A, first battalion cavalry, Lieutenant R. M. Skinner, commanding.—Killed—None.

Wounded.—Lieutenant Skinner, painfully.

Co. B, first battalion cavalry, Captain J. E Edwards, commanding.—Killed—Private A. S. Dukes.

Wounded—First Lieutenant P. D. Rush, slightly; Privates J. P. Dantzler, slightly; J. S. Funches, slightly; D. A. Irick, slightly; S. B. Mias, slightly; J. D. Rickenbacker, slightly; J. W. Thomas, A. H. Wannamaker, slightly.

Co. C, first battalion cavalry, Lieutenant A. O. Banks, commanding.—Killed—None.

Wounded—Private H. E. Crim, mortally.

Missing—First Lieutenant A. O. Banks; corporal J. G. Leaphart, privates K. P. Kyzer and Thomas Kleckley.

Co. D, first battalion cavalry, Lieutenant A. P. Grie, commanding.—Killed—Private J. J. Richardson.

Wounded—Privates W. W. Willis, painfully in face; A. N. W. Hartzog, slightly.

Charleston Light Dragoons, Captain B. H. Rutledge, commanding.—Killed—None.

Wounded—None.

Partizan Rangers, Captain M. J. Kirk, commanding.—Killed—Second Lieutenant W. T. Speaks.

Wounded.—Brevet Second Lieutenant P. E. Terry, painfully in face; Orderly Sergeant B. W. Davis, wounded in thigh.

The wounded are doing well. Private Crim, of company C, first battalion cavalry, may recover if he is able to bear the amputation of his leg.

Very respectfully,

W. N. TRENHOLM,
Captain Commanding Cavalry.

REPORT OF CAPTAIN HEYWARD.

CAMP WALKER, October 24th, 1862.

Lieutenant E. H. BARNWELL, A. A. A. G:

Lieutenant: I beg to report the casualties in my company as follows: one seriously wounded, three slightly, and one missing. The company went into action about fifty-five strong.

Respectfully,

D. B. HEYWARD.

REPORT OF SURGEON J. McP. GREGORIE.

Report of the casualties in the Charleston Light Dragoons, Captain B. H. Rutledge, commanding, in the engagement on the 23d instant:
Killed—None.
Wounded—Corporal J. A. Miles, slightly in the posterior; Privates E. W. Holland, in the head; G. E. Manigault, in the forehead; M. B. Pringle, in the foot; James Hopkins, seriously in the right shoulder; J. J. A. O'Neills, seriously in the left leg, (fracture;) J. M. Privoleon, seriously in the right thigh; J.D. Porcher, slightly in the right hip.
Respectfully submitted.

J. McP. GREGORIE,
Acting Surgeon, C. L. Dragoons.

REPORT OF W. W. ELLIOTT, ORDNANCE OFFICER.

Ordnance Office, }
Pocotaligo, November 17th, 1862 }

Brigadier General W. S. Walker :

General: I respectfully beg leave to submit a report of ammunition captured from the enemy, on the 22d of October, at the battle of Yemassee and Pocotaligo :
19 rifle (3 inch) shells, loose.
5 boat howitzers—cases of which
No. 1, contains 14 rifle (3 inch) shells for 6-pounders.
" 2, " 14 rounds fixed shot for 6-pounders.
" 3, " 2 canister, (12 pnds,) 9 cartridges, 1-12 pd. shot.
" 4, " 3 " " 26 pd shell and 1 pd shot.
" 5, " 4 " " 2 12-pd sph. case 1 6-pd shell.
Also 46 rifles and muskets of different make and calibre, some of which have been issued in the place of those injured in the fight.
I certify the above to be a true statement.
Very respectfully,

W. W. ELLIOTT,
Ordnance Officer Third Military District.

REPORT OF BRIGADIER GENERAL HAGOOD.

Headquarters Military District S. C., }
Adams' Run, 11th Dec., 1862. }

General: I have the honor to enclose, as directed in a communication received yesterday from Department headquarters, a list of casualties in Nelson Battery in the affair at Pocotaligo. Immediately after the event I caused the list to be sent to General Walker, and at his request sent a duplicate to your office.

Very respectfully,

JOHNSON HAGOOD,
Brigadier General Commanding.

By Gen. JORDAN,
Chief of the Staff, &c.

REPORT OF LIEUTENANT E. E. JEFFERSON.

CAMP ASHBY, October 24th, 1862.

Captain A. G. TALLEY, A. A.:

Captain: Below please find report of the losses of Captain Frank's Virginia battery, Nelson Light Artillery, in two battles of the 22d instant:

Killed—Privates Copeling Peters, John F. Fulcher, William A. Thacker, Thomas J. Allen.

Wounded—First Lieutenant Jefferson, concussion of shell, slight; Second Lieutenant F. T. Massie, shot in arm and head, slight; Sergeant-Major J. W. Eggleston, concussion of shell, suffering, but not serious; Fourth Sergeant George W. Eggleston, concussion, very lame; Privates Calvin H. Coffey, shot through the shoulders, seriously; M. W. Wright, in hips slightly; B W. Wright, shot through the shoulder; B. W. Goolsby, in calf of leg severely; E. W. Thacker, in foot, the ball ranging up, severely; George W Pugh, in abdomen, severe flesh wound; John Allen, in shoulder, very slight; E. T Bowling, in back, slight; Samuel Wood, spent ball in ankle, slight; corporal Salath Wood, spent ball in breast, slight; corporal R. H. Campbell, shot in breast, glancing ball in arm.

We have but seventeen sound horses left. We lost one caisson from the team running away with the limber, early in the action, and breaking it, the Yankees burning the rear chests and axle. One of our pieces and limber was struck sixteen times, another fourteen times. Splinter bar of one caisson nearly broken in two by a shell, or ball, through the chests, and several wheels injured. We had other men slightly injured, but as they are on duty, I did not think it necessary to report them.

Very respectfully yours,

E. E. JEFFERSON,
First Lieutenant Commanding Nelson Light Artillery,
Virginia Volunteers.

HEADQUARTERS IND. MILITARY DISTRICT S. C., }
Adams' Run, December 11, 1862. }

List of casualties in the seventh battalion infantry, South Carolina Volunteers, in the affair at Pocotaligo.

KILLED.

1 Private S. Fenbril, company C.
2 Corporal S. T. Folsom, company F.
3 Private G. Hale, company F.

WOUNDED—SINCE DEAD.

1 Private E. Turnipseed, wounded in lungs, arm and thigh, co. C.
2 Private G. Bruce, company F.
3 G. McGougin, wounded in neck, company F.

WOUNDED.

1 Private S. Sinclair, in thigh, company A.
2 First Sergeant W. D. Hill, in arm and breast, company C.
3 Fifth Sergeant Elisha Davis, in leg, company C.
4 Fourth Coporal R. Y. Neill, through chest, company C.
5 Private John Hawkins, through leg, company C.
6 Private James A. Davis, in thigh, company C.
7 Private G. Evans, in mouth, company C.
8 Corporal C. Faust, left shoulder, company E.
9 Private A. Ammond, in left shoulder, company E.
10 Private H. Dees, over left eye, company E.
11 Private R. Turner, left shoulder, company F.
12 Private B. Turner, left side, company F.
13 Private G. W. Horton, in neck, company F.
14 Private James Hopkins, in head, company F.
15 Private G. Smith, in arm, company G.
16 Private M. Gibson, both thighs, company G.
17 Private A. F. Hughes, in thigh, company G.
18 Private William Justice, in chest.
19 William A. Tiller, in thigh, company G.

HEADQUARTERS DEP'T OF S. CAROLINA, GEORGIA AND FLORIDA, }
Charleston, S. C., December 12, 1862. }

REPORT OF THE CASUALTIES in the command of Brigadier General W. S. Walker in the affair with the Abolitionits at Pocotaligo and Yemassee, October 22, 1862.

Name.	Rank.	Company.	Killed, wounded and missing.
C. Peters	Private.	Nelson Va. Battery.	Killed.
John F. Fulcher	"	" " "	Killed.
Wm. A. Thacker	"	" " "	Killed.
Thomas J. Allen	"	" " "	Killed.
E. E. Jefferson	1st Lieut.	" " "	Wounded slightly.
F. T. Massie	2d "	" " "	do slightly.
George C. Eggleston	Sergeant.	" " "	do severely.
J. W. Eggleston	"	" " "	do severely.
C. W. Coffey	Private.	" " "	do severely.
W. W. Wright	"	" " "	do severely.
B. W. Wright	"	" " "	do slightly.
B. W. Golsby	"	" " "	do severely.
E. W. Thacker	"	" " "	do severely.
G. W. Pugh	"	" " "	do severely.
John Al'on	"	" " "	do slightly.
C. T. Bowling	"	" " "	do slightly.
Sam Wood	"	" " "	do slightly.
Sa'ath Wood	Corporal.	" " "	do slightly.
R. W. Campbell	Private.	" " "	do slightly.
S. Fenbril	Corporal.	Co. C., 7th Bat. S. C. V.	Killed.
F. Turnipseed	Private.	" C., " " "	Wounded, since died.
S. F. Tolson	"	" F., " " "	Killed.
G. Hale	"	" " " " "	Killed.
G. Bruce	"	" " " " "	Wounded, since died.
G. McGougan	"	" F., " " "	Wounded, since died.
S. Sinclair	"	" A., " " "	Wounded in thigh.
W. D. Hill	Sergeant.	" C., " " "	do in arm.
F. Davis	"	" " " " "	do in leg.
R. Y. Neil	Corporal.	" " " " "	do in chest.
John Hawkins	Private.	" C., " " "	do in leg.
J. A. Davis	"	" " " " "	do in mouth.
G. Evans	"	" " " " "	do in shoulder.
C. Faust	Corporal.	" E., " " "	do in shoulder.
A. Ammond	Private.	" " " " "	do in eye.
H. Dees	"	" " " " "	do in eye.
R. Turner	"	" F., " " "	do in shoulder.
B. Turner	"	" " " " "	do in side.
G. W. Horton	"	" " " " "	do in neck.
J. Hopkins	"	" " " " "	do in head.
G. Smith	"	" G., " " "	do in arm.
M. Gibroin	"	" " " " "	do in thigh.
A. F. Hughes	"	" " " " "	do in thigh.
Wm. Gustice	"	" " " " "	do in chest.
W. R. Tiller	"	" " " " "	do in thigh.
J. A. Miles	Corporal.	Charleston Light Dragoons.	do slightly.
E. C. Holland	Private.	" " "	do slightly.
G. E. Manigault	"	" " "	do slightly.
M. B. Pringle	"	" " "	do slightly.
James Hopkins	"	" " "	do severely.
J. J. H. O'Neill	"	" " "	do severely.
J. M. Prioleau	"	" " "	do severely.
J. D. Porcher	"	" " "	do slightly.
Skinner	Lieut.	Co. A., 1st Bat. S. C. V.	do painfully.
A. S. Dukes	Private.	" B., " " "	Killed.
P. D. Rush	Lieut.	" " " " "	Wounded slightly.
J. P. Dautzler	Private.	" " " " "	do slightly.
J. S. Funches	"	" " " " "	do slightly.
D. A. Trick	"	" " " " "	do slightly.
S. B. Nias	"	" " " " "	do slightly.
J. D. Rickenbacker	"	" " " " "	do slightly.

REPORT OF CASUALTIES—(Continued.)

Name.	Rank.	Company.	Killed, wounded and missing.
J. W. Thomas	Private.	Co. A., 1st Bat. S. C. V.	Wounded slightly.
R. H. Wannamaker	"	" " " " "	do slightly.
H. K. Crisce	"	" C., " " "	do mortally.
A. O. Banks	Lieut.	" " " " "	Missing.
J. G. Reaphart	Corporal.	" " " " "	Missing.
H. P. Hyver	Private.	" " " " "	Missing.
Thomas Flockley	"	" " " " "	Missing.
J. J. Richardson	"	" D., " " "	Killed.
W. W. Willis	"	" " " " "	Wounded painfully.
R. N. W. Harkag	"	" " " " "	do slightly.
W. T. Speaks	Lieut.	Kirk's Co. Par. Rangers.	Wounded.
P. E. Terry	"	" " " "	do painfully.
B. W. Davis	Sergeant.	" " " "	do in thigh.
Jasper Johns	Private.	Co. F., 3d S. C. Cavalry.	do in thigh.
John Adams	"	" " " "	do severely.
L. Ritter	"	" " " "	do in thigh.
W. T. Remley	"	" " " "	do in arm.
W. D. Jordan	"	" " " "	Missing.
J. J. Tripp	"	Rutledge Mounted Rifles.	Wounded severely.
Sanders Glover	"	" " " "	do slightly.
T. O. Buckner	Lieut.	Co. K., 3d S. C. V. Cavalry.	do severely.
J. J. Harrison	Major.	" 11th S. C. V.	Killed.
G. W. Monroe	Private.	" C., "	Wounded slightly.
C. Rush	"	" B., "	Crushed by R. R. train, dead.
C. Cook	Sergeant.	" D., "	Wounded slightly.
G. E. Stanley	Private.	" " "	do slightly.
F. E. Grant	Sergeant.	" I., "	Wounded.
J. P. Campbell	Private.	" " "	Killed.
A. J. Smoke	Sergeant.	" " "	Killed.
S. Crosley	Private.	" " "	Wounded.
Wm. O. Bogan	"	" " "	Wounded.
H. Valentine	"	" " "	Wounded.
G. W. Way	"	" " "	Wounded.
James Warren	"	" " "	Wounded.
G. P. Warren	"	" " "	Wounded.
James Yarley	"	Co. I., 11th S. C. V.	Wounded slightly.
E. B. Loyless	Lieut.	" " " "	Missing.
K. Riller	Private.	" " " "	Missing.
J. Hiers	Corporal.	" H., " "	Wounded in shoulder.
J. M. Hickman	Private.	" " " "	do in shoulder.
J. Polk	"	" " " "	do severely.
W. J. Carter	"	" " " "	do slightly.
P. B. McDaniel	"	" B., 1st Bat. S. C. S. S.	Killed.
J. B. Alleton	Captain.	" " " " "	Wounded slightly.
M. Stuart	Lieut.	" " " " "	do slightly.
Capers	"	" " " " "	do slightly.
J. B. Attaway	Private.	" " " " "	do slightly.
W. Broun	"	" " " " "	do slightly.
E. Bootwright	"	" " " " "	do severely.
S. M. Smith	"	" " " " "	Wounded.
W. W. Long	"	" " " " "	Missing.
J. Walden	"	" " " " "	Missing.
J. P. Chapin	Sergeant.	Beaufort Light Artillery.	Wounded slightly.
Wm. Thompson	"	" "	do severely.
N. B. Fuller	Corporal.	" "	do severely.
E. E. Burban	"	" "	do severely.
J. J. Brown	"	" "	do severely.
J. E. Tripp	Private.	" "	do since died.
R. F. Sams	"	" "	do severely.
John Jenkins	"	" "	do slightly.
Daniel Jenkins	"	" "	do slightly.
A. Budden	"	" "	do slightly.
E. B. Trescott	"	" "	do slightly.
T. E. Cuthbert	"	" "	do severely.
S. A. Sams	"	" "	do slightly.
J. D. Richardson	"	" "	do slightly.

Total casualties. Killed 14; wounded 102; missing 9.

REPORT

OF THE

BATTLE NEAR COFFEEVILLE, MISS.

BRIG. GEN. TILGHMAN COMMANDING.

HEADQUARTERS 1ST DIV., 1ST CORPS, A. W. T.,
December 6th, 1862.

Lieut. Col. E. Ivy, *A. A. General:*

COLONEL: I have the honor to make the following report of the action of the 5th instant, between the Federal advance guard, near Coffeeville, and the troops, placed under my command by Major General Lovell, commanding 1st corps.

At about half-past two o'clock, P. M., on Friday afternoon, 5th instant, whilst engaged in the town of Coffeeville, with the various duties of my command, I learned that the enemy, emboldened by their successes heretofore, had pushed their advance within one mile of the town, and that having commenced skirmishing with our rear guard of cavalry, Major General Lovell, commanding 1st corps, had gone out with a portion of my division to check them, I immediately rode out, with a portion of my staff and body guard, to the point selected by General Lovell, on which to form, and found that he had pushed forward a portion of the 1st brigade, under Gen. Baldwin, on the right of the main road to Water Valley, whilst the 9th Arkansas, of Gen. Rust's division, commanded by Col. Dunlop, was placed in line of battle, on the left of the same road. Col. A. P. Thompson, commanding brigade, of the 2d division, had also been ordered to place the 3d Kentucky regiment, of his brigade, upon a road leading out from Coffeeville to the west of the main road spoken of, in order to watch our left flank. Upon the main road and in rear of the 1st brigade, upon a small eminence, four pieces of artillery had been placed, being part of Capt. Bouchard's company of the Point Coupe Artillery; whilst at three hundred yards to the rear of this battery, two Parrott guns from Capt. Hedden's battery, of my own division, were placed on a still higher point, and in a position not to endanger the infantry or the battery in front, should occasion present itself to open upon the enemy. Before reaching the point at which Gen. Lovell was stationed, I heard brisk cannonading, and on joining Gen. Lovell, near where the rear battery was placed, found that it proceeded from our advanced battery, which was being replied to by a rifle gun of the enemy.

I immediately reported for orders to Gen. Lovell, who directed me to ride with him to the position, held by the advanced battery. On reaching that point and finding that the enemy had obtained the exact range of our guns, I retired, with General Lovell, to the rear battery, and was immediately ordered to open fire with the Parrott guns, at short intervals. This was done, and in a few moments the fire of the enemy's battery ceased.

I then asked permission of the Major General commanding to press the enemy and drive them back, and upon receiving his orders to do so, with information that General Rust had been ordered to manœuvre on my right with part's of two of his brigades, rode rapidly to the front, ordering, at the same time, the 14th Mississippi regiment, under Major Doss, which had been held in reserve, to move up at double-quick and take position on the extreme right of my line. The cavalry, under Col. Jackson, numbering about seven hundred, were placed at my disposal also. The proper disposition of the forces was soon made; orders were given to Gen. Baldwin, on the right, and to Col. A. P. Thompson, of the 2d division, who had assumed the direction of the 9th Arkansas, of his own brigade, to deploy the right companies from each regiment, as skirmishers, one hundred paces in front of the main line. A greater distance was not deemed prudent, as the woods were very dense and the enemy known to be in close proximity. The cavalry was formed in the main road and ordered to move with caution in rear of the main line. The line of skirmishers being formed and everything prepared, orders were given to the men to hold their fire until within fifty yards; to move with caution until the enemy was reached, but then to press them with all their energy. The command, "forward," was given, and both skirmishers and the main line moved. The line had not advanced two hundred yards before the enemy opened on our left a brisk fire. This was answered first by a yell along our whole line, the men moving rapidly and with great enthusiasm until they were within good range, when the 9th Arkansas, directed by Col. A. P. Thompson, and the 8th Kentucky, under Col. H. B. Lyon, opened fire in return. Very soon the fire extended towards our right, along the 23d Mississippi, under Lieut. Colonel M'Carley, and the 26th Mississippi, under Major Parker. The order to press the enemy was fully carried out, and they were not allowed time to breathe, and though making two gallant stands in the first mile, they were driven from their positions, without our men faltering for a moment. The tactics of the enemy did them great credit; their whole force consisted of *mounted infantry*, armed with Colt's, Smith's and Sharp's most approved weapons, with two pieces of artillery. The country over which they had to pass was an alternate wood and field. On being driven to the edge of a field, they mounted and retreated across it, dismounting and sending their horses to the rear. They had all the advantage of position, being covered by the woodland, whilst our men advanced across the open field. At these points the fire of the enemy was terrific, but nothing could stop the onward movement, and our men moved forward without slackening their pace in the least. Having driven the enemy for more than a mile, it occurred to me, that should the troops of Gen. Rust's command not have moved to their left far enough to guard my right flank, that I might run some risk of being outflanked. To guard against this, I detached Lieut. Barbour, commanding my body guard, with a portion of his men, with orders to move at full speed to my extreme right and take position, with his men well extended, and watch my right flank. No sooner had he reached the point and commenced moving up with our main line than he was fired upon by the enemy. Lieut. Barbour immediately sent a courier informing me of the fact, when I ordered the 14th Mississippi, under Major Doss, to move at double-quick, by the right flank, until he reached the point occupied by Lieutenant Barbour; then to assume his original front and press them again. During all this time the enemy were interruptedly driven from every position, and forced back to a point three miles from Coffeeville, when on reaching a commanding position, they opened fire from their artillery again, supported by the severest fire of musketry we had yet encountered. The heaviest fire was encountered by the 9th Arkansas regiment and the 8th Kentucky regiment. Their efforts were, however, useless; nothing could check the advance of our men, and the position was carried without a moment's delay, just at dark.

It occurred to me a few moments before this, that a dash of our cavalry might have secured the piece of artillery in its last position; but it would have involved a heavy loss of life, not warranted, under the circumstances, and I did not give the order. Having already driven the enemy much farther than was ordered by a message from Gen. Lovell, I gave the order to halt and cease firing, very much to the chagrin of both officers and men, who, notwithstanding the severe duties and deprivations of the last week, seemed to forget everything but the desire showed by all to repay the injuries suffered by them during their long and barbarous imprisonment at the North.

The 14th Mississippi, Major Doss commanding, towards the close, became too far separated from the main command, but was abundantly able to take care of itself, and drove back the enemy in their front, killing and wounding a number, among them, Lieut. Col. McCullough, who was shot dead within twenty paces of our line. This regiment also captured seventeen prisoners, with all horses, arms and accoutrements. The loss on our part, as stated in my note to Major General Lovell, of the 6th inst., is known to be accurately as follows: *Killed, seven; wounded, forty-three.* That of the enemy, thirty-four killed; among them Lieut. Col. McCullough and a 2d lieutenant, who gave his name as Woodbury, (of the 3d Missouri) just before expiring. The wounded of the enemy could not be accurately ascertained, inasmuch as all who were not too badly wounded were removed on horseback as fast as they fell. Estimating their wounded by the number killed, in the same ratio as that known to exist on our part, the wounded may be given at two hundred and thirty-four, which, from the number seen in the act of being removed, is *under* rather than *over* the actual loss. Sixteen of their severely wounded fell into our hands. Thirty-five prisoners, with seventeen horses and all their arms and accoutrements, were captured.

Among the prisoners were one captain and several non-commissioned officers. The wounded on both sides were removed at once to Coffeeville, and every care taken of them. The dead were buried next morning. The body of the Federal lieutenant was decently buried marked on the headstone so that it could be recognized. The body of Lieut. Col. McCullouck was not secured. The command returned to its first position near Coffeeville, and bivouacked in line of battle. The whole affair was a complete success, and taught the enemy a lesson I am sure they will not soon forget. The troops behaved in the most gallant manner; officers and men emulated each other. All did their duty nobly. I take especial pleasure in mentioning the names of Brigadier General W. E. Baldwin, of my own division, and Col. A. P. Thompson, (commanding a brigade in Gen. Rust's division.) These officers in command on my right and left, displayed the greatest good judgment and gallantry. The brunt of the battle was borne by the 9th Arkansas, Col. Dunlop; 8th Kentucky, Col. H. B. Lyon; the 23d Mississippi, Lieut. Col. McCarley; and the 26th Mississippi, under Major Parker.

I have seldom seen greater good judgment and impetuous gallantry shown by any officers or men. The cavalry, under Col. Jackson, maintained the most perfect order, and were always in position to answer any summons. The batteries engaged rendered the most efficient service up to the time of my ordering to advance. The first shot fired from the Parrott guns of Captain Hedden's battery, under the direction of Captain Culbertson, chief of artillery of my division, wounded Col. Misner, and killed his orderly and three men. These facts were related by a non-commissioned officer among the prisoners.

My thanks are especially due to those of my personal staff, who were present. Major Watts, Inspector General; Major Halliday, Chief Commissary; Lieut. George Moorman, Aid-de-Camp; Lieut. Tilghman, Aid-de-Camp; rendered the most efficient and valuable service.

I notice with great pleasure, also, Lieut. Barbour, commanding my body guard, together with Lieut. Lundy, of that company. These officers and their men rendered me great aid. The timely service of Lieut. Barbour, on my right wing, may have saved us probably from serious injury. The whole force engaged on our side may be stated as not exceeding thirteen hundred men, whilst the enemy is known to have had not less than five regiments, numbering not less than thirty-five hundred men. Enclosed, I have the honor to submit a correct list of the killed and wounded on our side.

I regret the absence of Captain Powhatan Ellis, chief of staff, during the action. He was engaged at my headquarters in an important business, I was thus deprived of his valuable services. The same may be said of others of my staff who were absent on duty at various points.

               Respectfully, your obedient servant,
                           LLOYD TILGHMAN,
               Commanding 1st Div. 1st Corps Army of West Tenn.

CASUALTIES IN THE ACTION OF 5TH DECEMBER, 1862, NEAR COFFEEVILLE, MISS.

FIRST BRIGADE, FIRST DIVISION, FIRST CORPS, W. E. BALDWIN, BRIGADIER GENERAL COMMANDING.

Twenty-sixth Mississippi Regiment, Major Parke, Commanding.

KILLED.
Private J. C. Barret, company B.
Private W. L. McFarland, company C.
Private George Socum, company C—Total 3.

WOUNDED.
Sergeant H. L. Parker, company B.
Private J. H. Hill, company A.
Private Andrew Jackson, company H—Total 3.

MISSING.
Pravate W. L. Griffith, company B—Total 1.

Eighth Kentucky Regiment, Col. Lyon Commanding.

KILLED.
Corporal Talbot Hart, company A.

WOUNDED.
Lieutenant T. B. Jones.
Private John Sockney, company A.
Corporal A. B. Crawley, company B.
Private J. M. Mount, company B.
Private J. J. Turner, company C.
Private Jacob Campbell, company D.

MISSING.
Private J. R. Lavender, company A.
Private J. H. Roback, company A.
Private W. Davis, company C.
Private E. Davis, company I.
    Total—Killed, one (1;) wounded, six (6;) missing, four (4;)

Twenty-third Mississippi Regiment, Lieut. Col. McCarley Commanding.

KILLED.

Private D. L. Newlin, company A.
Private J. G. Eaves, company A.

WOUNDED.

Lieut B. Tapp, company E.
Private C. N. Simpson, company I.
Sergeant R. W. Roberston, company A.
Private D. T. Rutherford, company A.
Private P. Mahundro, company A.
Private A. J. Wildman, company B.
Private F. M. Jones, company D.
Private A. J. Ross, company D.
Private J. S. Doty, company D.
Private R. R. Bullock, company F.
Private J. F. Davis, company F.
Private John Baxter, company I.
Private John Beard, company I.
Private F. M. Barton, company K.

Total—Killed, two (2;) wounded, fourteen (14;) missing, four (4.)

Fourteenth Mississippi Regiment, Major W. L. Doss Commanding.

WOUNDED.

Sergeant W. W. Eggerton, company D.
Private B. F. Matthews, company I.
Private W. I. Gentry, company F—Total 3.

Grand Total—Killed, six (6;) wounded, twenty-six (26;) missing nine (9.)

SECOND BRIGADE, SECOND DIVISION, FIRST CORPS, COLONEL A. P. THOMPSON, COMMANDING.

Ninth Regiment Arkansas Volunteers, only regiment of said brigade under fire.

KILLED.

Private Henry Byers, company C.

WOUNDED.

Private James Craig, company A.
Private L. F. Taylor, company A
Private P. Holcombe, company A.
Private George Lepham, company B.
Private H. H. Pollard, company D.
Private C. C. Jones, company D.
Private John Walsh, company D.
Private Wm. Eubanks, company D.
Private G. W. Robertson, company E.

Private W. M. Purtle, company E.
Private J. Bono, company E.
Private E. D. Cozart, company F.
Private R. W. McCam, company F.
Private T. G. Ross, company K.
Sergeant A. Gainey, company H.
Corp'l Love, company H.
Private George Hudson, company H.

MISSING.

Private S. M. Crawford, company E.

Total—Killed, one (1;) wounded, seventeen (17;) missing, one (1.)

Grand total—Killed, seven (7;) wounded, forty-three (43;) missing, ten (10.)

I certify that the above is a correct return, as reported.

LLOYD TILGHMAN.
Brigadier General Commanding 1st Division.

FORT DONELSON.

REPORT OF THE ACTION AND CASUALTIES OF THE BRIGADE COMMANDED BY COL. J. M. SIMONTON.

JACKSON, MISS., September 24, 1862.

GEN. S. COOPER, *Adjutant and Inspector General, C. S. A.:*

GENERAL: I have the honor to submit a report of the action and casualties of the brigade I commanded at the battle of Fort Donelson on the 15th February, 1862. I have been prevented from doing so sooner from the discourtesy of the Federal authorities either to allow me to make it to a superior officer in captivity with me, (but in a different prison,) or in any other way; and I now make this report to you direct, because I do not know the whereabouts of the proper division commanders, and from a desire to do justice to the gallant officers and men under my command upon the bloody field; also,.that the government may know who not only bravely met the invading foe, but shed their blood in defence of the most holy cause for which freemen ever fought; and that their families, in after times, may reap the benefits of their noble deeds, and costly sacrifices.

On Saturday, February 15th, 1862, about one o'clock, A. M., I received a verbal order from Brigadier General Pillow to take command of the brigade, commanded up to that by Colonel Davidson, of the third Mississippi, (and properly the brigade of Brigadier General Clark of Mississippi,) composed of the following regiments, viz: third Mississippi, Colonel Davidson, Lieutenant Colonel Wells commanding; first Mississippi, Colonel Simonton, Lieutenant Colonel Hamilton commanding, seventh Texas, Colonel Gregg commanding, eighth Kentucky, Colonel Burnett, Lieutenant Colonel Lyons commanding, forty-second Tennessee, Colonel Quarles commanding. The last regiment named, however, was detached previous to going into the action, and from which I have received no report. In obedience to orders, the brigade was formed in column under the crest of the hill in rear of and to the left of the rifle pits occupied by our army, and in rear of the brigade commanded by Colonel Baldwin of the fourteenth Mississippi, in which position we remained until five o'clock, A: M. The enemy were in position behind the crests of a number of small hills in front, and to the right of our rifle pits, and encircling our entire left wing. At the hour above mentioned Colonel Baldwin received orders to move in the direction of the enemy and attack them on the right. I was ordered to follow with my command, which order I obeyed, but, owing to the ground and timber, we were compelled to march by the flank, and had not moved more than four hundred yards when the head of the column was fired upon. I immediately sent an order to Lieutenant Colonel Wells to face his right wing to the right, and wheel it to the right, so that I might occupy a position on Colonel Balwin's right, (the one General Pillow had directed,) but by some misunderstanding of the order, or its being miscarried, Lieutenant Colonel Wells charged his front forward on first company, breaking my line at the left of his regiment. I then ordered Lieutenant Colonel Lyon, of the eighth Kentucky, to file right, and move by the flank, at double time, which the gallant officer obeyed under a heavy fire of the enemy's musketry. Before they had completed the movement many of his noble men had bravely fallen, but they held the position determinedly, and immediately I ordered Colanel Gregg, of the seventh Texas, and Lieutenant Colonel Hamilton, of the first Mississippi, to move their respective regiments, at double quick, in rear and beyond the eighth Kentucky, which movement those officers executed with as much coolness, and their commands, in as good order as if they had been on review. I, at the same time, dispatched an order to Lieutenant Colonel Wells to occupy the position on the left of the eighth Kentucky. (I make this explanation to show how the regiments changed position in going into action, and that justice may be done to all as, near as possible.) This threw me in line of battle in the following order: Seventh Texas on the right, first Mississippi regiment, second; eighth Kentucky, third, and third Mississippi, on the left, and in front of the left of General McClearnand's division of the Federal army. During this entire time the enemy kept up a continuous volley of musketry, with, however, but little effect—most of the balls passing over us. I now ordered the entire command to advance and occupy the crest of the hill, which was executed with a coolness and steadiness that would have done honor to soldiers of an hundred battles. That heroic band of less than fifteen hundred in number, marched up the hill, loading and firing as they moved, gaining inch by inch, on an enemy at least four times their number. For one long hour this point was hotly contested by the enemy, and many gallant officers and brave men fell in the faithful discharge of their duty; among whom was the lamented and daring Lieut. Col. Clough of the seventh Texas, together with a number of company officers, whose names are mentioned in the list of killed and wounded.

At this moment I was informed by an Adjutant that the command was running short of ammunition. I immediately dispatched an aid, Captain Ryan, to General Pillow for reinforcements, and at the same time ordered Colonel Gregg to move his regiment further to the right to prevent a flank movement I discovered the enemy were attempting to make, and the remainder of my command to charge the enemy's lines, which movements were executed with a spirit and determination that insured success. The enemy's lines gave way, and the rattle of musketry was drowned by the shouts of victory that rose along the lines of men conscious of superiority and right. The enemy, however, again rallied and formed in line of battle a few hundred yards in rear of their first position, and in rear of *four* pieces of artillery, (of Swartz's battery.) The line of my brigade, in the charge over the hills and in passing through the enemy's camp, having become somewhat broken, I ordered the commandant to halt and rectify their allignments, which was quickly done; and being now informed by Captain Ryan that the fifty-sixth Virginia regiment was on my left, I again ordered an advance, which was promptly obeyed by all; and soon the enemy was again driven from his position, and four pieces of Swartz's battery in our possession. The enemy continued to fall back, contesting the crest of every hill, until we had driven them over one and a half miles, and had possession of the ground occupied by the left of McClernand's and Wallace's division of the Federal army. The enemy had disappeared behind the crests of a range of hills about half a mile in our front, and in the direction of their transports. At this point I was ordered to halt my command and await further orders. In the meantime the brigade was furnished with ammunition, (chiefly gathered from the slain of the enemy,) the lines rectified, and the command brought to a rest; in which position we remained for a considerable time, until orders came for us to march inside the rifle pits, which order was obeyed *without the fire of a gun* or even a sight of the *foe*, unless he was wounded or a prisoner. I had not fully occupied my position in the *rifle pits* when an order came to me to move at double quick to the right of our line. The men were again ordered into line, and moved in the direction indicated, but before arriving at the specified point another order was received to return. Thus ended the battle of February 15th, 1862, so far as the brigade I commanded participated.

The number killed, and in each regiment, as per Adjutants' reports, is as follows:

		Killed.	Wounded.
Third Mississippi Regiment, 546 men and officers		5	46
Eighth Kentucky " 312 " "		27	72
Seventh Texas " 305 " "		20	39
First Mississippi " 331 " "		16	61
1494		68	218

Making a total of 286 killed and wounded out of 1494 officers and men. I respectfully refer you to documents A, B, C, D for the names of the killed and wounded of the different regiments. I cannot call especial attention to one of the field officers under my command without doing injustice to the others. Lieutenant Colonel Wells, assisted by Captains Kennedy and Wells, of the third Mississippi; Lieutenant Colonel Lyon, assisted by Major Henry of the eighth Kentucky; Colonel Gregg, Lieutenant Colonel Clough and Major Granbury of the seventh Texas; Lieutenant Colonel Hamilton and Major Johnston of the first Mississippi, all won for themselves the confidence of their commands and are entitled to the highest commendation of their countrymen. Captain R. B. Ryan and Sergeant-Major T. H. Wilson, acted as my aids and discharged their duty gallantly. It would give me much pleasure to mention the names of company officers who distinguished themselves for efficiency and gallantry, but their conduct will be made known by their respective regimental commanders.

I am, sir, your obedient servant,
JOHN M. SIMONTON,
Colonel First Mississippi Regiment,
Commanding Brigade at Battle of Fort Donelson.

REPORT of the Third Regiment Mississippi Volunteers at the battle of Fort Donelson, on the 15th of February, 1862.

Letter of Company.	Men Engaged.	Killed.	Severely Wounded.	Slightly Wounded.	Surrendered.	Escaped.	Commanders.	Rank.
A.	60		2		70		A. J. Gibson.	Captain.
B.	54		3	1	52	2	R. J Hill.	"
C.	52		1	2	48		G. W. B. Garrett.	"
D.	40	1		1	85	12	R. B. Allen.	"
E.	81			3	79	4	A. D. Saddler.	2d Lieutenant.
F.	66	1	2		62	7	T. B. B Flint	Captain.
G.	48	1	2		45	15	J. H. B'dlespenger.	1st Lieutenant.
H.	45		3		46		J. W. Douglas.	" "
I.	59	1	1	4	64	2	W. O. Swindell.	2 1 Lieutenant.
K.	51	1			60	1	B. F. Saunders.	Captain.
Total...	546	5	15	11	561	43		

Captain J. H. Kennedy, of company "E," acted as Lieutenant Colonel; Captain E. M. Wells, company "H," as Major, and Lieutenant C. N. Simpson, company "I," as Adjutant, during the engagement of this day. The other officers who were absent from their post were either sick or wounded. This refers to both field and company officers. Surgeon N. W. Moody and his Assistant, J. N. Thompson, were at their posts and acted nobly.

From the above it will be seen that the number surrendered and escaped exceed the number engaged. The most of this surplus was on detached service, either as nurses in hospital, wagoners or with the artillery; the remaining number were reported sick. Below I give the names of the killed and wounded in full; those marked severely wounded were all sent to Clarksville, Tennessee.

Company A.—Privates George A. Green, and J. W. Hall, severely.

Company B.—Privates J. M. Bannill, B. F. Barton and David Jones severely, and R. M. Nelson, slightly.

Company C.—Orderly Sergeant J. E. Johnson, severely; privates William Ragan and D. A. Fowler, slightly.

Company D.—Private R. P. Lumpkin, killed; Corporal M. A. Cordod, severely and W. D. Deloach, slightly wounded.

Company H.—Lieutenant N. W. Roach and privates George Steel A. T. Wages, severely wounded.

Company K.—Private Philip Amel, killed.

Company E.—Sergeant B. T. Wallis, and privates Joseph Petty and J. C. Saylors, slightly wounded.

Company F.—Private W. R Campbell, killed; privates W. R. Skillman and W. A. Gentry, severely wounded.

Company G.—Private Tandy F. Bright, killed; captain More McCarthy and private John L. Rutherford, severely wounded.

Company I.—Private W. G. Williams, killed; privates Joseph Roach, severely, and L. Dunlop, J. H. Duff, W. H. Bailey and H. W. Mayes, slightly wounded.

Killed and wounded of the 8th Kentucky Regiment, commanded by Col. H. B. Lyon, surrendered at Fort Donelson, Tenn., 16th February, 1862.

Company A—Killed—Sergeant F. Bryant, Privates John Prather, John Buchanan, M. Hays and J. M. Thompkins.

Wounded—R. C. Clayton, Thomas H. Jones, W. H. Jones, seriously; E. G. Orr, I. H. Gates, H. Stodghill, A. Yarbrough and R. Night, slightly.

Company B—Killed—Privates L. C. McConnel, J. M. Howell, Robert Wilson, James Carney, J. W. Chapell.

Wounded—R. P. McAliston, N. B. Howell, J. S. Goodwin, G. W. Barnes, J. W. Thompson, severely; Captain, J. Bingham, 2d Lieut. W. L. Dunning, Privates C. B. Wolf and J. E. Smith, slightly.

Company C—Killed—Privates A. B. Son, M. B. Adkins, J. O. Stall, and Isaac Fulds.

Wounded—Sergeant H. T. Rowland, Privates Joseph Endfield, E. A. Edwards, J. F. Sinton, severely; J. Balentine, John Waltrip, slightly.

Company D—Killed—Privates H. B. Poston and J. J. Jones.

Wounded—E. Mitchell, C. Umphreys, Thos. Choat, A. E. Reese, L. L. Mashan, severely; Captain J. A. Buckner, Lieutenant F. G. Terry, Privates J. E. Strong and R. H. Greenwood, slightly.

Company E—Killed—Privates L. T. Perry, H. B. Reaves, J. L. Dent and H. R. McNeill.

Wounded—D. L. Lawrence, A. Simpson, J. D. Prior, severely; 1st Lieut. J. E. Burchard, Privates D. M. Russell, James Canady, J. F. Mason, B. C. Hall, slightly.

Company F—Killed—Privates R. M. Burnett.

Wounded—1st Lieut. G. H. Page, Sergeants J. F. Redford, J. A. Daniel, Privates William O. Anderson, C. F. Duerson, G. D. Edwards, J. Fry and J. N. Miller, severely.

Company F—Killed—Private A. Sutor.

Wounded—1st Lieut. A. J. Sish, Privates A. J. Lofton, N. W. Weathers, A. Ferril, J. W. Brock and W. Woodward.

Company H—Killed—Privates G. W. Doake, W. Eastwood. Wounded—1st Lieutenant J. N. Goodloe, 2d Lieut. J. J. Dennis, Corporal W. B. Worthington, Privates Stephen Pitts, James Bassett, L. Dorsett, W. P. Donnahoe, severely; Benjamin Johnson, slightly.

Company I—Killed—1st Lieut. W. J. Clements, Private John Clarke.

Wounded—Privates J. A. Thomas, mortally, (since dead;) G. Price, Sergeant B. D. Morton, Albert Hamkins, Privates S. D. Robertson, J. B. Sish, A. R. Walker, James Durlin, W. E. Price, W. J. Davis, slightly.

Total—Killed, 27; wounded, 72; aggregate, 99.

COUCH, *Adjutant.*

Killed and wounded of Col John Greggs Regiment of Texas Volunteers,
(unumbered by War Department.)

Field and Staff—Lieutenant Colonel J. M. Clough, killed on the 15th February.

Company A, McLelland county, Texas.
Captain C. N. Alexander, slightly wounded, (escaped.)
1st Lieutenant E. B. Rosson, killed on the 13th February.
2d " J. W. Nowlin, " " 15th "
1st Corporal W. Bennett, missing.
Private H. H. Dechered, severely wounded.
" R. W. Gray, " "
" B. F. Moffet, " "
" J. Rodgers, slightly . "
" C. B. Sledd, missing,

Company B, Upsher county, Texas.
2d Lieutenant John H. Corin, slightly wounded.
2d Sergeant D. Aaden, . " "
Private A. H. Appleton, " "
" T. B. Brooks, killed.
" Geoge Echols, " "
" G. T. Ford, " "
" James Roberston, killed.

Company C, Kaufman county Texas.
Private Charles Allen, killed.
" James A. Morris, "
" W. J. McDonald, "
" John H. Boykin, mortally wounded.
" J. H. Murdock, severely "
" J. L. Wells, slightly "

Company D, Harrison county, Texas.
3d Lieutenant A. G. Adams, slightly wounded.
Private Thomas J. Beale, " "
" C. Fisher, severely, "
" J. Stevens, " "
" B. F. Manson, " "
" B. A. Duncan, " . "
" John M. Cave, killed.
" James R. Hudson, "
" M. Karsch, "
3d Sergeant Thomas S. Jennings, killed.

Company E, Cherokee county, Texas.
Private J. Y. B. Atwood, slightly wounded.
" B. Gallagher, " "

Company F, Smith county, Texas.
Private John Moore, killed.
" Valentine, "
" Shackleford, "
" Delay, slightly wounded.
" Hicks, " "
" Harrison, " "
Company F had no commissioned officers present during the engagement, and for the time being was placed under the command of Captain Alexander, Company A.

Company G, Freestone county, Texas.
Private W. A. McIllveen, killed,
" J. N. Mayo, "
" W. F. Simms, "
" W. L. Neal, "
2d Sergeant C. W. Love, severely wounded.
Private J. L. Means, " "
" J. E. Smith, " "
" Robert A. High, slightly "
" Thomas A. Jordan, " "

Company H, Harrison county, Texas.
Captain W. B. Hill, killed.
Private R. O. Sheppherd, "
1st Sergeant J. M. Jones, slightly wounded.
Private B. C. Pleasants " "
" J. W. Rodgers, " "
" R. H. Walker, " "
" J. A. Turner, " "
" C. Ellis, severely "
" J. O. McCracker, severely "

Company I, Rusk county, Texas.
Private Charles Kavanaugh, severely wounded.
" D. M. McHinley, " "
" James Crocker, slightly "

RECAPITULATION.

	Killed.	Wounded.	Missing.
Company A.	2	5	2
" B.	2	5	
" C.	3	3	
" D.	4	6	
" E.		2	
" F.	3	3	
" G.	3	5	
" H.	2	7	
" I.		3	
Total,	20	39	2

Our regiment numbered 391 at "Donelson," of which number 305 were in the fight on Saturday. Sixty-one were killed, wounded and missing; 7 escaped, and 324 surrendered as prisoners of war.

W. D. DOUGLAS,
Adjutant.

Report of the killed and wounded, and number in action of the 1st Mississippi regiment at the battle of Donelson, fought February 15th, 1862.

Field and staff, in action, 7.

Company A, commanded by Captain G. M. Mosely; in action, 34.
Q. R. Snoddy, 1st Lieutenant, killed.
A. Arnaud, Sergeant,   "
Samuel Nesbit, Corporal,   "
Avon Glitzman, private, severely wounded.
E. J. Crenshaw, Sergeant,   "   "
L. H. Martin, private,   "   "
W. H. McRae, private, slightly "
I. F. Mosely,   "   "   "
C. J. Boyd,   "   "   "
J. Smylie,   "   "   "
J. Thompson,   "   "   "
T. A. Proctor,   "   "   " .
J. R. Howard, Corporal,   "   "
W. H. King, private,   "   "
Samuel Collins,   "   "   "
In action, 34; killed, 5; wounded, 12.

Company B, commanded by 1st Lieutenant H. W. Waldrop; in action, 32.
James L. Taylor, 2d Lieutenant, killed.
H. Livingston, private, killed.
L. W. McShan,   "   severely wounded.

G. R. Manseille, Jr., 1st Sergeant, slightly wounded.
J. A. H. Keys,   "   "   "   "
Joseph Ford, private,   "   "
T. W. Mills,   "   "   "
B. R. Price,   " .   "   "
Noah Webster, "   "   "
In action, 32; killed, 2; wounded, 7.

Company C, commanded by 2d Lieutenant J. N. Davis.
William Nixon, Sergeant, killed.
C. L. Billingsly, private,   "
W. L. Wilson, Sergeant, slightly wounded.
William Milan, private,   "   "
In action, 34; killed, 2; wounded, 4.

Company D, commanded by 1st Lieutenant J. C. Cubbertson.
J. G. Martin, private, killed.
R. D. Neighbors, private, killed.
Moses Johnson, private, slightly wounded.
John Scott,   "   "   "
Wm. Williams,   "   seriously   "
W. L. Carson, Corporal, slighhtly wounded.
In action, 33; killed, 2; wounded, 4.

Company E, commanded by 1st Lieutenant J. C. Wilbourne.
W. T. Simmons, 1st Sergeant, killed.
James Rayburn, private,   "
C. L. Dalton,   "   slightly wounded.
Q. T. Martin, '   "   "   "
T. F. Taylor,   "   "   "
W. L. Hargis,   "   severely   "
In action, 33; killed, 2; wounded, 4.

Company F, commanded by 2d Lieutenant W. D. Howdge.
James W. Wolfe, private, killed.
W. H. Neely,   "   severely wounded.
D. L. Wolfe,   "   "   "
J. Milam,   "   slightly   "
J. T. Meachem,   "   "   "
M. L. Mabley Brent, 2d Lieutenant, slightly wounded.
In action, 28; killed, 1; wounded, 5.

Company G, commanded by 1st Lieutenant J. C. Davis.
C. F. Davis, private, severely wounded.
W. L. Boyd,   "   "   "
Levi Magey,   "   slightly   "
C. F. Knight,   "   "   "
James Powell,   "   "   "
I. W. Shields,   "   "..   "
In action, 26; wounded, 6.

Campany H, commanded by Captain M. L. Alcam.
G. B. Dyer, 1st Lieutenant, killed.
T. T. Gilmour, Sergeant,   "

H. F. Brooke, private, severely wounded.
G. W. Crouch,   "   "   "
W. D. Allen,   "   slightly   "
R. L. L. Weaver, "   "   "
E. D. Sallis, Sergeant,   "   "
In action, 38; killed, 2; wounded, 5.

Company K, commanded by Captain O. D. Hughes.
W. E. Namy, Brevet 2d Lieutenant, slightly wounded.
J. W. Rhyme, Sergeant,   "   "
J. J. Cunningham, Sergeant,   "   "
R. S. Whittey, Corporal,   "   "
L. S. Johnson, private,   "   "
W. W. Whittey,   "   severely wounded.
In action, 24; wounded, 6.

Company I, commanded by Captain J. M. Puler.
James M. Fry, private, killed.
John B. Moore, private, killed.
T. C. Smith,   "   severely wounded.
D. H. Strickland, "   "   "
T. P. Butler,   "   slightly   "
W. P. Juniper,   "   "   "
John H. Maley,   "   "   "
J. W. Montgomery, "   "   "
J. F. Phelps,   "   "   "
In action, 42; killed, 2; wounded, 7.

Summary report of the 1st Mississippi regiment.

	Killed.	Wounded.	In action.
Field and Staff,			7
Company A,	3	12	34
Company B,	2	7	32
Comoany C,	2	4	34
Company D,	2	4	33
Company E,	2	4	33
Company F,	1	5	28
Company G,		6	26
Company H,	2	5	38
Company I,	2	7	42
Company K,		6	24
	16	61	331

Respectfully submitted to John M. Simonton, Colonel commanding brigade, by

Lieut. Colonel A. A. HAMILTON,
Commanding 1st Mississippi regiment.

G. V. SIMONTON, *per Adjutant.*

REPORT OF BRIGADIER GENERAL DANIEL RUGGLES OF THE PART TAKEN BY HIS DIVISION AT BATON ROUGE, LA.

HEADQUARTERS 2ND DIVISION, 1ST DISTRICT,
Army East of the Mississippi,
Camp Breckinridge, August 9, 1862.

SIR: I have the honor to submit, for the consideration of the Major General commanding the forces, the following report of the part taken by my division in the action of the 5th inst., at Baton Rouge. The second division was composed of two brigades, the first consisting of the third Kentucky regiment, Captain Bowman, sixth Kentucky, Lieutenant Colonel Cofer, seventh Kentucky, Col. Crossland and thirty-fifth Alabama, Colonel Robertson. The second brigade of the fourth Louisiana regiment, Lieutenant Colonel Hunter, battalion of thirtieth Louisiana regiment, Colonel J. H. Breaux, battalion of Stewart's Legion, Lieutenant Colonel Boyd, and Confederate Light Battery, Captain O. J. Semmes, with two companies mounted men and some two hundred and fifty partisan rangers, detached on scouting and outpost service.

On the night of the 4th August, this division proceeded from Corinth bridge, marching left in front; Semmes' light battery in the rear of left battalion fourth Louisiana volunteers, a detachment commanded by Lieutenant Colonel Shields; thirtieth Louisiana volunteers, consisting of one company from his regiment, commanded by Captain Boyle; one company partisan rangers, commanded by Captain Anuker; one company mounted rangers and a section of Semmes' battery, under Lieutenant Fauntleroy, had preceded the march of the division, having left camp at four and a half P. M., to operate on the plank road leading from Baton Rouge to Clinton, on our extreme right. The head of the division column, preceded by a company of mounted rangers and advanced guard, reached ward's creek bridge, on the Greenwell Springs and Baton Rouge road, about three o'clock A. M., where a temporary halt was called, preparatory to the formation of the division line of battle. During this halt, while the advance was driving in the enemy's pickets, some stragglers from the column were mistaken for enemy's pickets, and fired on. The mistake being mutual, in the darkness a few shots were exchanged, unfortunately disabling General Helm and killing Lieutenant Todd. This necessarily caused some confusion. Order, however, was soon restored and the column marched to the point whence the deployment was to commence. The line was formed a little before daylight. Colonel Thompson's brigade (the first) with the right resting near the Greenwell Springs road, Colonel Allen's brigade (the second) on the left, his left extending through a wood and resting on a large field. Semmes' battery (four pieces) in the centre, occupying the space between the two brigades; a squadron of cavalry, under command of Captain Augustus Scott, was ordered to proceed to the extreme left of the line, to observe and endeavor to prevent any attempt to outflank us in that direction. At a little after daylight, during the prevalence of a thick fog, the order was given to advance. The line proceded but a few hundred yards before it encountered a brisk fire from the enemy's skirmishers, strongly posted on our extreme right, in some houses surrounded by trees and picket fences. Almost simultaneously a battery of the enemy opened on our line from the same direction. Semmes' battery was ordered forward to our indicated position, to drive off the skirmishers and silence the enemy's battery, and the whole line moved rapidly forward firing and cheering. The effect was instantaneous. The enemy's skirmishers fled and his battery was compelled to change position and seek shelter under the guns of the arsenal to prevent being captured, where it remained, continueing to fire on our advancing line. Semmes' battery took position on the right of the division, to keep up the engagement with the battery of the enemy. Colonel Thompson's brigade continued to advance, under an occasional fire, across an open field and through some corn fields, just beyond which they encountered a heavy fire from the enemy, strongly posted in a wood. Here the contest was warmly maintained on both sides for a considerable time, during which the first division succeeded in entering a regimental camp on our right. The enemy were finally driven back into and through another camp immediately in our front. The enemy at this period were strongly reenforced, and a heavy battery a little to the left of the centre opened an oblique fire on both brigades. About the same time the enemy attempted to break our centre, by pushing a column between the two brigades. This movement being discovered, Semmes' battery was ordered forward and opened on this column at short range, with grape and cannister with marked effect, for a few rapid discharges scattered the enemy and drove him back in confusion. A similar attempt was made on the right of the division, which was defeated with equal success by a timely and well directed fire from the thiry-fifth Alabama and sixth Kentucky regiments. The two brigades, which, from the nature of the ground, had become separated, were ordered in, advancing, to gain ground, to the right and left respectively, in order to subject the enemy's position in front to a converging fire. In executing this movement the first brigade met a portion of the first division falling back in some disorder. Colonel Thompson halted and was attempting to reform them when he was informed by a mounted officer that the order was for the whole line to fall back. In obedience to this supposed order he fell back a short distance, but soon reformed his line and charged the enemy under a galling fire.

Unfortunately while leading his men in this charge, Colonel Thompson fell, severely wounded, and was borne from the field, and about the same time Colonel Allen, also fell, dangerously wounded, while leading, with unsurpassed gallantry, his brigade against a battery of the enemy. These circumstances prevented the further prosecution of this movement. About this time the Major General commanding arriving upon this part of the field, directed the final charge upon the enemy, which drove him in confusion through his last regimental encampment to the river, under the protection of his gun boats. His camps, containing a large quantity of personal property, commissary stores and clothing, were destroyed. Finding it fruitless to remain longer under the fire of the gun boats, and disappointed in the expected co-operation of the "Arkansas," the exhausted troops were withdrawn in good order to the suburbs of the town. The seventh Kentucky regiment and a section of Semmes' artillery being left on the field to protect the collection of the stragglers and wounded, which was thoroughly accomplished. Colonel Allen's brigade, on the left, moved forward through a wood and into some cornfields. They soon encountered the enemy in superior force, protected by houses and fences. They successively charged these positions, driving the enemy steadily back until within a few hundred yards of the river, where they were subjected to a destructive fire from the batteries before mentioned and the enemy's gunboats. They charged and took a section from one of the enemy's batteries, Colonel Allen leading the advance with the colors of one of his battalions in his hand. It was at this critical juncture that, as before stated, this gallant soldier fell from his horse severely wounded, and during the confusion which followed this misfortune, the enemy succeeded in recapturing the pieces.

The enemy pressed heavily upon this brigade, and poured into it such a galling fire from infantry and artillery that it fell back in some disorder. Colonel Breaux, who assumed command upon the fall of Colonel Allen, succeeded, with the aid of officers of the brigade and two officers connected with the staff, who were sent to his assistance, in rallying a sufficient number to show front to the enemy, until Semmes' battery was brought up, as already stated, to their support, and succeeded, by a well directed fire, in preventing the enemy's advance. This position was maintained despite the heavy firing on the brigade from the enemy's gunboats and land batteries, until the troops were withdrawn, with the rest of the army, to the suburbs of the town. Lieutenant Colonel Shields had been ordered, as already stated, to take position on the Plank road, leading from Clinton to Baton Rouge, and as soon as he heard the fire of our main body, to attack a battery of the enemy, said to be stationed at the junction of the Clinton and Bayou Sara roads. This service was promptly and gallantly performed. He drove in the enemy's pickets, followed them up, and opened fire on a regimental encampment to the right of the Greenwell Springs road, driving the enemy from it. He was here met by two regiments of the enemy, but succeeded in holding them at bay till he was fired upon by our own artillery, fortunately without injury. Four of the artillery horses, being disabled, and the infantry unable to withstand the heavy fire of the enemy, he withdrew to his original position, where the wounded horses were replaced by others, when he returned to his advanced position, which he held till General Clark's division came up on his left, when the two companies of infantry were, by order of the Major General commanding, attached to the twenty-second Mississippi regiment. The section of artillery under his command retained its position until the army retired, when it rejoined the battery in the suburbs of the town. In concluding this report of the battle, I have the satisfaction of stating that the conduct of both officers and men was gallant and daring, every movement being performed with characteristic promptitude. I respectfully commend the reports of the commanders of brigades, as well as those of regiments, battalions and independent companies, to the special consideration of the Commanding General, and also recommend the following officers and soldiers, specially named in these reports, to favorable consideration: 1st. Colonel A. P. Thompson and Colonel H. W. Allen, brigade commanders, both severely wounded. Fifth Kentucky, commanded by Captain Bowman. Seventh Kentucky, Colonel Crossland, and his color-bearer, James Rollins. Sixth Kentucky, Lieutenant Colonel Cofer; Captains J. Smith, Utterback, and Thomas Page, and first Lieutenant H. Harned. Thirty-fifth Alabama, Colonel Robertson and Lieutenant Colonel Goodwin. Of the second brigade, the fourth Louisiana, Lieutenant Colonel Hunter. In this regiment, Lieutenant Corkern, company B, Lieutenant Jeter, company H, and Sergeant-Major Daniels. Battalion of Stewart's Legion, commanded by Lieutenant Colonel Samuel Boyd, who was disabled by a severe flesh wound in the arm. Captain Chum also was wounded. The command devolved upon Captain T. Bynum, who acted with gallantry. The battalion thirtieth regiment of Louisiana volunteers, commanded by Colonel J. A. Breaux, who speaks in high terms of the officers and men of his regiment, especially Captain N. Trepagnier and Lieutenant Dapremont, both wounded. Lieutenant Colonel Shields, thirtieth Louisiana, commanding separate detachment, who speaks in high terms of the intrepidity of Lieutenant Fauntleroy, commanding section of guns in his detachment. Captain Semmes, commanding battery, and his officers, Lieutenants Barnes and J. A. West, performed gallant service. Captain Blount, brigade inspector of second brigade, rendered gallant service in the field, where it is believed he has fallen, as nothing has been heard of him since. I also have the gratification to name the members of my staff, who served with me on this occasion, viz: Lieutenant L. D. Sandidge, corps artillery Confederate States army, A. A. A. and Inspector General; Captain George Whitfield, chief quartermaster; Major E. S. Ruggles, acting ordnance officer, and acting chief commissary of subsistence, first Lieutenant M. B. Ruggles, aid de camp. Lieutenant Colonel Charles Jones, who was severely wounded, and Colonel J. O. Fuqua, Dist. Judge Advocate and Provost Marshal General, who were all distinguished for their efficiency, coolness and gallantry throughout the conflict. The following officers, attached to the general staff, also rendered gallant service: Captain Sam. Bard, on special service; Lieutenant A. B. DeSaulles, engineers; Lieutenant H. H. Price and Lieutenant H. C. Holt. Other officers on special service, amongst whom were Captain Augustus Scott, commanding squadron on temporary service; Captains Curry, Kinderson and Behörn, as volunteer aids for the occasion, and Captain J. M. Taylor served with zeal and gallantry. The entire division entering the fight numbered about nineteen hundred and fifty, infantry and artillery, with a few irregular cavalry and partizan rangers, numbering in all some three hundred and fifty or four hundred. The casualties, killed, wounded and missing being two hundred and seventy-seven, (277.)

Very respectfully, your obedient servant,
DANIEL RUGGLES,
Brigadier General Commanding Second Division.

Captain JOHN A. BUCKER,
A. A. Genneral.

REPORT OF A. A. GENERAL JOHN A. BUCKNER OF THE ENGAGEMENT AT BATON ROUGE.

HEADQUARTERS IN THE FIELD,
Corinth river, ten miles from Baton Rouge, Aug. 9, 1862.

GENERAL: In compliance with your request, I have the honor to submit the following report of the late engagement at Baton Rouge, so far as the first brigade of first division was concerned, after its commanders, Brigadier General Helm, and subsequently Colonel Thomas Hunt, were wounded, and I had the honor to receive the command at your hands. The enemy had been repulsed from one of his encampments, and the different regiments constituting the first brigade were drawn up in line in one of his camps, not, however, fully deployed. After moving the two regiments on the left of the brigade, by the flank to the left, the whole were formed in line of battle, and were ordered to advance. The movement was spiritedly made up to the second encampment, through a somewhat sharp volley of musketry, in as good style as the broken and confined limits of the ground would admit, and immediately the enemy was hotly and determinedly engaged. After a few volleys, I ordered the brigade forward, which order was being promptly obeyed by the fourth and fifth Kentucky, the other regiments being just in the act of advancing, when I received, from General Clark, the order to face about and retreat. This order was then given by myself and General Clark's aids. The troops fell back reluctantly and not in very good order, the General himself and a number of others being wounded in the retreat. I immediately reported to you to know whether you had ordered the retreat, and was informed that you had not. The second brigade of this division was then ordered by yourself to advance. It went up in good style, Captain Hughes, commanding twenty-second Mississippi regiment, leading them gallantly. By your presence and assistance, the first brigade was rallied and led by yourself, in person, to the same position from which it had fallen back, when it joined with the second brigade, and moved conjointly through the second encampment, driving the enemy before them through the third and *last* of their camps to the river, under cover of their gunboats. This being accomplished, which was all that was expected of the land force, the "Arkansas" failing to make her appearance, nothing remained but to destroy what had been captured, (inasmuch as no arrangement had been made for bearing it off, though the battle field was in our possession sufficiently long,) and retire from the range of the enemy's batteries on the river. Accordingly, you gave me the order to withdraw the division out of range of the fire of the fleet, to await the movements of the gunboat "Arkansas." This was done in good order, though with some degree of reluctance, the cause of the movement not being fully understood. Your order to fire the enemy's tents and stores was well executed. Their loss must have been very heavy in quartermaster and commissary supplies, and particularly so in sutlers' stores, considerable quantities of new goods and general equipments being burned. The position in which you left me near the house where General Clark lay wounded was held more than two hours after the main body of the troops were withdrawn, with a section of Semmes' battery and the remnant of the seventh Kentucky regiment, Colonel Crossland commanding, as support. Learning that Cobb's battery had left its position and been ordered to the rear, the section, with its support under my command, was removed to occupy the better position left by Captain Cobb, at which point it remained a half hour, and would have remained the whole evening, but for the erroneous information of the enemy's advance in force being given by a surgeon who was moving rapidly to the rear. Leaving pickets at this point, just in the edge of town, I withdrew the artillery and its support slowly back to the point at which you found me. A flag of truce was hoisted early in the evening by the enemy, and on being met by an officer whom I sent to the front, the privilege of bearing off the dead and wounded was requested and granted for four hours by yourself, upon condition that the agreement be reduced to writing. No communication being received in writing for sometime, twenty mintues longer were given, shortly after the expiration of which time, a note was received, signed by the commanding officer at Baton Rouge, disclaiming the flag of truce.

I cannot conclude my report without speaking of the cool courage and efficient skill with which Brigadier General Charles Clark led his command into the action, and the valuable assistance rendered him by his aids Lieutenants Spooner and Yerger; of the officiency of Major H. E. Topp, of the thirty-first Mississippi, in leading his regiment; of Major Brown, chief commissary of the division, whose fearless exposure of himself where the contest was hotest, in urging on the troops to a charge; of Captain J. H. Miller, commanding fourth Kentucky regiment, who displayed conspicuous gallantry in leading his regiment; of Colonel Crossland, commanding seventh

Kentucky regiment, whose regiment, after being in front and assisting in bearing the brunt of the battle, remained upon the field while the shells from the enemy's gunboats were falling thickly around them; and of the valuable service rendered me by Major O. Wickliffe, of the fifth Kentucky, towards the close of the engagement, where his constant presence at the head of his regiment, inspired confidence and courage, not only among his own men, but all who were near him in the closing contest, which decided the engagement so favorably and so gloriously for the Confederate arms. For list of casualties I would refer you to papers "A" and "B," concerning late battle.

I have the honor to be, General,
  Very respectfully, your obedient servant,
        JOHN A. BUCKNER,
         A. A. General.

FIELD REPORTS OF FIRST DIVISION AT THE BATTLE OF BATON ROUGE.

REPORT OF L B SMITH, COLONEL, COMMANDING 4TH BRIGADE.

HEADQUARTERS FIRST DIVISION,
Camp on Comite River, August 10, 1862.

To Major General BRECKINRIDGE:

SIR: The following is a correct report of the part the fourth brigade took in the late engagement in front of the city of Baton Rouge, on the 5th instant. By order of General Clark, I moved the fourth brigade across a corn field, perpendicular to the road, throwing the fifteenth Mississippi regiment in the woods, deployed as skirmishers, to protect the right. We then moved forward across several fields to the outskirts of the town, when the division was halted till I was ordered to move by the left flank to the road, and then by the front, till they fired on me, which was returned. At that moment, we were not more than twenty yards from their lines. About three rounds from our men put them to flight. The fog being so thick, we could not see more than twenty steps. We were then on a line with their camps on the left of the road, and the firing had ceased, when General Clark ordered me to fall back in the ravine, some hundred yards to the rear. I about faced the brigade, and marched back in good order, walking my men in a gully. Soon after, the second brigade moved obliquely to the left, and engaged them on the left of the road; the right of the second brigade began to give way, and in twenty or thirty minutes, I suppose, I moved forward to their support, and to their right, engaging the enemy, and a general forward movement was made by our division. About the time we had reached the tents and tops of the hills, orders came to fall back to the bridge, where the stampede had taken place that morning, which we did in as good order as we could after having so severely engaged them. I would beg leave to mention the names of Lieutenant Colonel Moore, of the nineteenth Tennessee, Captain Hughes, of the twenty-second Mississippi, and Adjutant Fitzpatrick, of the twenty-second Mississippi, as acting gallantly all through the engagement. Captain Hughes fell in the last charge at the head of his men. The fifteenth Mississippi was held in reserve with a battery, and was not in the fight. The men behaved well, and observed the commands I gave them.

Respectfully submitted,

L. B. SMITH,
Colonel Commanding Fourth Brigade.

REPORT OF COLONEL J. EDWARDS.

HEADQUARTERS THIRTY-FIRST ALABAMA REGIMENT,
Camp near Comite River, La., Aug. 8, 1862.

To Major JOHN A. BUCKNER,

Assistant Adjutant General:

SIR: I have the honor to make the following report of the part taken by the thirty-first Alabama regiment, in the action at Baton Rouge, Louisiana, on the 5th instant. At early dawn on the morning of the 5th instant, the different regiments, composing the second brigade, of which my regiment formed a part, were assigned their positions in line of battle. After having advanced for considerable distance over very difficult ground, my regiment, with the thirty-first Mississippi and fourth Kentucky, was ordered to commence the attack on the enemy's left, which order was executed vigorously, but cautiously, skirmishers being thrown out at different times and places. The fog hovering over the field rendered it impossible to discover what was in our front at a distance of but few paces. The enemy retired slowly before the well directed fire, which we constantly poured upon them, falling back from their first encampment. On reaching that encampment, my regiment was exposed to a galling fire in front and on the left flank, when we were ordered to fall back. At this point, Lieutenant Childress, of company "K," was mortally, and Lieutenant Hays, of company "G," and Sergeant Loughlin, of company "B," were severely wounded while gallantly fighting, and left on the field. Having fallen back to a small ravine, the line was reformed, and advanced to dislodge the enemy from their last encampment to our left, which was gallantly done after a severe contest. The order then being given for us to retire, it was executed in good order. Sickness and death had thinned my ranks to such an extent that I only carried into action ninety-seven, rank and file, of which number two were killed and nine wounded. I take pleasure in saying that, although neither of my field officers were with me, both being absent, sick, I found but little or no difficulty in rallying my men. I saw not a single instance in my regiment, amidst all the galling fires of the enemy, which they withstood, of any officer or soldier being disposed to shrink from his duty, but all seemed to vie with each other in the stern determination to conquer or die. In the last charge made upon the enemy, when they were driven from their last encampment, I am proud to say my regiment was side by side with the foremost in the charge, and when

the work was accomplished of driving the enemy from their position, and we were ordered to fall back, they did so in perfect order.
Very respectfully,
J. EDWARDS,
Colonel, commanding thirty-first Alabama regiment.

REPORT OF MAJOR TOPP.

HEADQUARTERS THIRTY-FIRST REG'T. MISS. VOLS., }
August 7th, 1862. }

Major JOHN A. BUCKNER,
A. A. General:

Dear Sir: I have the honor to make the following report. About the time, or immediately after the repulse of the second division, a portion of our brigade, of which the thirty-first Mississippi regiment was a part, under the command of Colonel Hunt, of the fifth Kentucky, was ordered forward through several corn fields, in which the enemy was discovered by my skirmishers, thrown out for that purpose, towards the second encampment, to which we approached within two hundred yards or less, driving constantly the enemy before us, when a terrific fire from the enemy in the direction of the second encampment checked our advance, and where well nigh all of my casualties occurred. At this point we were ordered to fall back, by Colonel Hunt, and the retreat had hardly begun when Colonel Hunt was wounded and taken off the field. Here I attempted to rally my regiment, but the confusion had become so general that I found it impossible to do so. We then fell back to the ravine in advance of the first encampment, and formed under the cover of the ravine. General Clark, commanding division, came up at this juncture. I told him that we were without a brigade commander, Col. H. having been wounded, and requested him to assign some one to the command of the brigade, Colonel Edwards, of the thirty-first Alabama, having lost his horse, and expressing an unwillingness to assume the command. General C. then left and very soon Major Buckner, as I was informed, took the command, and ordered us to march by the left flank in the direction of the enemy's second encampment, and having fairly gotten us in a position to advance, ordered us forward. The command was instantly obeyed, and the brigade, with the exception of the two regiments on the right, was soon engaged with the enemy. My regiment was lying down firing, with very little damage to themselves, and gradually approaching the encampment, when, to our surprise, we observed the right of our brigade falling back in disorder. I have no idea who gave the command as I was on the extreme left. I then ordered my regiment to fall back which it did, in confusion, to the cut in the road. At this time the regiments held in reserve were carried forward by General Clark, and we rallied again in the road under the direction of Major Buckner. We were a second time ordered to forward, and this time there was no halting or falling back. We advanced at a double quick to within seventy-five yards of the encampment, fired, and charged bayonets when the enemy began to give way, and finally ended in a route. We were entering the encampment when we were ordered to halt by Major B., and formed upon the color line of the second encampment. We remained in this position some five minutes or more, when the same officer called "attention," gave the command, "about face, forward, march," the whole line marching in admirable order.

Respectfully submitted.

H. E. TOPP,
Major Commanding thirty-first regiment Mississippi Volunteers.

REPORT OF MAJOR J. C. WICKLIFFE.

HEADQUARTERS 5TH KENTUCKY REGIMENT,
Camp near Comite river, La.,
August 7th, 1862.

Sir: I have the honor of submitting to you the following report of the part taken by the 5th Kentucky regiment in the action of the 5th instant at Baton Rouge.

The 5th Kentucky, with the commander of the brigade, was placed in line of battle early on the morning of the 5th of August. The line was advanced towards Baton Rouge steadily. In obedience to an order of my brigade commander, my regiment was held as a support to the battery attached to this brigade, where it remained until I received an order in person from Major General Breckinridge to post one company, as pickets, to the right and at some distance from the arsenal. In obedience to this order, I placed Captain Gillum, with his company, consisting of one lieutenant, four sergeants, one corporal and twenty-four men, upon the ground designated by the General; and in obedience to another order from him, left Capt. Gillum there, when my command was ordered to join the brigade and engage the enemy in their camps. Captain Gillum remained at his post until ordered away, when the brigade retired to the point where the line of battle was first formed. Thus this company was prevented from engaging in the battle, and this will account why none was killed or wounded in company A, of this regiment. When ordered by Major General Breckinridge to join the brigade to which my regiment is attached, I was placed on the left of the 4th Kentucky regiment, which was the first regiment in the brigade. Immediately after this, an order from you was given to advance. My command did so, and until the fire was drawn from the enemy, who were secreted in and about the tents of the third and last encampment. The fire was immediately returned by the men under my command. It continued warm and heavy for about twenty or twenty-five minutes, our line, as far as I could see, advancing very little, but steadily, and the enemy as slowly retreating. At this time an order was given by Brigadier General Clark, commanding the division, to fall back to a small ravine, a short distance in the rear, and reform, which was executed in good order. In a few moments we were again ordered to advance, and did so, never halting until the enemy had been driven from the last of their encampments. After the brigade line had been formed, in obedience to an order from you, we retired slowly and in good order. My command numbered 222, rank and file. From this deduct company A, numbering thirty-one officers and men, and seven detailed to carry off the wounded, thus reducing the number of men actually engaged in the fight, under my command, to 184 men.

The following is a list of the casualties which occurred in my regiment: In company A, none. In company B, L. P. Smith, mortally wounded and since dead; H. Osborne, slightly. In company C, Lieut. H. H. Harris, wounded; private R. S. Brooks, killed; privates J. S. Jackson, J. T. Taylor, D. Tinsley and J. B. Yonng, wounded. In company D, Lieut. Oscar Kennard, wounded; private Wm. Hicks, killed; privates John Essill and John Henry, wounded. In company E, Sergeant R. M. Hague, wounded; privates James Bowers and Isaac Rutledge, killed; privates Elbert Gramor, B. Logan and J. L. Thompson, wounded. In company F, A. P. Fowler, W. P. Ratliff, J. Leach, J. W. Wallace and D. P. Howell, wounded. In company G, Lieut. P. V. Daniel, privates N. M. Beauchamp, Thomas Stith, Miche Meardin, Allen Dereby, Frank Keath, Green Woorley and M. S. Newman, wounded. In company K, Sergeant John H. Hughes, Corporal Moses Lafeiter, privates Alexander Barry, Charles Freeburg and Thomas Lively, killed; Sergeant T. H. Atwell, privates Edmond Elliott, Peter Frilty, James Hunt, G. Polfers, L. Hotsenburgh, A. J. Williams and W. McFatridge, wounded.

I cannot close this report without stating that the officers and men, under my command, discharged their duties in the action at Baton Rouge in a manner creditable alike to themslves and the cause for which they are battling.

Very respectfully,

J. C. WICKLIFFE,
Major com'd'g 5th Ky. regiment.

REPORT OF CAPTAIN J. H. MILLETT.

Camp near Comite River, August 7, 1862.

Captain John A. Buckner:

Sir: Through an unfortunate circumstance I was placed in command of the fourth Kentucky at about three o'clock, A. M., on the 5th instant. After being placed in line, our brigade moved forward until it reached the outskirts of Baton Rouge, when we moved by the left flank as far as the camp of the fourteenth Maine regiment. We then moved forward; the smoke being so dense my command was here separated from the brigade. Having thrown out my right company as skirmishers I continued to move forward, but discovering that the enemy were on my left, supported by a battery, all concealed by the houses and fences, and not being able to change direction without placing my regiment immediately under the fire of our own troops, I rejoined the brigadg. I had just taken my position on the right when you took command, and ordered us forward. I moved my regiment obliquely to the left until my right had cleared the fence in front, when I ordered them forward in the direction of the enemy's camp, which they did with a cheer. We had advanced probably two hundred yards when an aid, whom I took to be on General Clark's staff, (not being personally acquainted with any of them,) ordered me to fall back. Seeing the balance of the brigade retiring, I gave the command to my regiment, which they were very unwilling to execute, seeing the enemy retiring from their camps. After reforming my regiment, I was again ordered by you to advance. In this charge the enemy were driven completely from their camps. It is not necessary, Captain, for me to say how my command acted in this charge. You, being in front of my left, could judge for yourself. I think that you will agree that they did not abuse the confidence the Commanding General has in "ragged Kentuckians." The fourth Kentucky lost in

Killed, 5
Wounded, 14
Missing, 1
—
20

Respectfully,

J. H. MILLETT,
Captain Commanding fourth Kentucky Regiment Volunteers.

REPORT OF LIEUTENANT COLONEL JOHN SNODGRASS.

HEADQUARTERS FOURTH ALABAMA BATTALION,
August 6, 1862

Colonel J. EDWARDS,
Commanding Second Brigade :

Sir : I have the honor to make the following report of the part taken by the fourth Alabama battalion in the battle of Baton Rouge on the 5th instant. In the accidental affair on the road before daylight the following are the casualties: Lieutenant W. B. Stokes; Privates, Morgan, O'Connel, Stephen Oliver, Y. Freeman, P. Andrews, M. Y. Haine, and P. Mattison, company C, slightly wounded. Private A. Lewis, company A, slightly. Privates M. L. Sewel, G. W. Lisk, company G, slightly. Private J. J. Carlton, company E, slightly. When the positions of the various regiments, etc., were assigned, the battalion with the fifth Kentucky regiment, was ordered to support the Hudson battery, which position it occupied until between seven and eight o'clock, A. M., when I was ordered to advance to the support of our forces then engaging the enemy at their second encampment. The battalion continued in the engagement until the enemy's infantry were driven from the field, and their batteries were playing heavily upon the position we occupied, when we were ordered to withdraw. The following is a list of the casualties during the engagement: Major G. L. Alexander, mortally wounded in left breast by minnie ball, died shortly after. In company A, wounded—private W. B. Moore, seriously, privates A. J. Allen, A. M. Cannon, J. P. Wilson, slightly. Company C, wounded—private W. T. Harbin, slightly. Company D, Captain Randall, slightly wounded, T. J. Love, mortally. Company E, private William Anderson, mortally wounded, since died. Company G, killed—private J. K. P. Jenkins; wounded, privates H. McCoy and William McBrown, severely, corporal A. T. Hannah and T. R. Moon, mortally.

Recapitulation—Killed, 3
Wounded, 22
——
25

I take pleasure in calling your attention to the gallant and enthusiastic conduct of private John Thompson, company F, and J. M. Byrd, company G, who boldly moved in advance of the command and discharged their arms with due caution and alacrity. They were the first to open fire, and last to quit the field, and I am happy, while reporting the especially worthy conduct of those two privates, not to have a solitary instance of cowardice or wavering to report, the whole command having advanced and stood under the fire from which older troops and greater numbers had retired.

Very respectfully,

JOHN SNODGRASS,
Lieutenant Colonel Fourth Alabama Battalion.

Report of killed, wounded and missing in the action at Baton Rouge.

HEADQUARTERS 1ST DIVISION, }
Camp on Comite River, August 10, 1862. }

To Captain A. BUCKNER, *A. A. General,*

SIR: I herewith submit the following report of the killed, wounded and missing in this division, in the action of the 5th inst., at Baton Rouge, Louisiana:

KILLED IN SECOND BRIGADE.

Fourth Kentucky Regiment.—Company "A," privates R. W. Hoffman and Joseph Stuffman; company "E," private John R. Bogette; company "H," private W. O. Daniel; company "I," Sergeant Thomas Hickley.

Fifth Kentucky Regiment.—Company "B," private L. P. Smith; company "C," private R. S. Brooks; company "D," private William Hicks; company "E," privates James Bowers and Isaac Rutlege; company "F," private J. W. Wallace; company "H," Sergeant John H. Hughes, corporal Moses Lassiter, privates Alexander Barry, Charles Furburg and Thomas Lurdy.

Thirty-first Mississippi Regiment.—Company "D," privates Wm. Sutton and J. T. Cain; company "F," First Lieutenant W. J. Monahan and Sergeant S. M. McNutt; company "I," private W. F. Gray; company "K," Second Lieutenant J. A. McBrayer, privates J. J. Barnett, J. W. Hampton, H. H. McWharton and Nathan Thompson.

Thirty-first Alabama Battalion.—Company "F," privates Isaiah Martin and O. Vincent Terry.

Fourth Alabama Battalion.—Major G. L. Alexander; company "G," private J. K. P. Jenkins.

Total killed, thirty.

WOUNDED.

Fourth Kentucky Regiment.—Company "C," Captain S. Higginson and private Thomas Pike, severely; company "D," Captain W. S. Roberts, severely, Sergeant John Yarbrough, private T. Stiger, slightly, and private John O. Lucas, mortally; company "E," privates R. R. Woodson, mortally, R. Railey, Jr., J. J. Price and H. Hancock, slightly; company "H," privates John Mahone, slightly, and Thos. Ruggles, severely; company "I," privates Douglas Camron, severely, and Nicholas Lyon, slightly.

Fifth Kentucky Regiment.—Company "B," private F. Osborne, slightly; company "C," Lieutenant H. H. Harris, dangerously, privates J. F. Jackson, J. J. Taylor, slightly, D. Tinsley, severely, and J. B. Young, slightly; company "D," Lieutenant Oscar Kinnard, slightly, privates John Estill and John Henry, dangerously; company "E," Sergeant R. M. Hayne, privates Elbert Grammer, B. Logan, and J. L. Thompson, slightly; company "F," privates W. P. Ratcliff and A. L. Fowler, slightly; company "H," private Josiah Heath, severely; company "G," Lieutenant P. V. Daniel, severely, Sergeant Thomas Strite and private William Beauchamp, slightly, privates Francis Keith, dangerously, Fred Moog, M. Nurman, Green Woolsey and Michael McCarden, severely; company "H," Sergeant L. H. Atwell, privates Edward Elliott, James Hunt, Godfrey Polpes, Lewis Stotsenberg, Willian McFudge, severely, Peter Fritz, slightly, and A. J. Williams, dangerously.

Thirty-first Mississippi Regiment.—Fitzpatrick, A. C. S., slightly, Sergeant-Major F. M. McEwin, severely, and Color Sergeant Peter Saunders, mortally; company "A," privates W. J. Private, J. W. Fiharty, J. H. Oowen and J. W. Newland, slightly; compamy "B," private W. A. McGowan, slightly; company "C," Corporal E. E. Smith, slightly, privates J. M. Gordon, Reubin Davis, severely, and G. W. Hill, slightly; company "D," privates G. L. Cain, F. M. Rayland, W. P. Kyle, severely, P. M. Cobbs, M. R. Beasly, slightly, and J. N. Brown, mortally; company "E," privates D. Mallins, mortally, H. A. Cockran and G. M. Vaughan, slightly; company "F," privates W. McFinly, mortally, H. Hubbard, severely, D. J. Ramsey and H. Phillips, slightly; company "G," privates D. Bowland, T. Kirkpatrick, W. A. Milan, severely, and A. G. Monahan, slightly; company "H," corporal T. N. Ross, severely, private J. C. Wickless, slightly; Company "I," private J. L. Johnson, severely; company "K," Corporal A. J. McGraw and private L. M. Free, severely, W. A. McDowell and J. P. McWhorton, slightly.

Thirty-first Alabama Regiment.—Company "A," private Madison Willis, severely; company "B," Sergeant W. R. Laughlin, severely; company "C," Color Sergeant J. C. Brownfield, and private J. A. Smith, severely; company "E," privates Watson Mizell and J. W. Walker, severely; company "G," Lieutenant J. L. Haye, severely; company "H," private W. P. Smith, slightly; company "K," Lieutenant H. M. Childress, mortally.

Fourth Alabama Battalion.—Company "A," privates A. Lewis, A. J. Allen, A. M. Cameron, J. P. Wilson, slightly, and W. B. Moore, severely; company "C," Lieutenant W. J. Stokes, slightly, privates M. O'Connell, S. Olliver, G. Keenan, J. Andrews, M. S. Harris, P. Mattison and W. J. Harbin, slightly; company "D," Captain W. M. Randle, slightly, private J. J. Love, mortally; company "E," privates Wm. Anderson, mortally, and J. J. Carleton, slightly; company "G," privates M. L. Lervell, G. A. Sish, slightly, D. F. McCoy, W. M. Brown, severely, corporals A. J. Hannah, and J. B. Moore, mortally.

The Hudson Battery.—Privates J. C. Bagley, severely and missing, John Connelly, Nath. Miller, Bennett Davis, slightly. M. R. Beasley. (of thirty-first Mississippi,) severely, and Fred. R. Hanson, stunned severely by shell.

Total wounded, one hundred and twenty.

MISSING.

Fourth Regiment Kentucky Volunteers.—Company "H," private Samuel Clark.

RECAPITULATION.

Killed thirty; wounded one hundred and twenty; missing one.
Total, one hundred and fifty-one.

KILLED IN FOURTH BRIGADE.

Twentieth Regiment Tennessee Volunteers.—Company "G," private A. W. Thaxton.

Forty-fifth Regiment Tennessee Volunteers.—Company "I," James F. Boreman.

Twenty-second Regiment Mississippi Volunteers.—Captain F. Hughes, commanding regiment; company "A," private John Gray; company "C," privates James Stine, Matthew Flaherty and Patrick Brady; company "D," Lieutenant Burke and Corporal Sharp; company "E," private J. F. Causey and J. P. Brown; company "F," private John F. Callicote; company "G," private Simmons; company "H," private T. King; company "I," privates I. Hickey and P. Honan. Total killed, sixteen.

WOUNDED.

Nineteenth Tennessee Regiment.—Company "A," Lieutenant N. P. Nail, severely.

Twentieth Tennessee Regiment.—Company "A," private M. Kennedy, Lieutenant Murphy, and private W. A. Hay, slightly.

Twenty-eighth Tennessee Regiment.—Company "H," private A. B. King, slightly; company "K," private C. Field, slightly.

Forty-fifth Tennessee Regiment.—Company "I," private Soloman Tuttle, seriously; company "C," private E. Matthews, slightly.

Twenty-second Regiment Mississippi Volunteers.—Adjutant Fitzpatrick, seriously; company "A," private B. Givens, P. Givens, W. C. Calhoun, seriously, Captain M. A. Oatis, Lieutenant Sutton and private Bozeman, slightly; company "B," Sergeant C. Brock, privates B. Williams, W. H. Baily, and H. Abbes, slightly; company "C," privates H. McMillen, and M. Fitzpatrick, seriously; company "D," First Sergeant H. Seger, seriously, Lieutenant Golden, and private P. McGrew, slightly; company "E," private W. G. Brown, slightly; company "F," privates H. C. Stone, and B. F. Pritchard, severely; company "G," Sergeants Jerritt, Duffie, Corporal L. Byrd and private Smith, seriously; company "H," Corporal McCullough, privates Campell and Collins, seriously, and Sergeant Wilds, slightly; company "I," private J. Pace, slightly; company "K," Sergeant Leater, privates E. Beard, seriously; company "I," private Ingraham, slightly; company "K," privates S. N. Harsh and Jeff. Sinclair, slightly.

Total wounded, forty-one.

MISSING.

Nineteenth Tennessee Regiment.—Company "C," private Emmet White.

Fifteenth Mississippi Regiment.—Company "F," sergeant E. Matthews.

Twenty-second Mississippi Regiment.—Company "I," private J. K. McDaniel.

Total missing, three.

SECOND BRIGADE.

Total killed, thirty; total wounded, one hundred and twenty; total missing, one.

Total one hundred and fifty-one.

FOURTH BRIGADE.

Total killed, sixteen; total wounded, forty-one; total missing, three.

Total sixty.

FIRST DIVISION.

Total killed, forty-six; total wounded, one hundred and sixty-one; total missing, four.
All of which is respectfully submitted,
JOHN WEBB,
Assistant Adjutant General.

T. B. SMITH,
Colonel, Commanding First Division:

RETURN of the Casualties in the First Division at the Battle of Baton Rouge, August 5th, 1862.

COMMANDS.	Killed.	Mortally Wounded.	Severely Wounded.	Slightly Wounded.	Missing.	
SECOND BRIGADE.						
5th Regiment Kentucky Volunteers,	9	2	9	13	1	
4th " " "	5	...	...	13	1	
31st " Mississippi "	10	6	15	16		
31st " Alabama "	2	...	...	9	1	
4th Alabama Battalion,............	3	3	3	16		
Hudson's Battery,.................	...	...	3	3		
FOURTH BRIGADE.						
19th Regiment Tennessee Volunteers	...	...	1	...	1	
20th " " "	...	...	1	1		
28th " " "	1	...	1	1		
45th " " "	1	...	1	1		
15th " Mississippi "	...	...	...	...	1	This Regiment was held in reserve.
22d " " "	13	...	18	16	1	
Cobb's Battery,...................						
Total..............................	44	11	52	89	6	

Respectfully submitted,

T. B. SMITH,
Colonel Commanding First Division.

To Captain BUCKNER,
Assistant Adjutant General.

Officers mentioned for Gallant Conduct at the Battle of Baton Rouge. Exhibit " A," Report of the First Division.

Captain Hughes, commanding 22d Mississippi Regiment.
Brigadier General Charles Clarke and his aids.
Lieutenants Spooner and Yerger.
Major H. E. Topp, of the 31st Mississippi Regiment.
Major Brown, Chief of Subsistence.
Captain J. H. Miller, commanding 4th Kentucky Regiment.
Colonel Crossland, 7th Kentucky Regiment.
Major C. Wickliffe, of the 5th Kentucky.
Privates John Thompson, Company H, and J. M. Byrd, Company G, 4th Alabama Battalion.
Lieutenant Colonel Moore, of the 19th Tennessee Regiment.
Adjutant Fitzpatrick, 22d Mississippi Regiment.

FIELD REPORTS OF SECOND DIVISION AT THE BATTLE OF BATON ROUGE.

REPORT OF BRIGADIER GENERAL M. L. SMITH.

Headquarters 3d District,
Vicksburg, August —, 1862.

Maj. M. M. Kimmel, *A. A. G.*:

Major : The following report of the attack and defence of Vicksburg is respectfully submitted to the Major General commanding the district of Mississippi:

I assumed command of Vicksburg and its defences on the 12th of May, in obedience to orders from Major General Lovell, and proceeded at once to prepare for the approach of the enemy, then known to have passed B.ton Rouge with a formidable fleet, having in view to open the river to Memphis and Fort Pillow, then in our possession. At the time of arriving, the State of preparation for defence was as follows : Of the ten batteries that have been in use, three were mostly completed, and a fourth begun. The armed troops present consisted of the remnant of the 8th Louisiana battalion, Lieutenant Colonel Pinckney, and the 27th Louisiana volunteers, Colonel Marke; both of my brigades which had preceded me some six or ten days. Colonel J. L'Antry, ordered here by General Bragg, was found in command, pushing the works forward vigorously through his chief engineer, Captain D. B. Harris, who afterwards remained with me in the same capacity until most of the works were completed. From the 12th until the 18th, the works were pushed forward night and day with all possible vigor, at the end of which the first division of the Federal fleet, together with transports, carrying some three thousand men, made their appearance and found us in a condition to dispute, with a fair prospect of success, a further advance; that is to say, six batteries were complete, the cannoniers at their posts and fairly drilled. The arrival of this advanced division was immediately followed by a demand for the surrender of Vicksburg and its defences, couched in the following terms.

" U. S. S. Oneida, near Vicksburg,
" May 18th, 1862.

" To the Authorities at Vicksburg :

"The undersigned, with orders from Flag Officer Farragut and Major General Butler, respectfully demand, in advance of the approaching fleet, the surrender of Vicksburg and its defences to the lawful authorities of the United States, under which private property and personal right will be respected.

      "Very respectfully, yours,
 (Signed)   "J. PHILLIPS LEE.
    "*U. S. N. Com. Advance Naval Division.*
"(Signed) P. WILLIAMS, *Brigadier General.*"

The subjoined reply was returned :

        "HEADQUARTERS VICKSBURG,
         "May 18th, 1862.

"SIR : Your communication of this date, addressed to the authorities of Vicksburg, demanding the surrender of the city and its defences, has been received. In regard to the surrender of the defences, I have to reply that, having been ordered here to hold these defences, my intention is to do so as long as it is in my power.

    "Very respectfully, your obedient servant,
 (Signed)   "M. L. SMITH,
     "*Brigadier General Commanding.*
"To PHILLIPS LEE, *U. S. N. Commanding Advance Naval Division.*"

I here remark that the citizens of the town had, with great unanimity, made up their minds that its possession ought to be maintained at all hazards, even though total demolition should be the result. This determination was enthusiastically concurred in by persons of all ages and both sexes, and borne to my ears from every quarter. Thus, cheered on and upheld, the defence became an affair of more than public interest, and the approving sentiment of those so deeply interested unquestionably had its influence on the ultimate result, as affairs stand to-day. Our cause probably needed an example of this kind, and assuredly a bright one has been given. The inhabitants had been advised to leave the city when the smoke of the ascending gunboats was first seen, under the impression that the enemy would open fire immediately on arrival; hence, the above demand found the city sparsely populated, and somewhat prepared for an attack, although, when it really commenced, there were numbers still to depart, besides many who had determined to remain and take the chances of escaping unharmed, a few of whom absolutely endured to the end. As bearing immediately upon the defence of this place, measures had also been taken to push the "Arkansas" to completion. It was reported the contractor had virtually suspended work ; that mechanics and workmen were leaving ; that supplies were wanting ; finally, that a very considerable quantity of iron prepared for covering her had been sunk in the Yazoo river. Steps were taken to promptly furnish mechanics and supplies, and bell-boat being obtained and sent up to the spot, the prepared iron was soon recovered. It was considered fortunate that soon after this, Captain Brown was assigned to the duty of completing the boat, as after his assignment this important work, gave me no further concern. The enemy remained apparently inactive until the 28th, during which time the advance division of the fleet was joined by other gunboats, making ten in all. My force had, in the meantime, been increased by the 20th and 28th Louisiana volunteers, numbering for duty some five hundred each, by five companies of Starke's cavalry; one battery; Wither's artillery, Captain Ridley; and four companies sixth Mississippi battalion, Lieutenant Colonel Balfour; but all were troops just mustered into service, and indifferently armed. These were thrown forward towards Warrenton, and disposed for disputing inch by inch, the approach by land. This force was subsequently increased by the 4th and 5th Louisiana. The ensuing ten days I consider the most critical period of the defences of Vicksburg. Batteries incomplete, guns not mounted, troops few, and both officers and men entirely new to service, and not a single regular officer to assist in organizing and commanding. Had a prompt and vigorous attack been made by the enemy, while I think the disposition made would have insured their repulse, still the issue would have been less certain than at any time afterwards. The enemy opened fire on the afternoon of the 25th for the first time, and continued about two hours, apparently with a view of getting our range. The orders given to the batteries were not to return their fire at extreme range, and at ordinary range only at considerable intervals. This policy was adhered to throughout, at first, because little ammunition had then arrived; afterwards, for the reason that our works could not be injured by direct firing, and by saving the men, they were fresh night and day to meet close and serious attacks, such as occurred before the termination of the bombardment; besides, the enemy were thus kept ignorant of our real strength as well as the effect of their own shot. It was not long before they apparently came to the conclusion that no impression could be made on our works by their gunboats, nor the erection of new batteries prevented whenever attempted; and the remaining six batteries, of the ten first mentioned, were constructed under their eyes.

From the 20th of May to the middle of June the firing was kept up at intervals, and more or less heavy the latter part of the time, directed mainly at the town, and at localities where they apparently thought troops were encamped. From the 14th to the 18th of June there was an entire cessation of the attack, the mortar fleet that had bombarded Fort Jackson and Fort Phillip being on the way here to join in the attack. They began to arrive on the 18th, and to the number of eighteen or nineteen were in position on the 20th, on the afternoon of which day the bombardment again opened. Prior to this, a new source of anxiety arose. Fort Pillow and Memphis had fallen, and in addition to the attack we were enduring, Vicksburg was threatened by a combined land and naval force from above. From the 20th to the 27th the bombardment was pretty constant during the day time, at times very heavy, but generally ceasing at ten or eleven o'clock at night. On the evening of the 27th the firing began to increase in fury, and, for some time, a shower of bomb-shells was rained upon our batteries that severely tried the nerve and courage of both officers and men, still the damage was quickly repaired, and the men held their places at the guns. At daylight, on the 28th, the enemy recommenced with the same fury, and it was soon perceived that the entire gunboat fleet was in motion, moving rapidly up in front of the batteries and city, and it became apparent that the decisive struggle was at hand. Some thirty-five vessels were soon firing as rapidly as possible, the mortars filling the air with shells, and the sloops-of-war and gunboats delivering broadside after broadside of shot, shell and grape, according to their distance. Our batteries opened as soon as the vessels were within range, and, for the first time, in full force. The roar of cannon was now continuous and deafening, loud explosions shook the city to its foundations, shot and shells went hissing and tearing through trees and walls, scattering fragments far and wide in their terrific flight. Men, women and children rushed into the streets, and amid the crashing of falling houses, commenced their hasty flight to the country for safety. This continued for about an hour an a half, when the enemy left; the vessels that had passed the lower batteries continuing on up the river, apparently as the quickest means of getting out of range; those that had not passed, rapidly dropping down. The result of this effort on the part of the enemy was most satisfactory. Not a single gun was silenced or disabled, and, to their surprise, the serious bombardment of the preceding seven days had thrown nothing out of fighting trim. It also demonstrated to our satisfaction that, how large soever the number of gun and mortar boats, our batteries could probably be successfully held, consequently that the ultimate success of our resistance hinged upon a movement by land. The enemy evidently came to the same conclusion, as, after one week's bombardment with their mortars, and the final attempt, on the morning of 28th June, to silence and take our guns, the attack sensibly decreased in vigor and persistency. Up to the 8th there had been a great pressure on my command, owing to the limited number of men. The situation of the enemy's fleet, and the peculiar shape of the river in this vicinity, combined with the proximity of the Yazoo and the expected descent of a large force from above, (as reported,) had necessitated a rather heavy line of pickets, extending along a distance of twenty miles. To keep up this line, and sustain a heavy attack at the same time, taxed the energies of my men to a great extent. The arrival of the advance brigade of Major General Breckinridge's reserve corps was a great respite, and, as the force was gradually increased, thus bringing us to an equality in numbers with that which accompanied the fleet, it was almost felt that Vicksburg was no longer besieged. The general command of these defences was assumed by Major General Earl Van Dorn, on the 28th of June, Major General Lovell having been relieved by him from the command of the Department. Being authorized to make requisitions on the reserve corps for whatever force was deemed necessary to carry out the plan of defence, the picket front was, after the 28th, divided into five divisions, the two extreme ones guarded, by detachments from my brigade, (third Louisiana) the remaining three by detachments from Brigadier Generals Preston, Helm's and Colonel Statham's brigades, reinforced by light batteries from Colonel Withers' artillery. The fleet from Memphis began to make its appearance above on the 26th of June, and continued to receive accessions until it numbered, in all, forty-odd gun-boats, mortar-boats, rams and transports. Firing commenced from this fleet on the 12th July, and although, at no time, as heavy as from the lower fleet, continued, with but little interruption, until the final bombardment of the attack. On the morning of the 15th, the daring passage of the ram "Arkansas," out of the Yazoo, through the enemy's fleet, seemed to necessitate a prompt descent of those vessels that had passed up on the 28th, and everything was accordingly placed in readiness for them. A new battery of twenty-four pounders, just erected, was manned by a light artillery detachment from Preston's brigade, under Lieutenant Gracy, and sharpshooters, from the same brigade, placed along the bank, wherever the ground was favorable. As conjectured, the enemy were in motion at sundown, and at dusk descended amid the roar of cannon, the flashing of musketry, the glare of lightning, and scenes in every respect such as had distinguished their passage up, except that the action was of shorter duration, and the "Arkansas" was on the river returning their broadsides. The firing was mainly over in the course of an hour, and, at the batteries, not a single casualty from the enemy's shot occurred. From the 15th to the 18th the enemy were mainly occupied in endeavoring to sink the "Arkansas" with their mortars, and on the morning of the 18th, a daring attempt was made to cut her out from under one of our batteries. It resulted, however, in no injury to the "Arkansas," but in the destruction of one of their boats. This was really the termination of the attack, although the bombardment was kept up until the 27th, when both fleets disappeared. It will thus be seen that the enemy were in front of Vicksburg sixty-seven days, during which the combined efforts of two powerful fleets have been foiled, and the accompanying land force from four to five thousand held at bay.

The number of shot and shells thrown by the fleets is unknown It has been estimated as high as 25,000 and put as low as 20,000. The number, however, is unimportant and mentioned only to illustrate the fact, that the loss to a land battery when attacked by one afloat is comparatively small. The casualties from the enemy's firing was seven killed, fifteen wounded. In the town two only are reported. The enemy fired at least ten shots to our one, and their number of killed and wounded can, from information, be safely put down at five times as great. It is a matter of surprise that not a single gun was dismounted during the whole time, and only two temporarily disabled, both being repaired in one night. The number of guns brought against us, including mortars, could not have been much less than three hundred. The number on our side, as you are aware, was considerably less. After this general description given, it would be great injustice not to mention the commands and their officers that have been instrumental in so signal a success. The batteries were manned by three companies of 1st regiment Louisiana artillery, two companies of the 22d, two companies 23d Louisiana volunteers, Major

Clinch; four companies heavy artillery from Fort Pillow, Major Headley; three companies 8th Louisiana battalion, Major Ogden. Col. Jackson and Lieut. Col. Sterling, both of the heavy artillery, were, respectively, in immediate command of the upper and lower batteries, and Col. Fuller, Chief of Heavy Artillery Lieut. Colonel Pinkney, 8th Louisiana battalion, in command of two of the lower batteries for a portion of the time, was temporarily relieved, under a special organization, which reduced the battalion to a major's command. The officers commanding these companies were as follows: Captains Capers, Grayson, Butler, Tissot, Purvis, Herrod, Todd, Disumkes, Parks, Morman, Postlethwaite, Durives, Kerr, and Lieuts. Eustis, Butler and McCrory. The names of the above-mentioned officers are given for the reason that in connection with their lieutenants and men, they have passed through an ordeal that troops are but seldom called upon to undergo ! For more than seventy-five days and nights have these batteries been continuously manned and ready for action at a moment's warning. During much of this time the roar of cannon has been unceasing, and there have been portions of it during which the noise of falling shot and the explosions of shells have been such as might make the stoutest heart quail. Yet none faltered. The blazing sun, the fatiguing night watch, the storm of battle—all were alike cheerfully endured, and whenever called upon, heavy and telling blows were dealt upon our foes in return. I feel a pride in having such officers and such men under my command, for they have nobly sustained our cause in time of need, have added to the country's glory, and deserve well of her gratitude. Some officers possibly attracted my attention more than others by their chivalric courage and inspiriting manner ; yet the conduct of all was so noble and unexceptionable that I do not venture to particularize. The distant picketing was most efficiently and faithfully performed by the cavalry, commanded at different times by Col. Starke, Lt. Col. Ferguson and Major Jones, according as they were present. The nearer picket duty, together with that of being at all times guarded against surprise and ready to meet an attack, was so patiently and carefully performed by the 26th, 27th and 28th Louisiana volunteers, under Colonels Declonet, Marks and Allen Thomas; the 4th and 17th Louisiana volunteers, Col. Allen and Col. Richardson ; also, by the 3d regiment and 6th battalion Mississippi volunteers, Col. Mellon and Lieut. Colonel Balfour, together with Wither's Light Artillery, under Lieut. Col. Parker, that I felt secure in giving most of my attention to the bombardment going on. Whenever events demanded a united movement of all, I found a most reliable and efficient officer to represent me and carry out my instructions in the person of my present Assistant Adjutant General, Col. Girault, whose judgment and zeal were never at fault. Of Captain Lockett, the accomplished engineer officer of my staff, I have to speak in terms of unqualified praise, both as regards skill in his profession and qualities as a soldier. The services of such an officer are so important and indispensable as to have all the effect of a positive increase of force in determining the issue of a contest. I most cordially recommend him to notice. Captain Mc-

Donald, brigade ordnance officer, and Captains Frost and Harrod, aids, have in turn performed almost every duty, during the siege, known to the service; always prompt, they are distinguished for intelligence and perseverance in the performance of duty that merits constant praise. To the Brigade Quartermaster, Major J. St. Patton, and Brigade Commissary, Major Reed, are due such mention as devoted attention to their duties and the interests of the service merits; both have performed all the duties pertaining to a department, and both have been compelled almost to create what they have had. The part borne during the latter days of the bombardment, by a detachment from Major General Breckinridge's division, requires special mention. Captain Cobb's company of light artillery, under Lieut. Gracy, manned a battery which was so spiritedly served as to attract attention on both occasions in which it was engaged, and was even noticed by the enemy. The sharpshooters, detailed from the same command, kept up a galling fire on the enemy during the passage of the vessels on the evening of the 15th and drove them from the tops. The lamented Col. Statham's brigade, under his own lead, showed a bravery in guarding the front of attack assigned him, that could not be surpassed. On one occasion, having forced his way through a swamp, deemed impassable, he made a rush upon the mortar boats moored to shore, driving the force guarding on board, and had the positions of the boats been accurately known, would have taken possession of and destroyed several. The engineer company under Capt. Winter was steadily occupied in the repairs of batteries and did admirable service.

The report of the struggle at Vicksburg would be incomplete without the following merited tribute: During the engagement of the 28th a most estimable lady, Mrs. Gamble, lost her life by the fragment of a shell striking her while leaving the city. This lady deserves more than a passing notice. Burning with patriotism, she inspired all around her with the noble spirit of resistance to oppression, and confidence in the success of our cause. Ever present in the hospitals, ministering to the sick and wounded soldiers, she was among the last of her sex to leave the desolated city, when she yielded up her life in attestation of her faith and devotion Though but the type of a class of which our southern land can boast, she is a martyr to the cause she loved, and without her name the history which Vicksburg has made for herself would be incomplete. To the citizens of Vicksburg a nation's thanks are due for their noble example in surrendering their property and homes to almost certain destruction, and that so little damage was done does not detract from the merit of the act, but rather serves to call for gratitude to the Supreme Being who has not only preserved from destruction the homes of a patriotic people, but in mercy granted a victory over their enemies. In conclusion, I deem it proper to remark upon the manner in which the bombardment was conducted. In locating the batteries, pains had been taken to place them without the limits of the town, advantageous positions even having been rejected with that view, so that in the approaching struggle, the fight might, if the enemy so chose, be confined to the armed points, and the city itself, which could have no bearing upon the ultimate result, be made to suffer as little as an enlightened and humane method of conducting war would lead us to expect and which, under the same circumstances, I think most enemies would have pursued. Events did not justify our expectations. The bombardment opened upon both batteries and town. This was expected, and could not be objected to, and no fault is found at its continuing so as long as the enemy had hopes of accomplishing their object, but when the attack on the batteries ceased, when the bombarding force began even to gradually leave, when it was notorious that they deemed their attack a failure, then to continue to throw shells into a beautiful town, as was done day after day, with the sole purpose of injuring it, of defacing it, and of destroying private property, indicated a spirit of wanton destruction, scarcely pardonable in the uncivilized Indian. This seemed to be the special mission of the upper fleet. Shame to the man who commanded it!

I am respectfully, your obedient servant,

M. L. SMITH,
Brigadier General Commanding Defences, Vicksburg.

REPORT OF COLONEL J. W. ROBERTSON, COMMANDING FIRST BRIGADE.

HEADQUARTERS 1ST BRIGADE, 2D DIVISION,
Camp on Comite River, August 7, 1862.

To Captain L. D. SANDIDGE, *A. A. A. General, 2d Division,*

CAPTAIN: On receiving the order to report the part taken in the action of the 5th inst., by the first brigade, I referred the order to Colonel A. P. Thompson, who commanded the brigade during the action, with the exception of the closing half hour that the troops were under fire, when he was borne from the field severely wounded, and I submit, by his request, the following report:

On reaching the angle of the main road leading into Baton Rouge, the brigade was formed in line of battle, in a common to the left of the main road, the right of the brigade resting on that road, and the left near a dense forest, into which Colonel Allen's brigade had passed. The brigade was composed of the following regiments, positioned from right to left in the order named: Third Kentucky, Captain J. H. Bowman commanding; seventh Kentucky, Colonel Edward Crossland commanding; thirty-fifth Alabama, Colonel J. W. Robertson commanding, and the sixth Kentucky, Lieutenant Colonel M. H. Cofer commanding. As soon as the line was established, the command, "forward," was given by General Ruggles in person, which was promptly obeyed by the brigade, moving forward beyond the dwelling-house immediately to the front. The line was at this time found to be somewhat deranged, caused by the numerous fences and houses, over and around which the troops had to pass. The brigade was consequently halted and the alignment rectified, when the command "forward," was again given. The brigade moved directly to the front, parallel to the main road, preceded by a company of sharp shooters deployed as skirmishers, and commanded by Lieutenant J. C. Hubbard. At this point the firing commenced first, the line of the enemy having been unmasked by the skirmishers. The firing was continued but a short time when an order was received for the brigade to charge, and the troops rushed forward with a cheer, the enemy breaking before them. Having reached the middle of the field, the brigade was exposed to a fire from the right which could not be returned without exposing the troops of General Clark's division to the fire of the brigade, and was consequently halted until the firing ceased. An advance was made, skirmishing covering the front. The second line of the enemy was thus unmasked and exposed to the fire of the brigade. They gave way precipitately before the steady advance of our troops. On clearing the fields and reaching the enemy's encampment, the right wing was found to be covered by a portion of Gen. Clark's division. An officer approached from the right and stated that friends were exposed to our fire, when the firing ceased and the charge ordered by Colonel Thompson, he leading the brigade into the encampment of the enemy to the left, which was nearly cleared by this brigade, when troops were met on the right returning without any apparent cause, and were ordered by Colonel Thompson to halt and advance, when a mounted officer informed Colonel Thompson that it was the order for all the troops to fall back. This movement became general in the brigade. In retiring the thirty-fifth Alabama, and sixth Kentucky, forming the left wing, became separated from the right and occupied a position in line one hundred yards to the left and rear. The enemy reformed in heavy force behind their tents rapidly advancing, firing and cheering. The third and seventh Kentucky regiments were thrown under cover and met this advance with a steady fire. The thirty-fifth Alabama and sixth Kentucky were ordered forward, but advanced before the order reached them, opening a heavy fire upon the enemy, whose advance was thus checked. At this point, Colonel Thompson was severely wounded and taken to the rear. The command devolving upon Colonel Robertson, who being, from complete exhaustion, in no condition at that time to assume command, and finding the right wing separated from the left, placed Colonel Crossland in command of the right and Lieutenant Colonel E. Goodwin in command of the left, with orders to maintain the line, which was firmly held for nearly an hour, in the face of a terrible fire from musketry and artillery, when the charge, which closed the action, was made in person by the Major General commanding. It is the request of Colonel Thompson, that his entire approbation of the conduct of all the field and acting field officers engaged, and Captain W. P. Wallace and Lieutenant Charles Temple, Aids, and Acting Adjutant R. B. L. Soney, of the third Kentucky, be specially expressed in this report. To the deportment of the thirty-fifth Alabama regiment, he desires attention to be called. This regiment, although for the first time under fire, on the 5th instant, proved itself a worthy comrade for the third, sixth and seventh Kentucky regiments, who in this action sustained the enviable reputation won by them on the field of Shiloh. Colonel Robertson would call special attention to the gallant conduct of Colonel E. Crossland and Lieutenant Colonel E. Goodwin, who, the first with his regimental colors in hand, and the second with his hat on his sword, led the brigade in the final charge. To the reports of regimental commanders you are referred for notices of gallant conduct in other members of the command. The medical staff deserve the highest praise for their prompt and unceasing attention to the wounded.

By order of
G. C. HUBBARD, Lt. and A. A. G.:

J. W. ROBERTSON,
Colonel commanding first Brigade, second Division.

REPORT OF COLONEL H. W. ALLEN, COMMANDING SECOND BRIGADE.

EAST BATON ROUGE, August 18, 1862.

Capt. BUCKNER,
Assistant Adjutant General:

SIR: On the morning of the 5th instant, in pursuance to orders of Brigadier General Ruggles, I formed the second brigade, second division, in line of battle; the left of the brigade resting upon Bernard's fence, in the rear of Magruder's Institute, and the right resting upon the first brigade. On the right was placed Colonel Breaux, of the thirtieth Louisiana; on the left Lieutenant Colonel Hunter, of the fourth Louisiana, and in the centre was the battalion of Lieutenant Colonel Boyle. At dawn of day I received orders to advance. The brigade was put in motion and advanced steadily through thick woods, underbrush, cornfields and picket fences. In the midst of the forest we encountered a battery supported by infantry. We halted and delivered several volleys in quick succession. The enemy fled in every direction, taking off his artillery with him. We started in pursuit, and after considerable desultory firing upon the retreating foe, I discovered a battery on the extreme left, (said to be Minnen's,) supported by a large amount of infantry. It was evident that this was a flanking movement, and required my immediate attention. I ordered a movement to be made to the left, and advanced in the direction of the battery. At the command, "charge," the whole brigade raised a shout and made as gallant a charge as was ever witnessed. Here I fell, my legs terribly shattered with cannister shot. What transpired after this on the battle field I do not know. The loss of blood and extreme pain had rendered me almost senseless. To my successor in command I must refer you for further particulars of the fight. The officers and soldiers of this brigade fought with much gallantry, and, with few exceptions, did their duty nobly. I have been informed that, upon my fall, the brigade could not be rallied. This has often happened with the best of troops and the bravest veterans, and should not attach any disgrace to the soldiers. No one charges that the brigade retreated from the enemy, or even retired from the place of danger. The enemy had been whipped, and had fled in every direction. Captain Semmes' battery came up, fired a few rounds upon the retreating foe, and all was over. To my adjutant, Lieutenant B. W. Clarke, and to my voluntary aid, Lieutenant H. H. Walsh, I am much indebted. They performed their duties with great gallantry, coolness and bravery. Captain Blount was assigned to duty as inspector of the brigade. During the journey from Camp Moore, he lost his horse, and had been relieved from duty as inspector by the commanding General. He, however, secured a horse, and, in the thickest of the fight, reported himself for duty to me. I gave him, from time to time, several orders to execute, which he did in a very prompt and gallant manner. I see that he is reported a prisoner in New Orleans. This is a mystery to me. Many acts of individual heroism came under my eye, and I shall ever feel proud that I had the honor to command the second brigade in the battle of Baton Rouge. Among all the officers and men who distinguished themselves in that battle, I shall mention only one by name, that is private Cedars, of the West Feliciana Rifles, fourth regiment Louisiana. He took the colors from me as I fell, and at the same moment received a terrible wound in the thigh.

With respect, I am, truly, your obedient servant,

H. W. ALLEN,
Colonel Commanding Second Brigade, Second Division.

REPORT OF COLONEL G. A. BREAUX, COMMANDING SECOND BRIGADE.

Headquarters Second Brigade,
Camp near Comite River, August 8, 1862.

Lieutenant L. D. Sandidge,
Acting Assistant Adjutant and Inspector General:

Sir: Colonel H. W. Allen, commander of the second brigade, second division, having fallen towards the close of the action of the 5th May, 1862, it becomes my duty, as next in command, to make the report, as far as my knowledge enables me to do so. My attention was exclusively directed to the action of the thirtieth Louisiana regiment, which I commanded, until the fall of the colonel commanding.

At 4 1-2 o'clock, A. M., our line was formed on the extreme left of the forces, in a point of woods, adjoining open and cultivated fields. The ground was broken. We advanced in conjunction with the entire line. As we were about passing out of a little field, we met the enemy, who at once opened a brisk fire upon us, which we returned with good effect, since, in a few minutes, they fled before us. We were ordered "forward." As the extreme right of the brigade was advancing on a line parallel to a fence, behind which sharpshoters lay in ambush, harassing our flank, the thirtieth Louisiana was constantly called on to dislodge them, which it did by occasional fires We soon discovered that the enemy were in considerable force behind a fence, awaiting our approach, at a point from which they fired on our line at an angle of about forty-five degrees. We faced the thirtieth regiment to them, and soon silenced them by a well kept up and directed fire. Meanwhile, the fourth regiment and Boyd's battalion advanced, driving, also, all obstacles before them. It became apparent that the exact location of a battery of the enemy, planted in our front, was not known, the fog was too thick to enable us to see well. We, however, advanced, having changed the direction of the line to the left. The fire of the enemy soon revealed its exact position, and to the charge, was sounded. The entire brigade advanced at a double-quick, and in good order, notwithstanding the galling fire poured into our lines. Th gallant Colonel Allen, whose bravery cannot be too much extolled, flew at the head of the men, flag in hand, on to the battery and was soon in possession of its guns, surrounded by his men, while the right drove the infantry away by a destructive fire. Unfortunately, Colonel Allen was wounded, and the shock was terrible among the men of the fourth regiment, whose confidence seemed to repose mainly on him, and they withdrew in disorder, bearing away their wounded chief. At a short distance, I rallied them partially on the line formed by the regiment, on the right of the brigade, but to no good, since enough could not be gathered to push on our advantage. Sometime previous to this charge, as I infer from not seeing him in it, Colonel S. Boyd had been wounded and removed from the field. His battalion, stripped of his influence, did not rally after the first charge on the battery. Previous to this, the troops had all behaved with great gallantry. It now became evident that fatigue and thirst were overpowering our men; they could scarcely answer the appeals made to them by courageous men, to whose names justice will be done by those who witnessed their conduct throughout, and which I cannot give, as I only saw them there for the first time. At this time, a second Federal battery entered the field, and was opportunely met by a section of Captain Semmes' Confederate States battery. It affords me pleasure to bear testimony to the cool and effective response made by Captain Semmes and Lieutenant West, whom the fourth and thirtieth Louisiana regiments fell back to support in this encounter. After a brief and quick fire of the opposing batteries, it was found necessary to withdraw, and the infantry left with it. From this time, there was no more fighting on the left. Coming into command of the brigade at the close of the battle, and after it became disorganized, I am unable to give any particulars beyond those which refer to my regiment. I cannot close, however, without bearing witness to the bravery and gallantry of Colonel Allen, so conspicuous to us all.

I am, very respectfully, your obedient servant,
G. A. BREAUX,
Colonel, Commanding Second Brigade.

HEADQUARTERS THIRTIETH LA. SUMTER REGIMENT,
In camp near Comite River.

Lieutenant L. D. SANDIDGE,
  Acting Assistant Adjutant General:

SIR: For the action of my regiment in general, during the battle of the 5th August, at Baton Rouge, I beg to refer you to the report, circumstances have compelled me to make in the stead of Colonel Allen. For troops who had never been under fire before, the thirtieth Louisiana acted with great bravery and gallantry. Conspicuous among the officers who distinguished themselves, I take pleasure in mentioning Captain Trepagnier who lost his life in all probability, and Lieutenant Dupremont, of Picket Cadets, who was also wounded. I have the satisfaction of stating that men and officers were zealous in their efforts to beat off a superior force. The regiment, throughout, rallied and presented a good line whenever called on. After the partial disorganization of the brigade, which the loss of its commander temporarily produced, and when it became evident that the left must fall back, this regiment did so in an orderly manner and under orders.

Very respectfully,
G. A. BREAUX,
Colonel, Commanding Thirtieth Louisiana.

REPORT OF COLONEL M. H. COFER.

HEADQUARTERS 6TH KENTUCKY REG'T VOLUNTEERS,
Comite River, August 7th, 1862.

To G. C. HUBBARD, *First Lieutenant and A. A. A. General:*

Sir: Pursuant to circular order, just received, I have the honor to submit the following report of the part taken by the sixth regiment Kentucky volunteers in the battle of the 5th instant, and the orders received from the commanding generals. This regiment occupied the extreme left of the first brigade, second division, Colonel A. P. Thompson commanding. At a little before daylight the troops were drawn up in line, this regiment in the open field, the left resting about two hundred yards to the right of a dense forest, in which Colonel Allen's brigade was formed. At daylight the command, "forward," was given by General Ruggles, and we moved forward a short distance and halted by the order of the same officer, who was present in person. We were very soon ordered forward again, when we moved, encountering rough ground, hedges, fences, ditches, and a luxuriant growth of weeds and grass, altogether rendering even tolerable alignment and steady marching impossible. Passing on over this character of ground for nearly one mile, the enemy's skirmishers fired on us, doing no injury, but falling back as we advanced, until we arrived immediately in front of the enemy's camp. Here he engaged us warmly from a strong position in a heavy forest, but charging forward we drove him from his position, and my regiment passed nearly through the camp, when we observed a battery on our left, say one hundred yards, and a little in front. This battery was nearly silenced by an oblique fire from my left wing, and would have been easily taken but for the fact that the right of the brigade was retiring. Seeing no cause for the retreat on account of any movement or fire of the enemy, my regiment was ordered back, presuming the brigade was ordered to retire, which I since learned to have been the case. This retreat enabled the enemy to regain his battery, which he did promptly, and opened a furious fire with grape, canister, and shrapnell, on our flank. From the nearness of the guns, he did no serious damage. We continued to move to the rear some two hundred yards, when we reformed and returned to a fence in front of a grave yard, where we halted and opened fire on the enemy who had reformed and reoccupied his original position, from which we had just driven him. This position both parties held with great stubbornness, and an almost incessant fire was kept up for one hour. At this place I sustained nearly all the loss of the day. My position was very much exposed during this time, having no shelter but a thin picket fence, and being on ground elevated some eighteen inches above any ground in front between my line and the enemy. This position was maintained until an order to charge was given, and the enemy driven under his gunboats, when the regiment returned with the brigade to camp, having sustained a loss of five killed and seventy-three wounded, several mortally. I cannot allow this opportunity to pass without returning my thanks to the officers and men of the regiment for the gallant manner in which they bore themselves during the whole engagement. From a want of commissioned officers, I caused the eight companies of the regiment to be consolidated into four companies, placed respectively under Captains Isaac Smith, Utterback, and Thomas G. Page, and First Lieutenant Frank Harned. It is proper for me to say that I was not in the last charge, having been carried off the field too much exhausted and overcome to be able to go forward.

I have the honor to be, sir, your ob't serv't,
M. H. COFER,
Colonel commanding sixth Ky. Reg't.

REPORT OF COLONEL CROSSLAND.

HEADQUARTERS SEVENTH KENTUCKY REGIMENT,
August 7th, 1862.

Lieut. G. C. HUBBARD, *A. A. A. General:*

LIEUTENANT: In obedience to an order from your officer, I return the following statements of the action of my regiment in the battle at Baton Rouge, on the 5th. The brigade was formed in an open field, and ordered to "march forward." My regiment crossed a lawn into a field, and received a fire from the enemy's skirmishers, when we were ordered to charge. The skirmishers were routed and the regiment halted in a pea patch and ordered to lie down. Here we received a heavy fire, wounding three men. We were again ordered to forward and to charge, which order was executed in gallant style. Passing over the ground occupied by the enemy, we saw the bodies of two dead and three wounded. Another charge brought us into a road near the enemy's camp, through which we charged, and were halted and ordered to fall back by Capt. Buckner, of General Breckinridge's staff, who received the order from General Clark, which would have been done in order, but for a regiment in advance of our right, which broke in wild confusion through my regiment, which caught the panic and retired disorderly for a short distance. Aided, however, by the coolness of my company officers and adjutant, I succeeded promptly in rallying and reforming them in front of the road. Colonel Thompson ordered me to fall back to the road, where we opened fire on the enemy, then advancing from their camps, and kept it up briskly for an hour. The enemy advanced cautiously from their camp, under cover of a grove of timber, with the evident intention of turning our left flank. I saw two lines of infantry, with cavalry in rear. They charged, and the thirty-fifth Alabama regiment opened and kept up a hot fire from our left, which broke the enemy's lines, and they retired in confusion. Our ammunition was nearly exhausted, the wagons not having come up. Gen. Breckinridge came up on our right, and I reported the want of ammunition to him, and he ordered me to charge the camp with my regiment and the third Kentucky. We went through the camp and were halted by Capt. Buckner, and ordered to retire, which was done in good order. Captain Buckner, by order of General Breckinridge, ordered my regiment to remain and support a section of Semmes' battery, which was posted and remained to protect those engaged in recovery of the wounded and retreat of the stragglers. Captain Wess Jetton, with five men, was sent back to fire the camps. A cloud of smoke soon told that his mission of destruction had been faithfully executed. He reports the burning of large quantities commissary stores and quartermaster stores, together with numerous boxes of guns and valuable camp equippage. With a single exception, the officers bore themselves gallantly, and too much cannot be said in praise of the conduct of the men. Our infirmary corps kept close at our heels and promptly removed and took care of the wounded.

I beg to mention the gallant conduct of Joseph Rollins, our color-bearer.

EDWARD CROSSLAND,
Col. Com'dg seventh Kentucky regiment.

REPORT OF LIEUT. COL. S. E. HUNTER.

CAMP NEAR COMITE, Aug. 7th, 1862.

Col. J. A. BREAUX:

Sir: At nine o'clock, P. M., of the 4th instant, pursuant to orders, I marched the fourth Louisiana regiment, left in front, from this place in the direction of Baton Rouge. Just before daylight, I was ordered to halt in an open field. Only a few minutes elapsed before firing began between our pickets and those of the enemy. We were then ordered to fall back behind a hedge, where we remained a very short while, when we recrossed the hedge, and marched by the left flank through a narrow strip of wood to a field, enclosed by a thick and impassable hedge fence. Here we formed our line of battle, and were joined by the remainder of the brigade. The word "forward" was given, and all moved off in gallant style. We had not proceeded far when we received a desultory fire from the enemy, which was promptly and effectively returned, causing the enemy to retire. The advance continued, with occasional firing, until we reached an open field on our left. Here the enemy was discovered in considerable force in front and to the left. We were marched by the left flank until our brigade had nearly cleared the woods when we filed to the left. The fourth Louisiana had thus filed expecting to meet the enemy at right angles to our original line, when a battery opened on us to our right, and in front of the original line. The order was given to charge this battery, which was done in gallant style, the brigade being in a sort of wedge shape, gradually assuming a line as it approached the battery. A heavy and galling fire was kept up on us by the enemy who were concealed in the rear of the battery. When within a few paces of the guns of the enemy, Colonel Allen, who was in front, bearing the colors of one battalion of the brigade, was severely wounded, and fell from his horse. Seeing him fall, the line faltered, and finally gave way, the troops on the right and centre giving way first. The brigade retired in confusion across the field, through which it had so gallantly advanced. Here, after some little delay, my regiment was reformed and remained so for some time. No order to advance was given. A section of Semmes' battery came up and prepared for action on our right, and the left of the brigade. We were ordered to form in its rear to support it. After great exertion a line was partially formed, but at this point the enemy's artillery opened on us at short range. The right again gave way, followed rapidly by the whole line. The troops, exhausted by fatigue and crying for water, were thrown into utter confusion, and all attempts to rally them were fruitless. From this time no more fighting was done by our brigade.

I would not close this report without mentioning among the names of those among my officers who were conspicuous for gallantry on the field, Lieut. Corkern, who was in command of company B; Lieut. Jeter, company F; Sergeant-Major Daniels, and Adjutant Clark. I

hear of others who distinguished themselves, but only these came under my special observation.
Respectfully submitted,

S. E. HUNTER,
Lieut. Colonel Commanding fourth Louisiana.

REPORT OF LIEUTENANT COLONEL TOM SHIELDS.

IN THE FIELD, August 7, 1862.

Lieutenant L. D. SANDIDGE, C. S. A. A. A. A. *and Inspector General:*

SIR: For the information of Brigadier General Ruggles, commanding second division, I beg leave to make the following report of the operations of the detachment under my command, in the battle of Baton Rouge:

In obedience to orders, I proceeded, with a section Semmes' Confederate States artillery, under command of T. K. Fauntleroy, two companies of infantry, (company E., Sumter thirtieth Louisiana regiment, Captain Roger T. Boyle, and Beaver Creek Rifles, Captain Amacker) and one company of mounted partizan rangers, Captain Beckham, the whole numbering about one hundred and fifty, rank and file, at about four and a half P. M., the fourth inst., to take position on the Clinton plank road, there to engage the enemy, supposed to be posted, with a battery of artillery, at the junction of that and the Bayou Sara road. After a fatiguing nights' march, we reached that desired point just at dawn of day, of 5th inst., prepared to execute orders at the given signal—the firing of small arms by the main body on my left. Exactly at four and a half, A. M., the sound of musketry being distinctly audible, I ordered the advance, at doublequick, of the entire command; having previously dismounted the rangers, with a view to greater efficiency. The enemy's pickets fled precipitately at our approach, leaving accoutrements and equipments hanging to the posts and walls of the house where they were stationed, and on the trees immediately around it, and sought shelter in the woods to the right of the Bayou Sara road; gaining which, they fired one feeble volley, but immediately retreated in confusion in the direction of the arsenal. The infantry was now posted in a corn field on the right of a street leading to a Federal camp, with instructions to advance closely in support of the artillery, which was placed at the same time in raking position at the head of the same street. The enemy here appeared in force; two regiments of infantry disputing our further advance. The artillery opening obliquely on the camp, enabled us, by its well directed fire, to advance within two hundred and fifty feet of the camps of the fourteenth Maine regiment, (judged to be so by papers, etc., found subsequently in the tents;) again opening a rapid fire of artillery in the direction of this camp, we maintained our position until the infantry, suffering before the overwhelming numbers of the enemy, we were compelled to fall back, and some four horses of the section becoming unmanageable and unserviceable from wounds received, I consented to the withdrawal of the section to the junction of the roads above mentioned, there to await reinforcements from the main body, then seen to be advancing in our direction. In this new position we were unfortunately taken for the enemy, and fired upon, but luckily without casualty of any kind. Disengaging the disabled horses, and supplying their places with others, the section was again placed in position, where it was kept until the termination of the engagement. The infantry force under my command, was attached, by order, to the twenty-second Mississippi regiment on the arrival of that regiment in the field, leaving me with the artillery, where I remained until releaved by one of the staff of Major General Breckinaidge, upon the withdrawal of the army. I cannot speak too highly of the conduct of the men of the command, artillery and infantry, and beg to commend to favorable notice, the officers of company E., Sumter regiment, (thirtieth Louisiana) Captain Boyle, Lieutenant H. C. Wright, D. C. Byerly and William B. Chippendall, for gallant behavior. To Lieutenant T. K. Fauntleroy, commanding section of artillery, I am indebted for valuable services. His conduct throughout being marked with coolness and decision, and worthy of the highest praise. His artillery, as efficient as it was, would have been more so but for the inferiority of the friction primers, nine out of ten of which proving worthless, rendering the working of the pieces, at times, difficult and unsatisfactory. Of the casualties, I have to mention the following: In the Beaver Creek Rifles, Lieutenant Amicker, severely wounded in the shoulder; Sergeant Wilson, wounded in the hand, slightly; private J. L. Perryman, in the back, dangerously. In Fauntleroy's section of artillery, Sergeant Bellum, severely wounded, and four horses killed. In conclusion, I have to state that my object was to obey to the letter instructions received, and every effort was made on my part to that end, and but for the inadequacy of my force, I believe more important results could have been obtained. I hope what we have been able to accomplish may meet the approval of the general commanding.

Respectfully submitted,

TOM SHIELDS,
Lieut. Col. Sumpter, thirtieth Louisiana, Regt., com'ng. detachment.

REPORT OF COLONEL J. H. ROBERTSON.

Headqauarters Thirty-fifth Ala. Vols.,
Camp on Comite River, La.,
August 8th, 1862.

Captain L. D. Sandidge, *A. A. A. General, second division:*

I have the honor to make the following report of the part taken in the action of the 5th instant, by the thirty-fifth regiment of Alabama volunteers, up to the moment I was relieved of the command of the regiment by assuming command of the brigade. Before leaving the Comite river, I deemed it advisable to consolidate certain companies in which there were but few men, and in two instances no commissioned officer, the regiment having been decimated by sickness, and accordingly divided the regiment, only one hundred and eighty five strong, rank and file, into four companies, placing them in command of the following officers, from right to left, in the order named: Captain S. S. Ives, Lieutenant Thomas E. Ellett, Captain John S. Dickson, and Lieutenant S. D. Stewart. The regiment thus organized, occupied the left centre of the brigade, and kept this position during the action, passing immediately to the front of the line first formed on the common, over and through many obstacles, to a position near the river, when the fight ended. The regiment never having been under fire, much anxiety was felt, by both myself and the brigade commander, as to the probable effect upon the men of a close fire of musketry. I am highly gratified to say that never once did the regiment, men or officers, falter; but when ordered to charge did, on three occasions, bear themselves most gallantly, and once obstinately held, for an hour, a position exposed to a fire from overwhelming numbers. On reaching the first encampment of the enemy, in the third charge made by the brigade, this regiment passed entirely through the camp, driving the enemy before them, when, on looking to right and rear, I found my command was not supported, but the right wing was falling back to cover. Receiving no order, and fearing the enemy would attempt to flank the left wing, I immediately ordered the regiment to retire, being followed in the movement by the fifth Kentucky on the left, and formed line of battle on the right of the cemetery in which the sixth Kentucky was formed. The regiments were immediately moved forward, and checked the advancing enemy by heavy firing. Being called to command the brigade, I, at this time, turned over the regiment to Lieutenant Colonel Goodwin, who reports its further action. I desire to say that I am greatly indebted to Lieutenant Colonel E. Goodwin, my only associate field officer, for the coolness and gallantry displayed by him during the action. The officers commanding the companies were conspicuous for coolness and courage Dr. J. F. Delany, a private of company D, was detailed to act as assistant surgeon, during the action, and deserves particular mention, he being up with the regiment at all times, caring for the wounded and encouraging the men. I respectfully ask that Dr. Delany be discharged, that I may contract with him as assistant surgeon.

Respectfully submitted,
J. H. ROBERTSON,
Colonel Thirty-fifth Regiment Alabama Volunteers.

HEADQUARTERS 1ST BRIGADE,
August 8th, 1862.

To Captain L. D. SANDIDGE, *A. A. A. General, second division:*

CAPTAIN: Colonel Robertson desires me to say that he wishes to amend his brigade report by stating that Major John Throckmorton, A. Q. M., rendered very efficient service in taking off the wounded from the field, showing great fearlessness of personal danger in the discharge of his duties.

G. C. HUBBARD,
A. A. A. General.

REPORT OF LIEUT. COL. GOODWIN.

HEADQUARTERS THIRTY-FIFTH REG'T. ALA. VOLS.,
Camp on Comite River, Aug. 7th, 1862.

Lieutenant GEO. C HUBBARD,
A. A. A. G., First Regiment Second Division:

LIEUTENANT: Colonel J. W. Robertson, who had so gallantly led on the thirty-fifth Alabama in two seperate charges, having been called to the command of the brigade, Col. A. P. Thompson, having been seriously wounded while cheering on his men, the command of the thirty-fifth Alabama was handed over to me.

I held the position which we were ordered to maintain, by Col. J. W. Roberston, in front of the enemy's encampments, for more than an hour, all the while under the most galling fire of the enemy. I learned that the enemy, both infantry and cavalry, were drawn up in line of battle on my left, as if preparing to charge over line on the right. I, therefore, directed my command to fire upon them, when, after three well directed volleys, the enemy fled precipitately. A charge was immediately ordered by Major General Breckinridge. We promptly replied to the command, driving the enemy from their encampments, under cover of their gunboats, when the order was given to fall back for ammunition.

I desire especially to call attention to the zeal and daring of the men, both officers and privates, under my command—the last charge having been made without a round of cartridges on hand.

Very respectfully,
EDWARD GOODWIN,
Lieut. Col. commanding 35th Regiment Ala. Volunteers.

REPORT OF CAPT. J. H. BOWMAN.

HEADQUARTERS 3D KENTUCKY REGIMENT,
August 7th, 1862.

GEORGE. C. HUBBARD,
Lieutenant and A. A. A. General:

LIUTENANT: In obedience to an order from your office, I return the following statement of the action of the third Kentucky regiment in the battle of Baton Rouge, on the 5th:

The brigade was formed in an open field, the third Kentucky regiment on the right flank, and ordered to march forward. The third crossed a lawn into a field, received a fire from the enemy's skirmishers, when we were ordered to charge. The skirmishers were routed, and the regiment halted in a "pea patch," and ordered to lie down here. We received a heavy fire, killing one man and wounding five men. We were again ordered forward and to charge, which order was executed in gallant style. Passing over the ground occupied by the enemy, we saw the bodies of a few dead of our enemy. Another charge brought us into a road near the enemy's camp, through which we charged and halted, and remained for some time; and seeing that our line, to the left, was not up on line with us, I placed Captain Edward in command temporarily, until I went to the rear to see where to form the line, with instructions to remain in position until I could return. After obtaining the necessary information, I started on my return, with the regiment falling back in good order. When I demanded to know why the regiment was doing so, I was informed it was by order of Brigadier General Clark. I then resumed command and formed on line with the brigade. Soon Colonel Thompson ordered me to fall back to a cut in the road, which order was promptly executed. We remained in this position for nearly one hour, firing nearly thirty rounds of ammunition at the enemy, at times they being in short range of our rifles. The regiment was then ordered to charge forward, by Colonel Crossland, which order was promptly executed, and again we passed through their encampment, and were ordered to fall back, which order was executed without any confusion or excitement. Without a single exception, the officers of the regiment bore themselves gallantly, and too much cannot be said in praise of the conduct of the men. Our infirmary corps kept close on our heels, and promptly removed and took care of our wounded.

J. H. BOWMAN.
Capt. Com. Third Kentucky Regiment.

REPORT OF CAPTAIN TOM BYNUM.

HEADQUARTERS BATTALION OF INFANTRY
OF STEWAT'S LEGION,
Comite Bridge, August 8, 1862.

Captain MORRISON,
  A. A. A. G., Second Brigade :

SIR: I herewith submit the report of the participation of this battalion, under command of Lieutenant Colonel Sam Boyd, in the action of the 5th inst. Its force consisted of the following: one field, three staff and nine company officers, and one hundred and ninety enlisted men. They composed the centre of Colonel Allen's brigade, the thirtieth Louisiana regiment, Colonel Breaux, on the right, and the fourth Louisiana regiment, Lieutenant Colonel Hunter, on the left. The line of battle was formed in the woods back and leftward of the residence of Captain E. W. Robinson, and about three fourths of a mile to the rear of the central portion of Baton Rouge. As soon as the line was formed, it was put in forward motion, feeling its way slowly through tall weeds, in the morning's haze, for the enemy's first line of force. Marching straight to the front through briers, hedges, and over picket fences, the brigade was halted in the face of a line of the foe drawn up to receive us, and after giving them two well directed volleys, charged upon them, when they fled. The brigade having paused a few moments, resumed its line as well as the nature of the undergrowth would permit, and marched some two or three hundred yards forward in a left oblique direction. Receiving reports of a battery of the enemy supported by a regiment right on our front, about a hundred and fifty yards distant, our commander, after calling for three cheers for the Confederacy, ordered us to charge. Alarmed at our shouts and dash, the enemy broke, taking off their battery, but leaving heaps of slain and wounded. It was here that Captain Chinn fell, from a wound in the leg, while gallantly responding, at the head of his company, to Colonel Allen's orders. Resuming our course, we soon found ourselves upon the edge of an old field, on the opposite side of which is the Benton Ferry road, and the enclosure of the race track Square in our front was posted, along the roadside, a number of the enemy's skirmishers or sharpshooters, and to their left a battery was planted at the mouth of a street in front of the outskirts of the corporation of Baton Rouge. A regiment (the sixth Michigan) supported the battery, and its men were placed behind the fences and houses in the neighborhood of Hockney's. Colonel Allen, taking the colors of this command in his hand, rapidly drew up his command in line, which, at his call and example, rushed, under a galling fire of grape, cannister and Minnie, across the field. There was not a shrub, even as a screen, upon it, and over the three hundred yards of that open space the foe sent many a missile of death and shaft of anguish within a hundred yards of the cannon.

Lieutenant Causey, of Buffington's company, and commanding it, fell, shot through the brain. No victim in this great struggle against fanaticism and the principles of rapine and spoliation, leaves to his family and friends a brighter memory for chivalrous courage and unsullied patriotism. A few yards further on Lieutenant Colonel Boyd fell, shot through the arm, and was borne off the field. In a moment or so after the enemy leaving two cannon and a lieutenant, and eight or ten privates prisoners in our hands. In passing beyond the fence enclosing Turner's house, and getting partially into the street, the gallant leader fell, helpless, from his horse into the arms of his trusty soldiers, and was by them carried from the field. His fall was peculiarly unfortunate. It completely paralyzed his old regiment (the fourth, at whose head he was) even in that moment of victory. Notwithstanding his repeated shouts to go forward, it became confused and huddled up, lost in a maze of stolidity and dismay. At this critical moment, the undersigned first became apprized, by Colonel Breux, now commanding the brigade, that it was his duty to assume command of this battalion. With serious misgivings in his capacity in this emergency, and sorrow felt at the necessity, he arrived to do his best in seconding the gallant fearlessness and conspicuous example of the commanding officer, to save his troops from a panic and to rally them into line. His efforts were supported by the daring courage of Lieutenant Barrow, commanding Captain Chinn's company, by the energy of Lieutenant Burnett, Captain Bynum's company, and by the cool and noble example of Lieutenant Brown, of the same company. A partial success only rewarded their exertions. We were saved a panic, but the annoying fire from the enemy's sharpshooters left them no other alternative but to fall back across the field to the shelter of the woods. Here another effort was made to rally the brigade into line, now massed confusedly. The commanding officer employed every incentive and expedient that courage could suggest, but with haggard results. The men made no response to his appeals. They were not cowed or panic-stricken. They were simply exhausted, hopelessly exhausted, and seemed to be staggering under the half of that last ounce which breaks the camel's back of endurance. Having been under arms for more than sixteen hours; having neither supper, breakfast or sleep; having marched over twelve miles, and having gone through four hours fighting, is it a matter of surprise or for blame that they paid but little heed to the rallying cries of their leaders? Their conduct was, however, only in accordance with the example of troops who had been under fire, and were reported veterans. Many vicissitudes of this battle must remain unnoticed. The undersigned was not called to command till a late hour, and many events, doubtless, noted by the experienced eye of Colonel Boyd, must be unchronicled because of his absence. While Colonel Boyd was in command, his promptitude and courage ably sustained the policy of Colonel Allen. His adjutant, Lieutenant Breeden, was conspicuous for daring devotion to duty throughout the trials of the day. The men generally behaved with coolness and courage. Upon returning to headquarters, near Ward's Creek Bridge, the undersigned was relieved of his command by Lieutenant Barrow.

Below is a statement of the day's casualties:

Lieutenant Colonel Sam Boyce, slightly wounded in left arm.

CAPTAIN TOM BYNUM'S COMPANY.

Killed.—Privates T. Josiah Brown and Hunter H. Hunstock.

Seriously Wounded.—Color-sergeant B. T. Reames, face, shoulder and thigh; privates William Forbes, belly; John Indicert, thigh and knee, in hands of the enemy; William Merchant, right shoulder; M. Spoerher, right shoulder.

Slightly Wounded.—Privates William Glass, hand, taken prisoner; Rufus Hopkins, thigh; Lewis Marble, reported wounded, in hands of the enemy; J. McIntosh, flesh wound in hip; T. A. Newson, right arm; H. Stanmire, right side; Theo. Walters, bayonet wound in leg; J. J. Wallace, shoulder and hand.

Missing.—Privates Patrick Cullen, William Indicert, William Smiley, Otto Stranbe and William Wilson.

CAPTAIN BUFFINGTON'S COMPANY.

Killed.—Second Lieutenant J. R. Consey.

Seriously Wounded.—Privates John Bennett, M. M. Dixon, A. Kirby and Henry Turner.

Slightly Wounded.—Privates J. G. Lathrop, in the right arm; John Beck, flesh part of right thigh, and prisoner of war; Elliot Beck, in left shoulder; William Banks, not known how, and prisoner of war; and James David, in the shoulder.

Missing.—Privates James Beck, Julius Le Blane.

CAPTAIN CHINN'S COMPANY.

Killed.—John Torpey and W. F. Haddick.

Seriously Wounded.—Privates H. Burnett, in arm and face; James Johnston, in the arm; John Taveran, in lower part of face; L. J. Thompson, in the leg below knee.

Slightly Wounded.—Captain B. R. Chinn, in the thigh; Privates B. Brady, in the arm; James Littleton, in the hand; and A. C. Howard, in the arm.

Missing.—Privates A. J. Patterson, William Erwin, James Dimond.

I am, sir, very respectfully your obedient servant,

TOM BYNUM,
Captain commanding Battalion Infantry, Steward's Legion.

REPORT OF CAPTAIN O. T. SEMMES.

IN CAMP, NEAR BATON ROUGE,
August 8, 1862.

SIR: I was ordered to take part in the action of the 5th inst., which I did. My men behaved well. The officers, Lieutenants J. T.

M. Barnes and J. A. West, acted with great coolness and bravery, at times firing their pieces personally. Lieutenant T. F. Fauntleroy was detached with a section, and I did not see him during the action. The casualties were five men killed, five severely wounded, five slightly wounded; nine horses killed, two badly wounded, two missing; one caisson exploded by an enemy's shell; the rear carriage of another rendered worthless and left on the field. Four sets of harness lost. I fired two hundred rounds of smooth bore six pounder ammunition, and one hundred and twenty rounds of six pounder rifled. Dr. Lewis, A. S., C. S. A., rendered efficient service to my wounded on the field.

I am, sir, respectfully,

O. T. SEMMES,
Capt. com. C. S. Light Battery.

At four and a half o'clock P. M., of the 5th instant, I took position between Colonel Allen's and Colonel Thompson's brigades, filling a vacancy of some eighty yards, moved forward with the infantry line half a mile, opened fire on an enemy's battery, driving them back, moved to the right of the second division, General Ruggles commanding, when I opened on a battery with effect, at about two hundred and fifty yards, then occupied my first position, opening on a column of infantry, doing much execution; was ordered to the support of Colonel Allen's Brigade. I took position on its right and silenced a battery. This was my last firing, after which I rejoined the main forces.

Report of killed, wounded and missing in the second division, commanded by Brigadier General D. Ruggles, in the Battle of Baton Rouge, on the 5th instant.

Command.	Killed.		Wounded.		Missing.		Killed, wounded and missing.	
	Officers.	Privates.	Officers.	Privates.	Officers.	Privates.	Total.	Aggreg.
First Brigade,...............	1	11	13	65	....	6	82	96
Second "	2	26	4	82	6	60	169	181
Cavalry,...............	.....	.....	.....	.....	.....	.....	.....	.....
Grand total,...............	3	37	17	148	6	66	251	277

DANIEL RUGGLES,
Brigadier General, commanding division.

R. M. HOOE,
  A. A. General.

	Killed.	Wounded.	Missing.
First division, - - -	40	141	6
Second division - - -	44	165	72
	84	306	78
		84	
		78	
Aggregate, - - -		468	

CASUALTIES IN FIRST BRIGADE.

HEADQUARTERS FIRST BRIGADE, SECOND DIVISION,
Camp on Comite River,
August 11th, 1862.

To Capt. R. M. HOOE, *A. A. General second division :*

CAPTAIN : I have the honor to submit the following as the report of killed, wounded and missing in the first brigade, in the battle of the 5th instant :

Col A. P. Thompson, commanding brigade, wounded in neck.
Captain W. P. Wallace, A. A. General, wounded by fall from horse.
Lieutenant Charles Semple, ordnance officer, wounded in leg.

THIRD KENTUCKY REGIMENT.

Adjutant R. B. L. Socry, wounded in shoulder.
Company A.—J. W. Shepherd, wounded in thigh ; M. Winchester, missing.

Company B.—D. C. Scarborough, killed.
Company C.—Lieut. R. S. Pool and private B. F. Rogers, both wounded in ankle.
Company D.—First Sergeant F. W. Thomas, wounded in side; Corporal John Leach, killed; privates John Duke and Julian Watkins, wounded in leg.
Company E.—Private J. D. Curd, wounded slightly.
Company G.—Sergeant J. M. Morgan, wounded in side, slight; Corporal H. M. Wade, wounded in both sides.
Company H.—Private M. G. Miller, wounded in side; private A. J. Ellis, wounded in thigh.
Company M.—Private J. P. McLaw, wounded in shoulder; private J. G. Vaughan, wounded in leg.

SEVENTH KENTUCKY REGIMENT.

Company A.—Private M. J. Rhodes, missing; private Henry Crutchfield, wounded.
Company B.—Lieutenant E. Ashley, killed; privates N. M. Malone and J. W. Conder, wounded.
Company C.—Private W. Brown, wounded; private John Heady, wounded.
Company D.—Private A. B. Morris, wounded.
Company E.—Sergeant J. K. Hatchel, wounded.
Company F.—Sergeant J. Helton, wounded; private W. Morris, wounded.
Company H.—Corporal J. S. Taylor, wounded; private G. C. Crider, wounded.
Company I.—Captain D. S. Campbell, severely wounded.

THIRTY-FIFTH ALABAMA REGIMENT.

Company A.—Captain S. S. Joes, wounded in shoulder; Second Lieutenant J. M. Clemmons, wounded in side; private James Price, wounded severely in chest; private Sullivan, wounded in ankle; private J. T. Robinson, wounded slightly; private George N. Rice, killed.
Company B.—Lieutenant L. D. Stewart, wounded in foot; private T. R. Ellett, wounded in ankle.
Company C.—Wm. Parker, killed.
Company E.—Corporal W. L. Martin, wounded in leg; private James Bibb, wounded severely in mouth; private F. O. Johnson, wounded severely in chest; private W. Giles, leg broken; private G. P. Frotinan, wounded slightly; private S. L. Ellidge, wounded severely in both ankles; Corporal R. H. Wilson, wounded slightly in hand.
Company F.—Private J. B. Guthrie, killed; private J. M. Pitts, wounded in hand; Corporal J. M. Tipton, missing.
Company G.—Private George S. Toom, slightly wounded.

Company H.—Private T. V. Carlock, killed; John Collier, private wounded in arm; private West Lemay, wounded slightly; private William Sledge, wounded slightly in arm.
Company I.—Private Henry Beard, wounded severely.

SIXTH KENTUCKY REGIMENT.

Company A.—Private W. H. Bluiss, wounded; private S. V. Sweasy, wounded; Lieut. W. W. Knott. wounded.
Company B.—Second Sergeant L. L. Duncan, wounded; Third Sergeant C. J. Hall, wounded; private M. J. Cifres, wounded.
Company C.—Private F. D. Nuckols, killed.
Company D.—First Sergeant W. B. Gawin, wounded; Second Sergeant D. W. Neal, wounded.
Company E.—Private W. H. Franklin, wounded; private W. N. Crane, wounded; private T. W. Spillman, wounded.
Company G.—Private R. J. Baugh, killed; privates John Colter and P. H. Jones, wounded, Sergeant J. H. Williams and Corporal A. M. Mininoway, wounded.
Company H.—Corporal John Clark and private John Smith, killed; privates J. W. Ross, John Viers and A. L. Harned, wounded.
Company I.—Third Sergeant Wm. Anthony, killed; private Sam'l Wilson, wounded.
Company J.—J. J. Moreton, wounded.

COMPANY OF SHARPSHOOTERS.

Corp'l John Owens, wounded in knee; private L. Stacey, wounded in arm.

RECAPITULATION.

Third Kentucky regiment—
    Commissioned officers wounded, - - 3
    Non-commissioned officers wounded, - - 3
        "   " killed, - - 1
    Privates killed, - - - - 1
       " wounded, - - - 9
       " missing, - - - - 1
                                        — 18
Seventh Kentucky regiment—
    Commissioned officers killed, - - - 1
        "   " wounded - - 1
    Non-commissioned officers wounded, - - 3
    Privates wounded, - - - 8
       " missing, - - - - 1
                                        — 14

                      Carried forward, - - - 32

                    Brought forward,   -   -   -   -   32
Thirty-fifth Alabama regiment—
    Commissioned officers wounded,   -   -   3
    Non-commissioned officers wounded   -   -   3
    Privates killed, -   -   -   -   4
    "   wounded, -   -   -   -   15
    "   missing, -   -   -   1
                                                       — 26
Sixth Kentucky regiment—
    Commissioned officers wounded,   -   -   1
    Non-commissioned officers killed,   -   -   2
        "   "   wounded   -   -   6
    Privates killed,   -   -   -   3
    "   wounded,   -   -   -   -   13
                                                       — 25
Company Sharpshooters—
    Non-commissioned officers and privates wounded - 2
                                                       — 2
                                                         ——
                                                         85
        Respectfully submitted.
                            G. C. HUBBARD,
                        A. A. A. General first brigade.

List of names of killed, wounded and missing, in the battle of Baton Rouge on the 5th inst., in the Fourth Regiment Louisiana Volunteers, Boyd's Louisiana Battalion and Semmes' Light Battery.

FOURTH REGIMENT LOUISIANA VOLUNTEERS, COMMANDED BY LIEUT. COL. HUNTER.

Company H.—Orderly Sergeant I. A. Morgan, Private John Atkins, killed; Lietenant A. P. Foister, Corporal L. K. Chaney, Private Joseph Murrin, wounded; C. J. Sparkman, missing.

Company B.—Private George Hath, killed; Private Fongeronsse, wounded; Privates C. Mabin, John Wiltz, Jack Evans, F. Shilling missing.

Company C.—Privates W. H. Simmons, Peter Lintz, missing.

Company D.—Sergeants Dawson, J. N. Bourgwin, Corporal R. Waldo, Private D. Lawrence, R. B. Seedam, wounded.

Compauy E.—Sergeant H. R. Bonner, wounded.

Company F.—Sergeant G. C. Laumon, Privates W. M. Adams, L. A. Bernard, W. Montgomery, Pierce Guy, wounded; R. Sanchery, missing.

Company G.—Privates P. M. Green, killed; L. M. Powell, wounded; M. Nash, missing.

Company H.—Privates Hilaire Souquepie L. Beleau, wounded; Corporal S. Miller, Sergeant T. White, Private S. Sireque, missing.

Company I.—Privates S. P. Hutchinson, killed; D. N. Morgan,

wounded, J. M. Blin, L. Carter, W. T. Bennett, J. C. Arbuthnot, W. A. Easley, wounded.
Company K.—Private T. B. Morgan, wounded.

THIRTY-NINTH REGIMENT MISSISSIPPI VOUNTEERS, TEMPORARILY ATTACHED TO FOURTH LOUISIANA.

Company I.—Privates Jonas Morgan, killed; H. F. Osborne, wounded.

BOYD'S LOUISIANA BATTALION.

Lieut. Col. Boyd, wounded.
Captain Buffington's Company.—Lieut. Z. R. Causey, killed; Privates William B. Banks, John C. Bennett, John Beck, M. M. Dicou, James David, Abe Kirby, J. G. Lothrop, Henry Turner, John Lee, wounded; N. D. Carputter, James Doloun, Aug. Deis, W. T. David, Thomas Field, T. Henry, R. J. Kerner, Jules DeBlanc, Arman Misserable, Jackson Ratcliff, Anthony Sanchery, B. B. Spears, Peter Weiss, James Beck, missing.
Capt. Bynum's Company.—Privates H. Heinstock, J. Brown, killed; J. J. Wallace, T. Walters, Wm. Forbes, T. N. Newson, L. Latel, J. McIntosh, W. Merchant, J. Stofford, M. Spoerecher, H. T. Stammire, B. Hopkins, wounded.
'apt. Chinn's Company.—Privates John Turpey, J. V. Haddick, killed; Capt. B. K. Chinn, Privates B. Brady, W. Bennett, C. Howard, J. Johnston, J. Littleton, J. Tabenon, wounded; L. J. Patterson, W. Ernir, missing.
Semmes' Battery.—Sergeant J. Dressing, Privates McNiel, McKitchen, Wolf, Hill, killed; Sergeant Bellum, Corporal Sawyers, Privates Slattery, Hall, wounded.

RECPITULATION.

Killed, - - - - - - - - - 16
Wounded, - - - - - - - - - 57
Missing, - - - - - - - - - 25

Total, - - - - - - - - - 98

The report of the Thirtieth Louisiana, remaining regiment of the Second Brigade, was handed to Captain Buckner the morning he left.

R. M. HOOE,
Assistant Adjutant General

List of the Killed, Wounded and Missing of Sumter, Thirtieth Louisiana Regiment, Commanded by Colonel G. A. Breaux, on the 5th day of August, 1862, at the Battle of Baton Rouge.

COMPANY A, CAPTAIN PICOLET.

Killed.—Corporal M. Mauricio, private F. Moussirie.
Dangerously Wounded.—Sergeant A. Dupuy, privates A. Fagot and M. Fernandey.

Slightly Wounded.—Sergeant Frinquieri.
Missing.—Privates A. Mesa, S. Pascual, J. Peritro, J. Rodriguety and C. Payelle.

COMPANY B, CAPTAIN DE LA BRETTONNE.

Dangerously Wounded.—Privates A. Clement and D. Rodrique.

COMPANY C, CAPTAIN C. W. CUSHMAN.

Killed.—Sergeant J. F. Deslier, privates J. L. Welse, F. Webre, Frank, Schuler, Duffard, Augan, and Buckley.
Wounded.—Privates Labin, Brown, Bramberg, Hirt, Reinhern, Hass and Kounswaller.
Missing.—Lieutenant A. Dapremount, and dangerously wounded; Corporals Stanley and Frederick; privates P. Blesey and William Stricker.

COMPANY D, CAPTAIN ROGERS F. BOYLE.

Missing.—Corporal Bangs, and dangerously wounded.

COMPANY E, CAPTAIN N. TREPAGNIER.

Slightly Wounded.—Corporals Duvillier and W. Schabel; private A. Lormand.
Dangerously Wounded.—G. Hatters.
Missing.—Captain N. Trepagnier, dangerously wounded; Sergeant Hymel, dangerously wounded; privates D. Blanchard, supposed taken prisoner, J. Thomas, supposed taken prisoner, and E. Nuee, supposed taken prisoner.

COMPANY F, CAPTAIN FORTIN.

Killed.—Privates O. Tellon and A. Aubert.
Slightly Wounded.—Corporal E. R. Barnett; privates C. Cavillier, H. Delery, J. R. Stanton and E. Tazende.
Dangerously Wounded.—Privates A. Castinede, A. Pence, A. Lornge and J. Kennie.
Missing.—Sergeant V. Pejois, slightly wounded; Private J. C. Villar, dangerously wounded.

COMPANY G, CAPTAIN BREAUX, LIEUTENANT REVIN COMMANDING.

Slightly Wounded.—Private F. Nicol.
Dangerously Wounded.—D. Pourrier.

RECAPITULATION.

Killed, 12; wounded, 28; missing 18; total, 58. Enlisted men, 16; officers, 2.

GUS. A. BREAUX,
Colonel.

Officers and Soldiers mentioned in the Report of Brigadier General Ruggles, Commanding Second Division.

Colonel A. P. Thompson and Colonel H. Wallen, Brigade Commanders, both severely wounded; fifth Kentucky regiment, Captain Bowman; seventh Kentucky, Colonel Crossland, and his color bearer, James Rawlings; sixth Kentucky regiment, Captains Isaac Smith, Utterback and Thomas Page, and First Lieutenant F. Harned; thirty-sixth Alabama, Colonel Robertson and Lieutenant Colonel Goodwin; of the second brigade, the fourth Louisiana, Lieutenant Colonel Hunter, Lieutenant Corkern, Company B, Lieutenant Jeter, Company F, and Sergeant-Major Daniels; Battalion of Stewart's Legion, Lieutenant Colonel Sam Boyd, who was disabled by a flesh wound in the arm. Captain Chinn also was wounded, the command devolved upon Captain Bynum, who acted with gallantry. The battalion thirtieth regiment Louisiana volunteers, commanded by Colonel G. A. Breaux, who speaks in high terms of the officers and men of his regiment, especially Captain N. Trepagnier and Lieutenant Dapremont, both wounded. Lieutenant Colonel Shields, thirtieth Louisiana, commanding separate detachment, who speaks in high terms of the intrepidity of Lieutenant Fauntleroy, commanding section of guns in his detachment; Captain Semmes, commanding battery, and his officers, Lieutenants Barnes and J. A. West, performed gallant service. Captain Blount, Brigade Inspector of second brigade, rendered gallant service in the field, where it is believed he has fallen, as nothing has been heard of him since. I also have the gratification to name the members of my staff, who served with me on this occasion, viz: Lieutenant L. D. Sandidge, corps artillery, C. S. A., A. A. A., and Inspector General Captain George Whitfield, Chief Quartermaster, Major E. S. Ruggles, acting ordnance officer, and acting chief commissary of subsistence, First Lieutenant M. B. Ruggles, aid-de-camp, Lieutenant Colonel Charles Jones, who was severely wounded, and Colonel J. O. Fuqua, District Judge Advocate and Provost Marshal General, who were all distinguished for their efficiency, coolness and gallantry throughout the conflict. The following officers, attached to the general staff, also rendered gallant service, Captain Sam. Burd, on special service; Lieutenant A. B. DeSaulles; Engineers, Lieutenant H. H. Price and Lieutenant H. C. Holt. Other officers on special service, amongst whom were Captain Augustus Scott, commanding squadron on temporary service, Captains Curry, Henderson and Lieutenant Behoum, as volunteer aids for the occasion, and Captain J. M. Taylor served with great gallantry.

www.ingramcontent.com/pod-product-compliance
Lightning Source LLC
Chambersburg PA
CBHW020306170426
43202CB00008B/519